West's Law School Advisory Board

SCHOLARLY WRITING FOR LAW STUDENTS

SEMINAR PAPERS, LAW REVIEW NOTES AND LAW REVIEW COMPETITION PAPERS

Fourth Edition

By

Elizabeth Fajans, Ph.D.

Associate Professor of Legal Writing
Writing Specialist
Brooklyn Law School

Mary R. Falk

Associate Professor of Legal Writing
Brooklyn Law School

WEST®

A Thomson Reuters business

Mat #40873693

610 Opperman Drive
St. Paul, MN 55123
1–800–313–9378

Printed in the United States of America

ISBN: 978–0–314–20720–3

This book is dedicated to William A. Falk, Mimi Rockmore, Bob Zimmerman, and to the memory of Omar Lerman.

It goes without saying.

Acknowledgments

Brooklyn Law School's Summer Stipend Program supported the development of this book; we are grateful to Dean Joan G. Wexler and former Dean (now Judge) David G. Trager. We are indebted to many others as well for their support and good ideas. In particular, thanks are due to Professors Margaret A. Berger, Eve Cary, Darby Dickerson, Anne Enquist, Maryellen Fullerton, Jessie Grearson, Bailey Kuklin, Ann C. McGinley, Leo Raskind, Mary Bernard Ray, Jeffrey Stempel, Carrie W. Teitcher, Marilyn R. Walter, and Kristin Woolever; Linda Holmes of the Brooklyn Law School library; Victoria J. Szymczak, Library Director at Brooklyn Law School; Kathleen Darvil, Reference/Access Services Librarian; and former law students Rhonda Panken, Anthony Ranieri, Angela Thompson, and Paul Zimmerman. Rose Patti, who saw the manuscript through the first three editions, was a perfect angel. And so was Golda Lawrence, whose Word wizardry was invaluable.

Table of Contents

SCHOLARLY WRITING FOR LAW STUDENTS

SEMINAR PAPERS, LAW REVIEW NOTES AND LAW REVIEW COMPETITION PAPERS

Fourth Edition

Chapter One

INTRODUCTION: SCHOLARLY WRITING IN LAW SCHOOL

"I believe scholarship to be an antidote to the cynical carelessness about truth that advocacy encourages. To be sure, any scholarly achievement is partial, one-sided, transient, and inevitably influenced in its inception and execution by the scholar's habits, preferences, values, and so on.... [H]owever, it is a more important fact that every scholarly endeavor, no matter what its subject, aims to state something true...."

-Anthony T. Kronman

"[S]cholarship and advocacy rely on and flow from the very same essential bedrock foundations for effectiveness and excellence: thorough research ...; open-minded consideration and logical analysis of all plausible perspectives on all issues; building on past precedents to develop new legal arguments that will support new legal doctrine and law reform; cogent presentation of analysis and conclusions; and scrupulous attention to details."

-Nadine Strossen

"Scholarship is, in a sense, an act of faith that writing can make a difference."

-Erwin Chemerinsky

A. LEGAL SCHOLARSHIP

In the course of your law school career, you should become a confident practitioner of both "instrumental" and "critical" writing.[1]

1. *See* Philip C. Kissam, *Thinking (By Writing) About Legal Writing*, 40 VAND. L. REV. 135, 138–41 (1987).

Instrumental writing is the basic stuff of everyday legal practice: routine litigation documents or simple wills and contracts. Instrumental writing may involve little more than putting relatively uncomplicated ideas into writing, often with the help of standard forms and boilerplate language. In contrast, critical writing is innovative and introspective, and the writing process generates as well as records the writer's ideas. To be sure, critical writing plays a necessary part in the creation of non-routine practice documents—appellate briefs, complex estate plans, and advice letters, for example.[2] But the purest form of critical writing is scholarly writing—the sharing within the legal community of new ideas about the law.

The traditional vehicle for such writing is the law review article, which also remains, after more than a century of existence, the gold standard of legal scholarship. The Internet Age has brought scholars new forums like "blawgs," blogs dedicated to conversations about the law; it has broadened both access to and audiences for published and unpublished scholarship; and it has opened the door to an ever-expanding universe of sources and data. Yet the law review article, much like the law itself, has thus far changed only slowly and slightly, as though it, too, were constrained by *stare decisis*.[3] As a genre, it retains certain defining characteristics: its normative focus, strict organization, and closely detailed and documented explanation of premises and theses.

The several hundred journals or reviews that constitute the major forum for legal scholarship are nearly all published by law schools. The majority of journals publish articles across a broad spectrum of legal topics, but there are a considerable and still growing number of specialist journals. Indeed, many law schools publish several specialist journals as well as a general interest journal. With the exception of some specialist journals edited by practitioners or faculty, law journals are edited by law students. Not only do these journal members select and edit outside articles, but nearly half the content of an average journal is made up of articles written and edited by them. Although the selection of law review members was once based exclusively on grades, the great majority of law journals now use a writing competition in the selection process. These

2. We believe that you will find the techniques and strategies of critical thinking, reading, and writing that this book describes—for finding inspiration, drafting, revising, editing, and polishing—as essential in the practice of law as they are to your success in law school. In fact, one study shows that former members value the law review experience at least as much for its enhancement of their writing skills as for its enhancement of their resumes. Max Stier, et al., *Law Review Usage and Suggestions for Improvement: A Survey of Attorneys, Professors, and Judges*, 44 STAN. L. REV. 1467, 1491 (1992).

3. The place of law reviews and law review articles in the Internet Age is itself the subject of debate among scholars, much of it appearing in ... law review articles. *See, e.g.*, Nancy Levit, *Scholarship Advice for New Law Professors in the Electronic Age*, 16 WIDENER L. J. 947 (2007); Eugene Volokh, *Scholarship, Blogging, and Tradeoffs: On Discovering, Disseminating, and Doing*, 84 WASH. U. L. REV. 1089 (2006).

competitions typically ask the candidate to write a short scholarly paper based on a "closed universe" of supplied readings.

Thus, as a law student, your first encounter with scholarly writing is likely to be the law review competition. If you are invited to join your journal, you will be further immersed in the writing and editing of scholarly articles. But whether you join law review or not, you will almost certainly be asked to write a seminar or term paper—almost all law schools now require such a paper in the second or third year, thus requiring you to demonstrate competence in critical writing.

Whether you are writing a competition paper, seminar paper, or law review article, this book can help you make the necessary transition from instrumental to critical writing. It proposes specific strategies and techniques for each stage of the writing process, from inspiration to final proofreading. We hope it will help you to minimize anxiety and wheel-spinning, to produce work you can be proud of, and even to enjoy the process.

Our first concern is to assure you that scholarly writing is neither boring nor irrelevant. Legal scholarship is increasingly pluralistic and lively, open to new voices, new concerns, and new approaches. The past decades have seen the emergence of many new directions—among them, Law and Economics, Critical Legal Studies, Legal Storytelling, Feminist Jurisprudence, Law and Literature, Law as Practical Reason, Law as Interpretation, and Empirical Legal Studies. Interdisciplinary studies, frequently relying on the concerns and methods of the social sciences, are increasingly common, even in non-specialist law reviews.

Although student law review articles and seminar papers have traditionally tended to be less ambitious and theoretical than the contributions of law professors, this seems to be changing, too. The importance of the opening up of legal education to new perspectives was underscored in a statement by the Executive Director of the Association of American Law Schools:

> The education of lawyers must not merely involve the acquisition of knowledge and skills; it must include the cultivation of creative thinking and imagination, an appreciation of the commonality of the human condition, and development of a sense of judgment and responsibility. Hence, lawyering includes the ability to understand and critique existing and emerging visions of the profession in relation to interdisciplinary and multicultural perspectives, the implications of technology, and the consequences of economic globalization.[4]

Moreover, as the preceding quotation suggests, legal scholarship has a real bearing on the future of the profession. Like other professionals, lawyers cannot in good conscience concern themselves only with what is,

4. Memorandum 93–32 from Carl C. Monk, Executive Vice President and Executive Director, *Association of American Law School*, to Deans of Member Schools 2 (May 18, 1993) (on file with authors).

or even with what works: in order to be creative and responsible members of the community, lawyers also need to think about what might, could, should, and should not be. Legal scholarship allows that free play of intellect and imagination out of which the future of a discipline emerges. Many modern tort and contract doctrines were first articulated in law review articles. Perhaps the most famous example of a scholarship-driven doctrine is the law of privacy, first formulated by Samuel D. Warren and Louis O. Brandeis in their 1890 Harvard Law Review article, *The Right to Privacy*.[5]

Appellate judges routinely cite law review articles (including student notes and comments) as persuasive authority, and look to them not just for information, but for new directions. Judith S. Kaye, former Chief Judge of the New York Court of Appeals, has written:

> I like starting an opinion with good briefs and articles.... I look to law review articles for ... the newest thinking on the subject, for a sense of the direction of the law and how the case before us fits within it, for a more global yet more profound perspective on the law and its social context than any individual case presents.[6]

Whether judges look to the work of legal scholars for new ideas or for support for their own conclusions, their reliance is obvious from the many law review citations in appellate decisions on new or vexed questions. What is less obvious, but essential to your understanding of critical writing in the law, is that much legal scholarship is implicitly directed to the decision-makers in our society—legislative and executive as well as judicial. In other words, it is characteristically normative (informed by a social goal) and prescriptive (recommending or disapproving a means to that goal).[7] The goals may be as disparate as economic efficiency and equal distribution of wealth, and the suggested courses of action equally varied, but browsing through the introductions to any random selection of law review articles will reveal legal scholarship's normative/prescriptive core. It is thus a fundamentally rhetorical discourse, seeking to persuade its audience of the rightness of its conclusions. While meticulous description and interpretation play important roles in legal scholarship, they are most frequently subordinated to the enterprise of pointing the way to a good goal. Thus, whether you are writing a seminar paper, competition paper, or law review article, a purely descriptive or interpretive approach will only rarely be successful.

B. SEMINAR PAPERS, STUDENT LAW REVIEW ARTICLES, AND LAW REVIEW COMPETITION PAPERS

This book is designed to help you with scholarly/critical legal writing in all of the three formats you will encounter in law school: law review

5. Samuel Warren & Louis Brandeis, *The Right to Privacy*, 4 Harv. L. Rev. 193 (1890).

6. Judith S. Kaye, *One Judge's View of Academic Law Review Writing*, 39 J. Legal Educ. 313, 319 (1989).

7. Edward L. Rubin, *The Practice and Discourse of Legal Scholarship*, 86 Mich. L. Rev. 1835, 1847, 1851 (1988). The discussion of the normative/prescriptive nature of legal scholarship that follows is inspired by Professor Rubin's article.

competition, student law review article, and seminar or term paper. However, for the most part, the three are not treated separately here, because the processes of inspiration, drafting, revising, and polishing are the same for all.

Moreover, the same qualities that make a winning competition paper also characterize an "A" paper and a publishable article. Successful scholarly writing is first of all *original*, in that it says something about the law, no matter how modest, that has not been said before. Second, a good scholarly piece is *comprehensive*—it provides sufficient background material to enable any law-school-educated person to understand it and evaluate the writer's thesis. In this sense, legal scholarship always takes the reader from the known (background) to the unknown (the writer's analysis). Further, any strictly factual or descriptive material must be meticulously *correct*, and the writer's analysis must be *logical*: well reasoned, adequately supported, and divided into mutually exclusive, yet related, sections. Finally, a good scholarly paper is *clear* and *readable*, written in a somewhat formal style that avoids both the pompous and the colloquial.

The only real differences among the three formats are in manuscript preparation (e.g., footnotes vs. endnotes) and, more importantly, in scale. Law review notes range in length from 10 to 50 printed pages—approximately 30 to 150 manuscript pages. Seminar papers are typically 20 to 40 manuscript pages long, and competition papers shorter still. Whatever its length or immediate purpose, however, almost all student scholarly writing follows one of two patterns: the analysis of one judicial opinion or the analysis of a development or controversy in the law. The next two sections of this chapter describe these two basic patterns.

Preliminarily, though, a note on terms seems in order here. Some law reviews call a student article analyzing one case a "casenote," while others call it a "case comment," or just a "comment" or "note." Further, some reviews call the analysis of a development or controversy a "comment," and others call it a "note." Faced with this confusing terminology, we decided to call one-case analyses "casenotes" and development/controversy analyses "comments." We refer to casenotes and comments collectively as "articles." We also use "paper" to refer to all three formats covered by this book.

1. THE COMMENT: EXAMINING ONE ASPECT OF THE LAW

Scholarly comment on the law covers a wide spectrum: depending on your interests and skills, one place will be right for your contribution. Professor Richard Delgado has usefully identified ten sub-categories of the comment. We have added our own footnotes to each of his categories, directing you to examples of successful student articles.

First, there is the "case cruncher"—the "typical" article. This type of article analyzes case law in an area that is confused, in conflict, or in transition. Doctrine is antiquated or incoherent and needs to be reshaped. Often the author resolves the conflict or problem by reference to policy, offering a solution that best advances goals of equity, efficiency, and so forth.[8]

[2] Next, there is the law reform article. Pieces in this vein argue that a legal rule or institution is not just incoherent, but bad—has evil consequences, is inequitable or unfair. The writer shows how to change the rule to avoid these problems.[9]

[3] There is also the legislative note, in which the author analyzes proposed or recently enacted legislation, often section by section, offering comments, criticisms, and sometimes suggestions for improvement.[10]

[4] Another type of article is the interdisciplinary article. The author of an interdisciplinary article shows how insights from another field, such as psychology, economics, or sociology, can enable the law to deal better with some recurring problem. . . .[11]

[5] There is the theory-fitting article. The author examines developments in an area of law and finds in them the seeds of a new legal theory. . . .[12]

[6] Discussions of the legal profession, legal language, legal argument, or legal education form yet another category of law review writing. . . .[13]

[7] There are the bookish, learned dialogues that continue a preexisting debate. These pieces take the following form: "In an influential article in the W Law Review, Professor X argued Z. Critics, including Professor Y, attacked her view, arguing A, B, and C. This Article offers D, a new approach to the problem of Z (a new criticism, a new way of defending X's position in the face of her critics, a way of accommodating X and her critics, or something of the sort)."[14]

8. *E.g.,* Matthew Harte, Comment, *A Critical Analysis of the Bankruptcy Code's Exception to Discharge for Debts Arising From Wrongful Conduct,* 4 Brook. J. Corp. Fin. & Com. L. 113 (2009).

9. *E.g.,*. Joshua Kleinfeld, Comment, *Tort Law and In Vitro Fertilization: The Need for Legal Recognition of "Procreative Injury,"* 115 Yale L. J. 237 (2005).

10. *E.g.,* Joanne Barkin, Comment, *Judging Gina: Does the Genetic Information Non-discrimination Act of 2008 Offer Adequate Protection?*, 75 Brook L. Rev. 545 (2009).

11. *E.g.,* Jason D. Medinger Comment,, *Antitrust Leniency Programs: A Call for Increased Harmonization as Proliferating Programs Undermine Deterrence,* 52 Emory L. J. 1439 (2003).

12. *E.g.* Nathaniel C. Guest, Comment, *Putting History on a Stone Foundation: Toward Legal Rights for Historic Property,* 18:2 Temp. Pol. & Civ. Rts. L. Rev. 699 (2010).

13. *E.g.,* Steven Keslowitz, *The Transformative Nature of Blogs and their Effect on legal Scholarship*, 2009 Cardozo L. Rev. De Novo 252.

14. This type of article is usually written by a law professor. However, students as well as seasoned scholars write book reviews. A good student example is *By Night She Fought for Fair Use: Restoring the Integrity of Copyright Law, One Comic–Book Reader at a Time*, by Jessica Sawyer

> [8] Another category consists of pieces on legal history. The origins and development of a legal rule or institution may shed light on its current operation or shortcomings.[15]
>
> [9] Similarly, comparative law articles are often valuable and engrossing for many of the same reasons: it will sometimes happen that other legal systems treat a problem more effectively or more humanely than does ours.[16]

Finally, there is the empirical research article, which Professor Delgado deems "in some ways, the most useful of all, if one can manage the logistical problems it presents, because it enables the writer to expand knowledge beyond the armchair confines limiting most legal writing."[17]

The majority of legal scholarship and almost all student scholarly work fits into Professor Delgado's first three categories. These are the traditional modes of scholarship, and work in them is the most appreciated by judges and practicing attorneys. Although as a beginning scholarly writer you will most probably write a "case cruncher," law reform, or legislative comment, you should not rule out the other genres, especially if you have relevant pre-law-school training. In particular, if you have been trained in gathering and analyzing data, an empirical study might be appropriate; Professor Delgado is one of a growing number of scholars who are eager to see legal scholarship venture beyond its traditional "armchair confines." Similarly, if you have a background in history, literature, psychology, philosophy, or political science, an inter-disciplinary study might be right for you, especially if you have the added freedom that seminar papers provide.

Although the ranges of appropriate approach and subject matter are very broad, the scholarly comment itself is increasingly narrow in its focus. So much has been written, so many articles appear each month, that comments on general trends or overviews of entire areas of the law are usually redundant—unless, of course, you are the very first person to see the trend or to propose a new perspective. Thus, the most successful comments tend to be specific, rather than general.

Despite the many and varied approaches to the scholarly comment, its format is surprisingly unitary. The same simple organization underlies articles and papers in every one of Professor Delgado's ten categories. It is a basic four-part structure consisting of an introduction, a background section, an analysis section, and a conclusion. The obligatory

Wang, in 105 MICH. L. REV. 1213 (2007) reviewing KEITH AOKI, JAMES BOYLE & JENNIFER JENKINS, BOUND BY LAW? (2009).

15. *E.g.*, Sean W. Kelly, Note, *Black and White and Read All Over: Press Protection After* Branzburg, 57 DUKE L.J. 199 (2007).

16. Richard Delgado, *How to Write a Law Review Article*, 20 U.S.F. L. REV. 445, 446–47 (1986). A good example of this category is *Lessons from the British and American Approaches to Compelled Decryption,* by Brendan M. Palfreyman, in 75:1 BROOK. L. REV. 345 (2009).

17. Delgado, *supra* note 16, at 448. A good example of the last of Professor Delgado's categories is *Much Ado About Twombly? A Study on the Impact of* Bell Atlantic Corp. v. Twombly *on 12(b)(6) Motions*, by Kendall W. Hannon in 83 NOTRE DAME L. REV. 1811 (2008).

introduction of one to several pages describes the subject matter of the comment and plainly states the author's thesis, most commonly, the problem the author proposes to solve and its proposed resolution. The introduction also provides an explicit roadmap to the rest of the comment: "Part I sets out X. Part II analyzes X and concludes Y." After the introduction, a second section of the comment provides whatever background a law-school-educated person will need to understand the third, most important, section: the writer's original analysis of the subject matter. A short conclusion, often less than a page in length, summarizes the writer's views; the conclusion also may suggest related issues or ramifications, inviting the reader to further reflection.

Of course, background and analysis may each require more than one section. Background may need a review of relevant literature as well as a narrative history or an explanation of methodology, for example, or the analysis may consist of both a critique of existing approaches and a proposed solution. What is essential to a successful scholarly comment, however, is that the proportions of background and analysis be appropriate to the subject matter. The background section should be specific and comprehensive and not assume any but the most general knowledge of the law, on the one hand, but on the other hand, it should not drive the reader away by unnecessary length and irrelevant detail. The analysis section should be the focal point of the comment; it should be original and closely reasoned, building to a convincing conclusion—not trailing off as the exhausted writer sees the deadline (or the dawn) approaching.

In addition to their basic four-part structure, all scholarly comments on the law share another defining characteristic: the extensive use of footnotes, a distinctive and controversial feature of legal scholarship. Footnotes serve three separate functions in scholarly legal writing, which may help to explain why most writers use so many. First, they document the text, providing both authority and bibliography. Second, footnotes serve to attribute borrowed texts or ideas to their sources, avoiding plagiarism. Third, "textual" footnotes permit the writer to express ideas that do not quite fit the straight and narrow path of traditional legal reasoning. Many footnotes serve the first and second function at once; some serve all three.

Textual footnotes are used for creative digressions, for displays of erudition, and sometimes for personal, even humorous, asides to the reader. Some readers and writers are partial to such footnotes, while others denounce them indignantly as pretentious and distracting. The choice of whether to use textual footnotes copiously or sparingly seems less a matter of principle, however, than simply a matter of personal style.

Readers who are impatient with extensive footnoting, most often practitioners and judges, also tend to find that the length, dense reasoning, and detailed documentation of scholarly comments make them demanding and time-consuming reading. Thus, good ideas too sturdily packaged may not easily find an audience outside of academia. One response by law journals to this problem has been the creation of a new format, the "essay" or "commentary." This is a short, informal, sparingly documented article expressing the author's views, usually on a current controversy. This useful format tends to be the province of well-known scholars, however, and is not (at least not yet) an option for most student scholarly writers. However, even within the more rigorous technical and intellectual constraints of the traditional scholarly comment, it is possible to write a lively and original paper that holds the reader's attention.

2. THE CASENOTE: ANALYZING ONE OPINION

Unlike the scholarly comment, the one-case analysis or "casenote" is most often written by law students. It was originally a vehicle for informing law review readers that a significant case had been decided. Traditional casenotes were brief and did little other than describe the case and speculate as to its likely practical impact. Today, however, online and looseleaf services perform these functions more quickly and efficiently than a law review can, and the casenote has become vastly more substantial and sophisticated. Its function now is to provide thoughtful and original evaluation of the decision.

Whether written for a law review competition, as a term paper, or for publication, a successful casenote always looks beyond a court's articulated reasons for its decision and beyond the dissent's articulated reasons for disagreement. It is, therefore, never sufficient to argue that the majority is correct for the very reasons the majority advances, nor is it sufficient to argue that the majority is wrong for the very reasons advanced by the dissent. In sum, your casenote must go beyond paraphrase to analysis. Paraphrase is case-briefing, that important form of "instrumental" legal writing mastered during your first year of law school. Casenote analysis is critical writing—writing about what lies between the lines.

A casenote evaluates both the result and the reasoning of a judicial opinion. The following are some of the theses that close analysis can yield. Footnotes provide some successful examples that you may find helpful.

- The result was correct, but the court proposed no clear standard for guidance in future; XYZ would be a workable standard.[18]
- The result was incorrect; the court creates an exception to a constitutional provision that could swallow the rule.
- The result was incorrect; the court failed to look to the larger social context.[19]

18. *E.g.*, Jason E. Zakai, Note, *But Can I Say No: The Future of Third Party Searches After* Georgia v. Randolph, 73 Brook. L. Rev. 421 (2007).

19. *E.g.*, James Forman, Jr., Note,, *Driving Dixie Down: Removing the Confederate Flag from Southern State Capitols,* 101 Yale L.J. 505 (1991).

- The result is incorrect; the court's interpretation is at odds with the goals of the statute.[20]
- The result was incorrect; further, the court's standard is so complex that the outcome of future cases cannot be predicted; ABC would be a better standard.
- The result was correct, but the ruling protects one constitutional guarantee while endangering another.[21]
- The result was correct, but the court's reasoning obscured the proper inquiry.[22]
- The result was incorrect; the court failed to consider a significant issue which would have been dispositive.[23]
- The result was correct; however, the decision appears to overrule *sub silentio* an important line of cases.
- The result was incorrect; it will result in an inefficient allocation of resources.
- The result was incorrect; the court misconstrued or misused precedent.[24]

Like the scholarly comment, the casenote has begun to incorporate a broader range of perspectives and interdisciplinary approaches. Successful casenotes have used Feminist, Law and Economics, and Law and Literature analyses, for example. Indeed, one casenote effectively used Legal Storytelling, employing a personal narrative to help explain why a federal court wrongly refused to prohibit state display of the Confederate flag.[25]

Like the comment again, the casenote follows a virtually unvarying four-part pattern: introduction, background, analysis, conclusion. The introduction describes the case and its holding very briefly and plainly states the writer's thesis: "In this note (paper), I argue that. . . ." It also provides a roadmap: "Part I describes X; Part II analyzes Y." As with the comment, background sufficient for a law-school-educated reader follows. In some cases, a careful summary of the facts of the case, its procedural history, and the reasoning of majority, concurrence and dissent is sufficient background. Others may require more, a survey of prior cases for example, or an explanation of the writer's approach or

20. *E.g.,* Rachel Green, Note, *Treating Section 303(b) of the Bankruptcy Code as Subject–Matter Jurisdictional*, 75 BROOK. L. REV. 865 (2010).

21. *E.g.,* Gregory W. Jones, Note, *Free Speech & Tainted Justice: Restoring the Public's Confidence in the Judiciary in the Wake of* Republican Party of Minnesota v. White, 85 CHICAGO-KENT L. REV. 441 (2010).

22. *E.g.,* Richard M. Re, Note, United States v. Ankeny*: Remedying the Fourth Amendment's Reasonable Manner Requirement*, 117 YALE L. J. 723 (2008).

23. *E.g.,* Christopher Vidiksis, Book Note, *How to Buffer Your Way Out of a Scrape: Potential Abuse of the* Cartoon v. Cablevision *Decision*, 4 BROOK. J. CORP. FIN. & COM. L. 139 (2009).

24. *E.g.,* Robin J. Allan, Note, *After* Bridgeman*: Copyright, Museums, and Public Domain Works of Art*, 155 U. PA. L. REV. 961 (2007).

25. Forman, *supra* note 19.

methodology. The heart of a casenote, however, is the analysis, and it too may require more than one section—for example, one section that criticizes the decision and one that outlines a solution. A short conclusion summarizes the analysis and may invite the reader to take up the issues raised where the writer ended. Finally, like scholarly comments, casenotes use footnotes for authority, attribution, and supplementary discussion. The sample paper in Appendix A is a casenote.

3. THE LAW REVIEW COMPETITION PAPER: A SPECIAL CASE

The majority of law review competitions require students to write casenotes, and thus you should read carefully the immediately preceding section. There are, however, some important differences between competition papers and other casenotes. Not only are law review competition papers much shorter than articles and seminar papers, but they ordinarily require no original research. Thus, you can skip the first part of Chapter Three, "Gathering Information." (But you should read the second part, "Assimilating Information.") The most important distinction between competition papers and the other scholarly formats, however, is a scary one: competition papers are most often written in a short period of time, sometimes in as little as four days.

Your task will seem less overwhelming and your paper will be better if you focus your analysis on one aspect—even one narrow aspect—of the materials. Do not be too general (unless of course the instructions ask you for an overview), and do not skip around from subject to subject. Do try to find something to say that is both original (not a paraphrase) and logically supportable. Chapter Two is designed to help you find something to say.

A tight schedule requires special writing strategies. First, start writing your draft much earlier than you would start any other assignment, as soon as you can; writing generates ideas. (Of course, you should never begin a draft after just one reading of the materials. Competition entries that are excellent in all other respects will almost certainly be disqualified if the writer misread or misunderstood the materials.) Chapter Four proposes strategies for a getting a draft down on paper.

As you revise your draft, pay particular attention to organization and the use of transitions: this will improve the reader's attitude by making your analysis easy to follow. (See Chapter Four, Part B and Chapter Five, Part D.) If you must choose between polishing your prose and putting your ideas in logical, reader-friendly order, spend the time on organization. Above all, be sure that the proportion of background material to analysis is appropriate: be sure you do not end up with eight careful pages of background and two hasty pages of analysis.

If Bluebook or ALWD style is required for citations and footnotes (or endnotes), make a serious effort to get it right, but do not become obsessed. Neatness and consistency are impressive qualities even if you do not have your citation style down perfectly. (See Chapter Six for footnoting tips.)

Save at least an hour for a final careful proofreading. Careless mistakes turn your reader off. Put a ruler or sheet of paper under the first line, read it, then move the paper down to the next line. This will force you to read slowly and thus to catch mistakes your eye would otherwise rush by. *Never* count on your computer's spell-checking program to catch all mistakes.

Finally, be certain that you have followed all of the competition instructions: you do not want to be disqualified after all your hard work.

Appendix A is a focused and cogent competition paper—you may want to read it before you begin work on yours.

C. THE PROCESS OF SCHOLARLY WRITING

The first two sections of this introductory chapter described the enterprise of legal scholarship in general and the particular forms and formats that characterize student scholarship. At least as important as this introduction to the finished products of scholarship, however, is an introduction to the process of scholarly writing. The chart that follows describes the process, and the first thing you should notice is that it is not quite accurate—it describes in linear fashion a process that is really recursive and that often entails going back and forth between stages.[26] Nonetheless, the chart is helpful because it shows the basic progression from complex and lengthy writer-centered activity to more straightforward reader-centered activity.

THE PROCESS OF SCHOLARLY WRITING WRITER-CENTERED → READER-CENTERED						
STAGE	PREWRITING: READING, NOTETAKING & THINKING			WRITING AS LEARNING		WRITING AS COMMUNICATION
PURPOSE	1 FINDING A TOPIC	2 NARROWING THE TOPIC	3 CREATING A THESIS	4 GETTING STARTED	5 WRITING DRAFTS	6 REVISING AND POLISHING

In the writer-centered part of the writing process, the author is working on figuring out what he or she wants to say. This stage has two distinct phases. Writing specialists call the first stage *Prewriting*[27]—the stage of research and inspiration. *Prewriting* itself has three stages, as our chart shows: *Finding a Topic*, *Narrowing the Topic*, and *Creating and Developing a Thesis*. After *Prewriting* comes the second writer-centered phase, *Writing as Learning*. This is where the thesis is elaborated and problems solved as the writer writes. *Writing as Learning* can be usefully divided into two components: *Getting Started* and *Drafting*

26. This chart elaborates on one that appears in Jessie Grearson, *Process to Product: Teaching the Writing Process in Law School*, 9 SECOND DRAFT 1, 7 (1993).

27. See, e.g., ROBERT SCHOLES AND NANCY COMLEY, THE PRACTICE OF WRITING, 2d ed. 15–18 (New York, 1985).

and Revising. In the scholarly writing context, the *Writing as Learning* stage culminates in a complete draft considerably revised by the writer, the first "submitted" draft. By this point, the writer has already begun to take the reader into account, but it is in the last phase of the process, *Writing as Communication*, that reader expectation becomes the writer's paramount concern. Here, the task is *polishing* the final draft—burnishing the prose, providing helpful signposts, and conforming to the conventions of legal scholarship.

As the chart shows, the writer-centered phases, *Prewriting* and *Writing as Learning*, are the most complex and creative parts of the scholarly writing process. In order to produce work that you can be proud of and justifiably hope to see in print, you need to put most of your efforts into the crucial first stages—finding and narrowing a topic, developing your thesis, and generating ideas on paper. This is the single most important piece of advice this book has to offer: do not skimp on the creative stages. If you do, you will find yourself facing a blank screen in the last days before your draft is due, with little to say, and nothing more than a summary of your research to show for your time. Such a draft provides your teacher or editor with no basis for helpful feedback, and your final draft is unlikely to be much more satisfying for writer or reader.

This book is designed to take you through all the stages of the scholarly writing process. Chapters Two (finding and narrowing your topic and developing your thesis) and Three (research strategies) offer assistance in the *Prewriting* phase. Chapter Four (getting it down on paper) and the first half of Chapter Five (revising content and organization) take you through the *Writing as Learning* phase. The second half of Chapter Five (polishing and proofreading), Chapter Six (footnoting), Chapter Seven (writing with care), and Chapter Eight (writing with style) address the last phase, *Writing as Communication*. Finally, Chapter Ten offers suggestions on how to maximize the results of your labor by submitting your paper to a national writing competition or journal.

For those of you who are journal members, Chapter Nine introduces some issues and skills basic to the law review process.

Chapter Two

INSPIRATION: CHOOSING A TOPIC AND DEVELOPING A THESIS

"When inspiration does not come to me, I go halfway to meet it."

-Sigmund Freud

This chapter is designed to help you with the most difficult and most crucial part of writing your paper: finding something worth saying, a process that entails choosing an interesting and significant *topic*, narrowing it to manageable proportions, and then developing an original *thesis*.

The topic of your paper is, of course, the case or issue it discusses. The topic, generally an area or aspect of law, will probably need to be narrowed so that the task is less daunting and mastery possible. The thesis is your own analysis of the topic, usually an identification of a problem and viable solution, each supported respectively by evidence and arguments.

Imagine for example that the topic you have chosen (or which has been assigned) is the rights of voluntarily committed mental patients in your state. Through some preliminary research and the use of some of the brainstorming strategies described later this chapter, your first task is to narrow this topic—deciding, for example, to focus on the source of those rights. You would then develop your thesis—determining that the appropriate source of such rights is the common law, not the federal or state constitution.[1] Or assume you choose to write about federal asylum laws. You must first narrow that topic, concentrating perhaps on the denial of asylum when persecution has not resulted in physical injury. You must then take a position on that trend. You could perhaps argue

1. *See* Judith S. Kaye, *Foreword: The Common Law and State Constitutional Law as Full Partners in the Protection of Individual Rights*, 23 RUTGERS L. REV. 727, 746–47 (1992).

that "until courts enforce the human rights purpose of the asylum statute to include non-physical harm as persecution, there will be no safe haven for refugees in America."[2] Or suppose that your interest in health law leads you to explore the practice of medicine on the internet. Because this topic is too broad, you identify and focus on one problem: the tenuous relevance of traditional malpractice principles to a cyber-medicine paradigm. Ultimately you try to resolve that problem by concluding that physicians and patients need the creation of a uniform "virtual" national standard of care in the cybermedicine field.[3]

You should choose your topic and develop your thesis with a view toward writing a paper that expresses original, useful, and timely ideas about an important topic. The first criterion, originality, merits special discussion given that scholarship is so often indebted to the work that precedes it. In fact, so much has been thought and said on so many topics that there often seems to be little room for newcomers. So what do we mean when we say a paper must be "original"? One obvious thing we mean is that the work should not be duplicative of another's work. But this is only a beginning. There are different ways in which scholarly work can be original.

A work might be original if it identifies for the first time a new issue, a true problem in the law that needs fixing. Some problems may stem from disputes about law—that is, from conflicting interpretations or lines of authority. The classic example is a "split" among the United States Circuit Courts of Appeals. You need to think creatively about such conflicts, however, looking not only for differences among the Circuits, but also for conflicts among state courts, between state and federal courts, or between the laws of different countries.[4] Remember that even one contrary decision creates a split and that there is no presumption that the majority view is correct. Even the voice of a single dissenting judge can suggest a problem worth exploring. To find divisions of opinion and authority, look at *United States Law Week*, the editors' comments in casebooks, petitions for certiorari, annotations on uniform laws and on the various Restatements, and the annual survey issues published by many law reviews. Treatises also identify splits in authority, as do full-text computer searches.[5] Beyond conflicts between jurisdictions, there are also times when changes in law and society suggest a rule is no longer practical or equitable. Such situations are ripe for articles suggesting a new solution.

Then there are disputes about the direction law should take in new situations. This kind of problem raises new legal issues and requires

2. *See* Wendy B. Davis & Angela D. Atchue, *No Physical Harm, No Asylum: Denying Safe Haven for Refugees*, 5 TEX. F. ON C.L. & C.R. 81 (2000).

3. *See* Kelly K. Gelein, Comment, *Are Online Consultations a Prescription for Trouble? The Uncharted Waters of Cybermedicine*, 66 BROOK. L. REV. 209 (2000).

4. Heather Meeker makes many useful suggestions about this in *Stalking the Golden Topic: A Guide to Locating and Selecting Topics for Legal Research Papers*, 1996 UTAH L. REV. 917, 921 (1996).

5. *Id.* at 922–27. One example is a full-text search for "split w/5 circuits" in an online federal-courts database.

examining whether there should be new law for this situation or whether there is existing law that can be extended. News searches, online searches for first-impression cases,[6] looseleaf services, computer hot-topic databases, and internet searches are useful for finding new legal problems.

But it is not necessary for the problem to be new or never previously identified for an essay to be original. An essay may be original for other reasons—because, for example, its approach to a problem is original—the author comes at the problem from an original direction.

The clearest examples of this are in articles that recognize the need for a paradigm change and propose a new way of thinking about an issue. For example, one article notes that suits arising out of *in vitro* fertilization procedures have too often been shoehorned into traditional civil actions such as breach of contract or infliction of extreme emotional distress, sometimes by resort to legal fictions.[7] These actions most often end in defeat for plaintiffs, even those who have suffered the most heart-rending injuries through the most egregious conduct. The author goes on to propose an entirely new cause of action for such cases, the tort of "reprogenetic malpractice."[8]

An original approach may also stem from the context in which a problem is placed. For example, comprehensive legislative histories may shed light on a law, as might an exploration of analogous areas of law or approaches in various jurisdictions. Equally, an interdisciplinary or empirical approach might provide a fresh perspective, or even challenge basic assumptions about the law. For example, although popular wisdom holds that plaintiffs in malpractice and products liability actions are grotesquely over-compensated, empirical studies suggest that, on the contrary, the majority of victorious plaintiffs are indeed undercompensated for their injuries.[9]

Then again, perhaps neither the problem nor the approach is original; instead it is the solution that is new—recognizing marital status not on the basis of a single ceremony but on long-term objective manifestations of commitment, for example. Thus when we talk about "originality," we may be talking about an essay that raises a new issue, takes a new approach, or proposes a new solution.

Originality is one of the most important traits of good academic writing, but it is not the only trait. A work might be original, but the problem addressed might be trivial. Thus, importance is another major substantive criterion. An issue can be important because of its breadth—it has international or national impact, like many environmental issues—or because it is of interest to a broad audience—it matters to the

6. For example, try this search in Westlaw's allfeds and allstates databases: first impression /5 (case issue matter).

7. Joshua Kleinfeld, Comment, *Tort Law and In Vitro Fertilization: The Need for Legal Recognition of "Procreative Injury,"* 115 YALE L. J. 237, 237–238 (2005).

8. *Id.*

9. *See generally* Deborah L. Rhode, *Legal Scholarship*, 115 HARV. L. REV. 1327, 1357 n.119 (2002).

courts, to practitioners, to scholars, to the general public, like human rights abuses. Or an issue can be important because of its depth—it affects only one group, perhaps even a small group, but in profound and far-reaching ways, as in death penalty cases.

A solution grows in importance if it is long lasting. Interim solutions that are likely to be pre-empted or superseded may be of immediate interest, but are of less importance than solutions that promise permanence.

A paper may also be important if it is useful—if it provides a needed overview of an area of law or an efficient, equitable solution to a pressing problem. That is why so much legal scholarship is normative, that is, it has a social goal and is prescriptive, recommending a means to that goal. Courts and practitioners are especially grateful for practical articles: practitioners read articles looking for litigation strategies, and judges read articles seeking perspective on the cases before them. These readers appreciate articles that solve problems by advancing reasonable interpretations of authoritative texts or that place problems in context. Moreover, law students are well-situated to write these kinds of essays and often have an easier time with them than with the more theoretical, jurisprudential, or "law and" topics to which a third audience is partial, namely, highly specialized academics monitoring the law's intellectual climate.

Of course, ground-breaking new theories and strategies are also important. While as a novice scholarly writer you might not feel confident in taking on the burning issues or theoretical debates that engross legal academics, neither should you be too timid in your choice of topic, especially if you have a theoretical bent. Although only you can assess the needs and interests of your immediate audience—your professor or your law review editors—beware of adopting a too narrow view of what this audience wants to read or publish and be aware of the larger reading community. For example, there is a broad audience for articles suggesting new strategies in toxic-tort litigation, partly because causation has been so difficult to prove. Thus, an article urging plaintiffs to abandon their personal injury suits and base their suits on violations of dignitary interests—for example, on defendants' failure to inform them of possible risks—provides an important new strategy that will be welcomed by plaintiffs and their attorneys.[10] Moreover, as the preceding chapter suggests, legal scholarship has become increasingly pluralistic, and you should not feel entirely restricted to traditional topics. Do not rule out an interdisciplinary study, for example, especially for a seminar paper and especially if you have relevant educational background.

Finally, timeliness joins originality and importance as another oft-cited criterion of good papers. Obviously, new and emerging issues pique interest, cry out for solutions, and reduce the chances a paper is duplicative. But timeliness is not absolutely necessary. There are issues

10. This idea was put forward by our colleagues Professors Margaret Berger and Aaron Twerski during a faculty forum at Brooklyn Law School in March, 2004.

that have lingered in the legislatures and courts for decades—clearly articulated, but never adequately resolved. Thus, although you may have a harder time, it would be silly to ignore a fresh look at an old problem.

Indeed, timeliness may even be problematic for some topics. For example, a ground-breaking judicial decision may provoke so much online discussion, so many blog-posts, that there seems nothing more to say even before you begin to say it.[11] But don't give up too soon: writing a law review article gives you more space and more time to develop your ideas, and you may well be able to make a serious contribution to the conversation after the initial Internet chatter has died down.

Originality, importance and (though less so) timeliness are three key traits of a good topic and thesis. Yet you also need to pay attention to your own interests and instincts. For instance, writing about an area in which you would like to practice has obvious advantages since it will increase your expertise and thereby enhance your qualifications. Or you might use your scholarly writing project to explore an area of secondary interest to you. But no matter how timely and profound (or simple and do-able) a topic may be, if you do not feel passionately about it—or any way at all about it—then let someone else write about it. Writing about something that simply does not interest you is an invitation to procrastination and mediocrity. Although rocky patches are inevitable, scholarly writing should be overall an enjoyable journey of discovery—not a long dull commute.

This is not to say that all is lost if you are assigned a topic that does not interest you or if none of the available topics seems thrilling. Knowledge invariably creates interest. Even the least promising topic can eventually yield an interesting thesis and an "A" paper, but you will have to work harder and longer at the brainstorming stage.

Choosing and narrowing a topic is the easier process; developing your thesis is trickier and more creative. In neither phase, however, do you need to wait nervously, hoping that inspiration will strike before your first draft is due. This chapter proposes strategies for *finding* inspiration. As you read this chapter, however, keep in mind that inspiration and research are not neatly separable stages. Some preliminary research is necessary to find a topic, and more focused research is necessary to narrow your topic and find a thesis. Conversely, preliminary brainstorming is necessary to focus your research. Thus, the advice on research offered in Chapter Three complements the techniques described here.

A. CHOOSING A TOPIC

If you are hoping to write a paper of high quality, you must be satisfied that the topic you choose lends itself to authentic, original, and useful discussion. Ideally, your choice of topic will also be informed by your own interests and by your audience's needs and concerns.

11. *See* Stephen I. Vladeck, *That's So Six Months Ago: Challenges to Student Scholarship in the Age of Blogging*, 116 YALE L. J. POCKET PART 31 (2006).

1. FINDING A TOPIC

Like so many good things, good topics often begin in conversation. Talk to your professor, employer, or other mentor. Talk to other students. Find out what issues are "out there," what the current concerns of academics and practitioners are. Your course books may also provide good topics. The notes and comments that follow the cases are a rich source of open questions. Most important, use your experience. Perhaps an aspect of your moot court topic lends itself to scholarly discussion, or perhaps you worked on a project in a clerkship, clinic, or law firm that has the seeds of a good scholarly paper. It is helpful to choose a topic of which you have some prior knowledge—you will have an easier time narrowing your topic and arriving at a thesis.

Legal writing competitions are another good source of topics, since they reflect a current interest of the sponsoring organization (while providing you with an opportunity to distinguish yourself). The career center at your law school probably compiles a list of competitions, and you may be able to find others on the Web. Using a search term like "legal writing competitions" will get you to a number of law school websites that list competitions. Since each website has selective lists, you need to cast your net widely. (See Chapter Ten.) Yet other possible sources of topics are blogs—there are hundreds devoted to legal topics—and electronic discussion groups or "listservs." A threaded discussion online might suggest something to you, or you could take advantage of its informed audience to put out a general inquiry about unresolved questions in that area. (See Chapter Three.)

United States Law Week, in particular, its "Summary and Analysis" section, is a useful and wide-ranging guide to current trends in the law. Try the new-developments features of WESTLAW, LEXIS, and other online legal research sites. (See Chapter Three.) A good newspaper or news magazine in print or online is another excellent source, because it makes up in context what it might lack in legal analysis. On just one day during the writing of this chapter, *The New York Times* contained some twenty stories that raised legal issues. Among others, there were articles suggesting the following significant topics, a list that seems broad enough to provide something to interest everyone.

- A proposed ordinance requiring contractors on county projects to extend benefits to the domestic partners of employees.

- A death-row prisoner's election of death by firing squad.

- The legality of a law enforcement database containing the names and addresses of millions stopped on the street but determined to be innocent of any wrongdoing.

- A state law requiring police officers to question people they stop for a "legitimate reason" about their immigration status if the officers have "reasonable suspicion" the person is in the U.S. illegally.

- The effect of a government beach-replenishment program on the rights of waterfront property-owners.
- Privacy fears raised by the revelation that in gathering pictures for Googlemaps, Google "harvested" data from private wi-fi networks.
- The legal ramifications of an environment-threatening oil spill

2. NARROWING YOUR TOPIC

A topic that is original, significant, timely, and fascinating must also be *manageable* in order to be appropriate. One difficulty in writing a publishable student piece or a satisfactory seminar paper is that your audience is more experienced and more knowledgeable than you are. But if the issue is sufficiently narrow, you can read everything and become, in relatively short order, an expert in that one area.

The first step in narrowing your topic is deciding whether to take an "internal-to-law" or "external-to-law" approach—that is, a primarily legal or primarily interdisciplinary approach.[12] Examples of traditional "internal-to-law" analyses are statutory interpretation or the evaluation of a judicial opinion within its common law context. In contrast, an "external-to-law" topic might look to history (the effect of law on the American labor movement, for example) or it might take a "law and" approach (the relevance of economic analysis to the determination of whether zoning laws are racially or ethnically discriminatory, for instance).[13] As noted above, one increasingly common and valuable subset of the interdisciplinary topic is the empirical study, which employs social science methodology, to analyze data and statistics.[14] For example, one scholar took an empirical approach to confidential settlement agreements in Title VII actions alleging gender discrimination by employers, concluding that the data showed a "reasonable degree" of success for plaintiffs, while largely refuting the popular perception of such settlements as "windfall" to "whiners and complainers out to make a quick buck" on frivolous claims.[15]

This basic decision made, if your topic still seems dauntingly broad, three other techniques can help you narrow your topic through systematic exploration. One is to use your imagination like a zoom lens, moving

12. Richard Markowitz, *Legal Scholarship: The Course*, 48 J. Legal Educ. 539, 541 (1999).

13. *Id.*

14. " '[S]tatistics' does not simply mean a citation to data published by a survey organization or government agency.... [E]mpirical studies ... 'involve the application of statistical techniques of inference to large bodies of data in an effort to detect important regularities (or irregularities) that have not been previously identified or verified.' " David A. Hollander, *Interdisciplinary Scholarship: What We Can Learn From Princeton's Long-Standing Tradition*, 99 Law Libr. J. 771, 786–87 (2007) (quoting Peter H. Schuck, *Why Don't Law Professors Do More Empirical Research?*, 39 J. Legal Educ. 323 (1989)).

15. Minna J. Kotkin, *Outing Outcomes: An Empirical Study of Confidential Employment Discrimination Settlements*, 64 Wash. & Lee L. Rev. 111, 113, 117 (2007).

from a "macro" focus on your topic at its greatest level of generality to a "micro" level of greatest detail and specificity.[16]

For example, if you were interested in the newspaper story about providing benefits to domestic partners, you might first take a "macro" approach and ask why it is in the first instance that the law privileges some relationships over others. At the level of greatest magnification and specificity, you could focus on the very language of the proposed ordinance. In between, you might examine the rights and benefits accorded to domestic partners in different jurisdictions or in various legal contexts—insurance, succession to leaseholds, or prison visitation, for example. In other words, move up and down the ladder of abstraction to see if one rung seems right.

Another technique for narrowing is based on the "topics," or categories of argument, of *Aristotle's Rhetoric*, which include some of the most basic ways of thinking about subjects: definition, comparison, causation, and substantiation.[17] If you use these categories to explore systematically an interesting but too broad subject, you may well find a manageable aspect of it. For example, consider again the status of domestic partners, analyzed this time by Aristotle's categories.

Category	Narrowed Topic
Definition	**What constitutes a domestic-partner relationship? How is the family being redefined?**
Comparison	**Compare the proposed domestic-partner rights and benefits to those in other jurisdictions, to those flowing from other relationships, etc. Compare the proposed ordinance with other possible judicial, legislative, or executive solutions.**
Causation	**What is the likely effect of the proposal? Of the ordinance itself? What prompted it?**
Substantiation	**Local ordinances are a good (bad) approach because....**

A related third technique is to explore the topic by asking a series of questions. As you ask these questions, bear in mind that you are systematically exploring your topic to find an unresolved issue or an inadequate solution. In other words, you are trying to identify a problem in the law that you may be able to resolve.

- Can the topic be divided into parts or aspects?

16. *See* Sarah W. Sherman, *Inventing an Elephant: History as Composition*, in ONLY CONNECT: UNITING READING AND WRITING 217–20 (Thomas Newkirk ed., 1986).

17. ARISTOTLE, THE RHETORIC, (Lane Cooper trans., 1932); *see also* LINDA FLOWER, PROBLEM SOLVING STRATEGIES FOR WRITING 74–75 (1981).

- Can the parts be grouped in any way?
- Are there analogous topics?
- Are there competing schools of thought about the topic?
- Is there controversy concerning terminology?
- Are there disputes concerning theory?
- Is a definitive solution possible?
- What future events might affect the topic?
- Who is affected by the topic?
- Is the topic affected by political or public pressure or vested interest?

Once you have settled on an important and manageable topic that interests you, you will need to do a careful search of legal periodicals to determine what has already been written that may "preempt" your piece. Be sure to do a thorough job. (See Chapter Three, "The Mostly Research Stage.") But remember: another writer's superficial treatment of a topic will ordinarily not preempt your own more thorough and thoughtful treatment. Nonetheless, if a truly daunting amount has already been written on your topic, capitulation might be in order. On the other hand, it is almost always possible to carve out a niche for yourself by developing a novel thesis.

Even if your initial preemption check gives you a green light, proceed with caution. Keep up your research, even as you write and revise, being sure to keep up with informed electronic conversation on relevant blogs and blawgs. You may be able to save an article otherwise threatened by preemption if you stay current and know when and how to reframe the topic if another journal publishes a piece similar to yours in substance. Finally, if you are writing a casenote, check to see whether further litigation or legislative or executive action threatens your paper with mootness, or whether you can use later developments to enrich your basic thesis and arguments.

B. DISTINGUISHING TOPIC AND THESIS

"Any one topic lends itself to many possible theses."

-Jacqueline D. Lipton

Once your preliminary research has enabled you to narrow an interesting and significant topic to manageable proportions, the next major step—perhaps the hardest step—is to find a thesis, an original and supportable proposition about the topic.

The thesis of a typical student casenote or comment is prescriptive, that is, it articulates a problem and tries to resolve it. This is true regardless of whether you are writing a common law comment, legislative note, or interdisciplinary article. For instance, if your topic is litigation arising out of *in vitro* fertilization procedures, you can narrow your focus to why such actions, most often framed as breach of contract or infliction of extreme emotional distress, typically fail.[18] The problem is that the law lacks a category of injury fitted to the harm suffered when IVF goes wrong. The solution to the problem—the thesis—is the recognition of a new category of injury: the procreative injury.[19] To take another example, the topic of one legislative note was the Lilly Ledbetter Fair Pay Act and Amendments, which expanded the statutory limitations period for Title VII gender discrimination claims alleging "a discriminatory compensatory decision or other practice." The author narrowed the topic by focusing on the term "other practice," asking whether it extended the limitations period to discriminatory employment practices like denials of promotion or training opportunities. She concluded that the lower courts should answer that question by balancing the remedial purpose of the statute against the need to prevent stale claims.[20]

The problem/solution thesis also arises in the interdisciplinary context. For instance, the topic of one student comment focused on historic preservation, specifically the preservation of Independence Hall. The problem posed was how to make informed decisions about what to preserve and what to surrender. The author, who was at the time of writing earning a M.A. in historic preservation and a J.D., used various interdisciplinary materials to propose historic resources be given a presumptive, but rebuttable right to exist, drawing upon two legal theories: the public trust doctrine and the concept of cultural patrimony.[21]

The same kind of normative thesis is often found in articles tracing the legal history of an issue or practice. One law student focused on a defendant's right to allocution, in today's courts an opportunity for a defendant, unsworn, to present mitigating information to the judge at sentencing. However, when allocution first originated in 17th century England, it was the defendant's *only* opportunity to present arguments in his favor, as he had no right to counsel and was not allowed to testify. If a defendant could convince the judge of the applicability of one of five reasons for leniency, sentence would be suspended. The student author concluded from her historical survey that the rationale for allocution has changed. Today's defendant has ample opportunity to present a defense, so allocution serves only to assist the court in imposing an accurate and fair sentence. To ensure a determination is fair and accurate, the student went on to argue, the defendant should be sworn and subject to cross examination at allocution. Thus, in this article, the history of a sentencing practice revealed a problem for which the author proposed a remedy.[22]

18. *See* Kleinfeld, *supra* note 7.

19. *Id.*

20. Carolyn E. Sorock, Note, *Closing the Gap Legislatively: Consequences of the Lilly Ledbetter Fair Pay Act*, 85 Chi.-Kent L. Rev. 1199, 1214–1215 (2010).

21. Nathaniel C. Guest, Comment, *Putting History on a Stone Foundation: Toward Legal Rights for Historic Property*, 18 Temp. Pol. & Civ. Rts. L. Rev. 699 (2009).

22. Celine Chan, Comment, *The Right to Allocution: A Defendant's Word on its Face or Under Oath?*, 75 Brook. L. Rev. 579 (2009).

Empirical studies might also result in findings that point to a problem for which the author proposes a fix. The topic of one such study was an exemption in the Fair Housing Act and Amendments that permits senior citizen housing to bar dependent grandchildren. Analysis of data from the U.S. Census Report led to the conclusion that the exemption had a disparate impact on minorities because the grandchildren of minority groups reside with grandparents in greater numbers than do the grandchildren of majority groups. The comment went on to propose several ways to lessen or eliminate the differential treatment.[23]

The theses of empirical articles are not inevitably prescriptive, however. Some articles may instead raise an issue for empirical study and simply report the findings. The findings may or may not indicate a problem requiring reform, and the author may or may not suggest a remedy. For instance, we saw earlier that data on confidential settlement agreements in Title VII actions did not confirm the popular perception that these settlements confer a "windfall" on undeserving plaintiffs.[24] Thus, there were interesting findings to discuss, but no problem the author needed to resolve. The topic of another empirical study was the effect of *Bell Atlantic Corp. v. Twombly*, 550 U.S. 544 (2007), on pleading practice. The student conducted empirical research on whether there were more successful 12(b)(6) motions to dismiss for failure to state a claim as a result of attorneys failing to adhere to the seemingly more stringent pleading requirements of *Twombly*. The author found that there were more dismissals in civil rights and anti-trust actions, but the decision had little impact in other areas. The author speculated that since the effects of *Twombly* were still nascent, it might have greater impact in other areas in the future. The author also cautioned that *Twombly* imposed a high, possibly unfair, burden on civil rights plaintiffs, but he proposed no remedy.[25] Some readers might think the author, having identified a problem, should have suggested a remedy. Yet, as one teacher reminds us, "there are multiple stages to legal scholarship and to addressing legal issues. These include identification of problems, exploring possible ways to address these problems, critiquing proposed remedies, revising suggestions, and more."[26] At times, an analysis of findings or the identification of a problem may be a sufficient first step in an unfolding inquiry.

Similarly, there may be times when it is enough of a contribution to suggest a new framework for addressing a problem—even if a solution isn't proposed. One student did this in a scholarly review of a book justifying China's human rights performance. The student put the book's arguments in an international relations context, explaining the

23. John Nelson, Note, *The Perpetuation of Segregation: The Senior Housing Exemption in the 1988 Amendments to the Fair Housing Act*, 26 T. JEFFERSON L. REV. 103 (2003).

24. Kotkin, *supra* note 15.

25. Kendall W. Hannon, Note, *Much Ado About* Twombly*? A Study on the Impact of* Bell Atlantic Corp. v. Twombly *on 12(b)(6) Motions*, 83 NOTRE DAME L. REV. 1811 (2010).

26. Rachel J. Anderson, *From Imperial Scholar to Imperial Student: Minimizing Bias in Article Evaluation in Law Schools*, 20 HASTINGS WOMEN'S L. J. 197, 236 (2009).

two competing approaches to measuring human rights performance. The "offender model," preferred by the United States, assesses a country's record in terms of fixed standards of conduct. The "contender model," preferred by developing countries, assesses performance by comparing only similarly situated countries. The student author of the review argues that this framework helps a reader to appreciate the book's insights and properly focuses the debate over China's human rights record on how to balance of the competing standards of assessment.[27] Although he doesn't do the balancing, he reframes the debate helpfully. In developing a thesis then, keep in mind that while most law review articles have a problem/solution bent, other original, supportable propositions are permissible.

In addition to finding a supportable thesis, you need to find a manageable thesis. Few students do empirical research, for example, because the process threatens to go way beyond the writer's deadline. But if the research can be sufficiently focused, an empirical study is possible. Perhaps you can use data someone else has compiled, like the U.S. Census Report one student relied upon, or perhaps there are easy ways to collect a manageable body of data, as in the *Twombly* casenote where the issue was so new that there was limited caselaw to examine. Moreover, it is important to remember that you do not need to resolve an entire area of law that is in turmoil. Your goal can be more modest. Professor Delgado suggests that you "find one new point, one new insight, one new way of looking at a piece of law, and organize your entire article around that. One insight from another discipline, one application of simple logic to a problem where it has never been made before is all you need."[28]

It is reassuring to realize that papers are often built around a single insight. It is equally reassuring to realize that insights are usually not the fortuitous product of inspiration. Rather, insight begins in simple observation, in noting the obvious—that the courts will need to interpret the term "other practice" or that it is unclear how, or if, *Twombly* will effect general pleading practice. These observations—not the Muses or Fates—are, most normally, the sources of a thesis, of insight and understanding.

Yet, however modest the origins of your eventual thesis, it is helpful to begin thinking about possible theses as early as possible. Although many people seem to separate the research stage from the thinking and writing stages, this is an artificial, and perhaps even destructive, distinction. If you have been taking notes that summarize your research, but do not include in your notes observations, tentative thesis possibilities, gut reactions, and reflections, your final job of selecting a thesis and synthesizing your research may seem overwhelming. Moreover, a provisional thesis can provide helpful direction to your research, although you must

27. Yang Wang, Book Note, *China Reexamined: The Worst Offender or a Strong Contender?*, 106 MICH. L. REV. 1143 (2008).

28. Richard Delgado, *How to Write a Law Review Article*, 20 U.S.F. L. REV. 445, 448 (1986).

be careful to prevent a tentative thesis from blinding you to contrary evidence that requires you to refine or abandon it.

Because a thesis is so central to the enterprise of scholarly writing, the rest of this chapter describes brainstorming techniques that may help you find a thesis and supporting arguments.

C. FINDING AND DEVELOPING A THESIS

"The impulse to write comes from the discovery of a comment worth making."

-Richard L. Larson

The path to finding and supporting a thesis usually begins with reading and browsing texts to achieve an overview of a topic, moves to a more selective compilation of relevant materials as a particular area of interest forms, and ends with critical reading and synthesizing. This process allows a writer to probe for unresolved issues, contemplate practical consequences, or evaluate law in interdisciplinary or empirical contexts.

During this process, reading journals can be an immeasurable help because when you read, thoughts begin to percolate. At first, this thinking may be subliminal. But as you get into topic and text, as you read closely and critically, thoughts erupt into consciousness. When this happens, reading is no longer simply about parsing out the arguments of the ideas of author you are reading; it is also about your reactions to those ideas, the connections you can make, the problems you can identify, and, ultimately, your own original ideas on the topic. It is important to preserve the thoughts generated by both your initial and critical readings of a text because a thesis may emerge from them. Therefore, you may want to keep a reading journal while you are researching your project.

1. KEEPING A READING JOURNAL

"The meaning of what [one] reads or writes resides not in the page nor in the reader but in the encounter between the two."

-Mina P. Shaugnessy

Journals differ from note-taking in that notes typically tend to be summaries of what an author says, rather than a record of what the reader thinks about what the author is saying. But a reader who focuses exclusively on what a text says will never produce a paper which is more than a readable paraphrase or summary of his or her research. In fact, if you find that you are always attributing your analysis to another, there is a good chance your paper lacks original arguments and an original thesis. To write a critical analysis, you must begin preserving your own thinking about the ideas of another.

A double-entry journal is one useful kind of reading journal. On the left-hand page of a notebook, summarize the substance of the piece. On the opposite page, record your responses and reactions to what is said. The example below is an excerpt from a reading journal kept by the writer of the sample law review competition paper in Appendix A. In it, the writer takes notes on and records her ideas about *Sherman v. Community Consolidated District 21*,[29] where the Seventh Circuit held that recitation of the Pledge of Allegiance by willing public school children does not unconstitutionally coerce children who wish not to pledge.

Notes	Reactions
U.S. Sup. Ct. held gov't. can't compel recitation of Pledge (Barnette, 1943). But 1979 Ill. Stat. says "Pledge of Allegiance shall	Shall = duty?
be recited each school day by pupils in [public] elementary educational institutions...."(439).	Very young children... does it matter?
Ct. says stat. O.K. because "pupils" means "willing pupils." Then it frames the issue here: whether	Statutory interpretation O.K.?
child who objects to reciting pledge can "prevent others from reciting it in his presence?" (Id.) Ct. says no....	Is this how plaintiff framed the issue?

Another technique is to use loose-leaf paper to take notes. Then file your ideas and reflections in a separate section of a three-ring binder. If you take notes on your computer, you could use a different font or color for your own ideas and reactions. What is essential, even at this early stage, is to distinguish your ideas from your meticulously quoted sources, and thus avoid the risk of inadvertent (but no less inexcusable) appropriation of words or ideas that are not your own. (See Chapter Six, Part B.)

29. Sherman v. Community Consol. Dist. 21 of Wheeling Twp., 980 F.2d 437 (7th Cir. 1992).

Whatever method you use, the important task is to record your thoughts as you read, jotting useful phrases, sentences, even whole paragraphs that come to you. Do not censor yourself, and do not discard any of your raw material. These notes could be the seeds of your thesis, and even find their way into the paper itself. Writing can, even should, begin with your research, with your reading.

Finally, you may find it helpful to reread your journal on a regular basis in order to determine whether any dominant themes, questions, or arguments are emerging. If so, note them down. For example, a reading journal that contains many personal associations or gut reactions may indicate that the text makes or fails to make sense depending on whether you share the value system of the author. You might then want to probe whether there are other reasonable perspectives that make the text less plausible than it first seemed. If, on the other hand, the reading journal is full of references to logical inconsistencies, or to gaps or ambiguities in the law or in an argument, you could try to write out the missing arguments. If you are able to fill the gaps in the argument or explain away the inconsistencies (as a matter of semantics, perhaps), you have potentially found the "thesis" that the paper can explicate. For example, the majority decision was correct but the court's reasoning obscured the inquiry. Your next step would be to supply the reasoning that justifies the result. If the gaps cannot be filled or inconsistencies resolved, you have grounds for a critique. Perhaps the inconsistencies show a different approach was needed. Or, to take another example, perhaps you have recorded a number of factual questions about your case or topic; the next step might be close examination of, say, the lower court proceedings or even of the historical or sociological context. This might develop into an empirical or interdisciplinary study.

The important thing at this stage is to delve into the texts and their contexts to find something original to say.

2. PROBING TEXT

"Analysis is always an account of what is not visible in the text."

-Joseph M. Williams

One of the best ways to search for an original thesis is to be a critical reader. Critical reading requires you to do more than summarize. It demands more than basic understanding of the author's ideas and arguments. Finding something original to say requires you to take a critical attitude towards texts—ask questions, play devil's advocate, look for contradictions, omissions, mistakes. You should use this approach with everything you read—caselaw, statutes, treatises, law review articles.

a. Ask Questions

One of the best ways to probe a text is to ask questions about it. It may help to use the template below to focus your analysis.

- Articulate and evaluate the purpose of the text. Is the purpose of the author well-stated or clearly implied? Is it justifiable?
- Articulate the key question that the text answers. Is it clear and unbiased? Does the expression of the question do justice to the complexity of the matter at issue? Does the writer address the complexities of the issue?
- Focus on the important information presented by the writer. Does the writer have a comprehensive grasp on the literature, *i.e.,* does the writer cite germinal and recent sources, as well as other relevant evidence, experiences, and/or information essential to the issue? Is the writer aware of relevant theoretical and jurisprudential concepts? Is the information accurate and directly relevant to the question at issue?
- Focus on the most important concepts at the heart of the writer's reasoning, that is, the ideas you have to understand to follow the reasoning. Does the writer clarify key ideas when necessary?
- Focus on the writer's assumptions, on the often unstated generalizations that the writer does not think he or she needs to defend in the article. Do these assumptions need defending?
- Focus on the important inferences or conclusions in the piece. Do the inferences and conclusions clearly follow from the information relevant to the issue, or does the writer jump to conclusions *without supplying adequate support*. Does the writer consider and justifiably dismiss alternative conclusions where the issue is complex? In other words, does the writer use a sound line of reasoning to come to logical conclusions, or can you identify flaws in the reasoning?
- Focus on the writer's point of view. Does the writer show a sensitivity to alternative relevant points of view or lines of reasoning and respond intelligently?
- Focus on implications. Does the writer display a sensitivity to the implications and consequences of the position taken? What consequences are likely to follow if people take the writer's line of reasoning seriously? What consequences are likely to follow if people ignore this line of reasoning? Are there implications that the writer does not state?[30]

30. This list is a composite of two templates in RICHARD PAUL & LINDA ELDER, A MINIATURE GUIDE FOR STUDENTS ON HOW TO STUDY AND LEARN A DISCIPLINE USING CRITICAL THINKING CONCEPTS AND TOOLS, 16–17, 32 (2001).

These questions, and others like them, will help you to perform a critical analysis, to consider what is not said in a text as well as what is said. In addition to helping you probe the text itself for hidden meanings, these questions may direct you beyond the text, requiring you to locate it in legal, historical, social, and political contexts that may help you to better understand it. Moreover, you can eventually use questions such as these to help you refine and strengthen your own text. Asking these questions may, for example, force you to notice that you have not responded to relevant objections in your article or seminar paper. In a scholarly article, you may have no strict ethical duty to do so, unlike your duty to disclose binding negative authority in a brief, but your article will be stronger if you do.

Asking these questions is not the only way to read critically, however. Other techniques for exploring the textual and contextual implications of an article follow.

b. Read for Argument Type

One skill is fundamental to the close reading of legal sources and thus to all the text-probing techniques described in this section: reading not just for the content of argument, but for argument type as well. Noting the types of arguments advanced in a judicial opinion or law review article can put you on the road to a thesis. For example, the kinds of arguments an author uses often reveal the author's jurisprudential approach. You might then want to consider other jurisprudential approaches and assess which is more sensible. In addition, identifying arguments also identifies counter-arguments and helps in testing the validity of conclusions. You might, for instance, decide that the majority's failure to respond to important criticisms in the dissent compromises the court's decision in surmountable or insurmountable ways. Finally, reading for argument type can reveal missing arguments—often a promising start for a thesis. An important missing argument might convince you that the court reached the right result but for the wrong reason, or that the decision may have harmful results because it failed to account for important considerations.

Familiarity with a typology of legal argument can help you classify and evaluate argument. Because law lacks the precision of formal logic, there is no one definitive classification of legal argument. Nonetheless, we can usefully divide argument into four basic categories: argument from precedent, interpretive argument, normative argument, and institutional argument. Argument from precedent and interpretive argument form the meta-category of "rule-based" argument. Normative and institutional arguments are rarely free-standing, but rather, most often buttress rule-based arguments. They explain why existing common law should or should not extend to a new factual situation, why a novel application of a constitutional provision is or isn't appropriate, or why a particular statutory interpretation has desirable or undesirable consequences. Within each category of argument, traditional arguments are complemented by traditional counter-arguments.

The quintessential argument from precedent is, of course, that a prior binding decision compels the result in the case at bar because the two cases are identical in all meaningful respects. Related arguments, usually buttressed by normative arguments, hold that precedent should be extended, that persuasive precedent should be adopted, or even that precedent should be overruled.

Interpretive argument parses the fixed language of constitutions, statutes, and regulations. It traditionally begins with the plain meaning of the statute, but moves on to legislative intent if the statutory language is deemed ambiguous. Legislative history—committee reports, floor debates, drafter's comments—informs some interpretations, while legislative activity—earlier statutes or later amendments—informs others. The purpose of the statute, its place in a regulatory scheme, and its economic, political, or social context are also relevant. In addition, interpretive argument is informed by the traditional "canons of construction"—rules of interpretation. There are textual canons like expressio unius est exclusio alterius (the express mention of one thing excludes all others), substantive canons like the rule of lenity (statutory ambiguities should be resolved in favor of a criminal defendant), and deference canons (like deference to administrative interpretations). Further complicating statutory interpretation is that each canon has a "counter-canon," so that their use has been likened to the "parry" and "thrust" of a fencing match.[31] For example, although one canon commands respect for "plain meaning," another holds that plain meaning may be disregarded if it is contrary to legislative intent.

Normative arguments may be grounded in morality, in social policy, in economics, or in justice between the parties, and assert that a rule or result benefits society or, conversely, harms it. Normative arguments require discussion of how a proposed rule will achieve or undermine a goal. Like any other legal argument, normative arguments must be supported. It may be hard to find primary authority since policy arguments are typically made when promoting a new rule or application, but there may be helpful secondary sources: statistical data or economic, sociological, or psychological theory, for example.[32] Like the canons of construction, policy arguments can also be likened to a fencing match: freedom versus security, fairness versus efficiency, economic benefit versus costs of implementation.

Institutional arguments assert the appropriateness or practicality of a rule or result. Two common types of institutional argument concern the roles of judiciary, legislature, and executive, and the relationship between state and federal law. Other institutional arguments consider the practical effect of a rule or result on the administration of justice.

31. Karl Llewellen, *Remarks on the Theory of Appellate Decisions and the Rules or Canons About How Statutes Are To Be Construed*, 3 VAND. L. REV. 395 (1950).

32. *See* Ellie Margolies, *Closing the Floodgates: Making Persuasive Policy Arguments in Appellate Briefs*, 62 MONT. L. REV. 59 (2001).

The checklist below shows some of the most common arguments and counter-arguments. Of course, not all types of arguments are available in every context. More importantly, not all arguments are created equal. In addition to learning to identify argument, you should train yourself to remain unmoved by the over-certainty that characterizes much of legal argument. Try to be both rigorous and fair-minded when evaluating the strength of arguments, checking for logical fallacies and other flaws.

Checklist: The Varieties of Legal Argument

Argument	*Counter–Argument*
A. Argument from Precedent	
1. Precedent must be followed; the facts are meaningfully identical.	1.a) The facts meaningfully different 1.b) Precedent should be overruled.
1. Precedent should be extended from an analogous situation.	1. The situation is not sufficiently Analogous.
2. There are 2 competing lines of persuasive precedent: line A is better.	3. Line B is better.
B. Interpretive Argument	
1. The plain meaning of the statute should be applied.	1.a) The statute is ambiguous. 1.b) The plain meaning conflicts with legislative intent, creates an absurd result, etc. 1.c) The language must be read in context.
C. Normative Arguments	
1. Morality requires this result. (E.g., "Innocent victims must be compensated.")	1. The result is not moral (E.g., "It is wrong to impose liability Without fault.")
2. Good social policy requires this result. (E.g., "It will deter anti-social behavior.")	2.a) Society will not benefit. (E.g., "This kind of behavior cannot be deterred.") 2.b) There may be some benefit, but there will be more harm.
3. Economic concerns support this result. (E.g., "The loss will be shifted from the victim to the negligent homeowner.")	3. Economic concerns do not support this result. (E.g., "The homeowner's innocent spouse will be impoverished.")

4. Justice between the parties justifies the result. (E.g., "Defendant's egregious behavior here warrants extending the statute of limitations.")	4. Justice between the parties requires the opposite result. (E.g., "Plaintiff should not be rewarded for 'sleeping on her rights.' "

D. Institutional Argument

1. This is the kind of decision courts are best-equipped to make.	1. This is the kind of decision best made by the legislature.
2. This is an area where the state is free to make law.	2. Federal law preempts state law.
3. This rule would "open the floodgates."	3.a) Few litigants would/could invoke this rule. 3.b) The gates are already open. 3.c) There can't be too much justice.
4. Courts/Juries would have difficulty with this vague standard.	4. Courts/Juries use standards like this all the time.
5. This is a bright-line rule, easy to apply.	5.a) The rule is inflexible. 5.b) Draw the line somewhere else.
6. This rule creates a "slippery slope."	6. The rule is narrow and precise.

c. *Read for Inconsistency, Logical Error, and Omission*

Sometimes there are incompatibilities between what a text promises and what it delivers. The writer may spend more time on what she wants to reject or eliminate than on what she claims to resolve, or she may neglect an important aspect of the problem. For instance, a writer may purport to show that warrantless administrative searches of Blackberries issued by federal agencies do not violate the Fourth Amendment, but all that writer actually shows is that the government has a substantial interest in such searches. Noticing an inconsistency like this might lead you to a thesis.

Logical fallacies form another type of problem. One common fallacy is argument based on an unargued premise. In the sample casenote/competition paper in Appendix A, for example, a thesis is built on the court's unsupported assertion that the pledge of allegiance in school is a curricular activity, with no religious aspects. Since the issue was whether the flag salute statute violated the religion clauses of the First Amendment, the unargued premise weakened the court's conclusion that the statute was constitutional.

False dichotomy is another fallacy to beware. For example, a state supreme court concluded that social hosts should be liable for the injuries caused by their drunk-driving guests. It justified this decision on the ground that such a rule would shift the burden of loss from the victims to the social hosts, implying that victims of drunk driving must be compensated by the alcohol-provider or not at all.[33] This is a false dichotomy, however, because victims are compensated by the driver's insurance. False analogy is a similar failure of logic. In *Holder v. Humanitarian Law Project*,[34] where the Supreme Court upheld against constitutional challenge a statute making it a crime to provide "material support or resources" to foreign terrorists, the dissent in essence accused the majority of supporting its ruling with a false analogy. The majority held that like financial aid to a charitable arm of a terrorist group, human rights advocacy was properly criminalized because such ostensibly peaceful aid was fungible—it would free up resources for illegal activity. The dissent saw a weakness in the Court's reasoning here: while funds to one part of an organization could conceivably free up other funds, it is difficult to see what resources advocacy would free up for the terrorist organization.[35]

Another all-too-frequent problem in judicial argument is the unsupported empirical claim. An infamous example occurs in *Romer v. Evans*, where the dissenter asserts on no cited evidence that homosexuals live disproportionately in some areas, that they care more about politics than do heterosexuals, and that they have political influence disproportionate to their numbers.[36] Logical fallacies like these would support a thesis that the dissenting opinion was poorly reasoned.

Errors also result when arguments are not legitimately supported by the authorities cited. For example, in holding that religious beliefs did not excuse the respondents from compliance with an otherwise valid and generally applicable law, the Supreme Court in *Employment Division v. Smith*[37] cited as binding precedent an overruled decision, neglecting to indicate that it was overruled. This misuse of authority became the thesis of an article arguing that the Court's real reasons for changing First Amendment free exercise of religion doctrine were buried under a misleading "adherence-to-precedent" rationale.[38]

Indeed, judicial opinions often fail to set out the real reasons for a decision. As Robert A. Leflar observed, overcrowded dockets often prevent judges from thinking through ground-breaking decisions, and this prompts them to offer "authority reasons" where substantive reasons would be more appropriate.[39] Substantive reasons go to the ultimate merits of the controversy and fall into one of two primary categories.

33. Kelly v. Gwinnell, 476 A.2d 1219, 1229 (N.J. 1984).

34. Holder v. Humanitarian Law Project, No. 08–1498, slip op. (U.S. June 21, 2010).

35. *Id.* at 13–14 (Breyer, J., dissenting).

36. Romer v. Evans, 517 U.S. 620, 645–646 (1996) (Scalia, J., dissenting).

37. Employment Div. v. Smith, 494 U.S. 872 (1990).

38. *See* Michael W. McConnell, *Free Exercise Revisionism and the Smith Decision*, 57 U. Chi. L. Rev. 1109 (1990).

39. Robert A. Leflar, *Honest Judicial Opinions*, 74 Nw. U. L. Rev. 711, 721 (1979). *See also* Robert S. Summers, *Two Types of Substantive Reasons: The Core of a Theory of Common–Law Justification*, 63 Cornell L. Rev. 707 (1978).

"Goal reasons" justify a decision on the ground that it will promote desired social ends like public health or fair labor practices. "Rightness reasons" justify a decision on the basis of accepted socio-moral norms and look to such equitable matters as culpability and fair dealing.

Often a thesis will emerge if you can articulate the court's unspoken, but real, reason for a decision. Your paper can focus on the impact these unspoken reasons have on the argument's viability or the decision's usefulness. For example, in *Braschi v. Stahl Associates*,[40] the New York Court of Appeals held that the term "family" in a non-eviction provision of the rent-control laws includes adult life partners unrelated by blood or law whose relationship is characterized by emotional and financial commitment and interdependence. The court offered "goal reasons" to support its redefinition. It said it was bringing rent control law in line with the reality of contemporary family life. In so doing, the court almost invited the legal community to expect this definition to be extended to allied areas of law, although it thwarted those expectations in the end.

A close reader might have anticipated this by noticing that the Court of Appeals, unlike the lower courts, nowhere mentioned that the tenant of record died of AIDS in a city in which thousands of other HIV-positive unmarried life partners also lived in rent-regulated apartments to which only traditional "family" had previously had succession rights. A reader alert to the court's silence might have wondered whether compassion for AIDS victims was in any way behind the court's surprising judicial activism—whether, in other words, "rightness reasons" rather than "goal reasons" were the true basis of the court's decision. And if the redefinition of family *was* motivated largely by sympathy for desperately ill people facing eviction, rather than an interest in making law more responsive to contemporary notions of family, your paper could examine whether the court would be likely to extend that definition to other contexts. A reader who questioned *Braschi* thus could have correctly predicted in a casenote that the court would not extend its remarkable decision in *Braschi* beyond the housing context.

Finally, you should always do research to check an author's accuracy. Did an author ignore fundamental premises or texts or depend on unreliable sources or mischaracterize an author, argument, or fact? For example, the court in *United States v. Dickerson* said that without defendant's confession, which was obtained before he had been mirandized, the defendant might be acquitted.[41] Yet there was actually considerable evidence of guilt. A bank robber was seen leaving the scene of the crime as a passenger in Dickerson's car. Tangible evidence was found in Dickerson's apartment and car—a gun and leather bag described by eyewitnesses, marked money, and the fluid used to clean marked money. The actual robber confessed, implicating Dickerson. This kind of conflict between fact and assertion can provide grounds for a fertile critique.

40. Braschi v. Stahl Assoc. Co., 543 N.E. 2d 49 (N.Y. 1989).

41. United States v. Dickerson, 166 F.3d 667, 672 (4th Cir. 1999).

d. *Take a Problem–Solving Approach*

Karl Llewellyn believed that the best way to analyze a judicial opinion was not just to extract issue-holding-reasoning, but to imagine the case as a problem to be solved—that is, to go back and recreate the litigation in your mind, imagining every possible argument that could have been made by the parties.[42] If you are writing a casenote, this process can help you find something to say about your case. Of course, unlike in Llewellyn's day, writers now have instant electronic access to the briefs filed in most appellate cases, and thus, access to arguments that did not make it into the judicial opinion. These briefs can be a useful resource as you look for a thesis, but bear in mind that the issues in an appeal have already been extensively sifted and narrowed, and there may well be important considerations that do not make it into the briefs—whether for tactical reasons, length restrictions, or because the lawyers simply did not think of them. So Llewellyn's idea is still an excellent technique for getting beyond the reasoning of the court.

Imagine for example that you are writing a casenote on a California Supreme Court case holding that a convicted defendant who wishes to make a personal oral statement to the trial judge at sentencing requesting mitigation of his punishment may only do so under oath and subject to cross examination.[43] The appellate court's decision is based on statutory interpretation. Imaginatively recreating the arguments that might have been made by prosecution and defense at the trial level will take you far beyond the relatively few arguments and counter-arguments appearing in the decision. When the defendant made his request, the prosecution in this case would have argued that the statutory language plainly limited unsworn statements by defendants to requests for arrest of judgment, not requests for mitigation of sentence. It would have further argued that any change should be made by the legislature. In support of these statutory arguments, the prosecution would have placed great weight on the importance of oath and cross as evidentiary safeguards in the truth-seeking process. The defense could have argued that application of the canon of lenity, which favors interpreting statutory language in a criminal defendant's favor, required permitting an unsworn request for mitigation. The defense might note that given that cross-examination is a shield guaranteed to the defendant by the Confrontation Clause, it would appear unfair to use it as a sword against him. The defense might also point to many practical questions. Would other rules of evidence, like the rule against hearsay, apply? If the defendant expressed remorse, could the prosecutor challenge the defendant's sincerity, possibly bringing in a rebuttal witness? These are just some of the avenues to a thesis that a problem-solving approach would open up.

42. *See* Karl Llewellyn, *The Current Crisis in Legal Education*, 1 J. LEGAL EDUC. 211, 213 (1948).

43. People v. Evans, 187 P.3d 1010 (Cal. 2008).

e. Read for Jurisprudence

Reading for jurisprudence—analyzing the way the writer looks at law and justice, legal interpretation, or adjudication—is another way of probing a text. Every age has a roughly definable mainstream jurisprudence. Early in the twenty-first century, that mainstream is the convergence of Formalist,[44] Legal Realist,[45] Legal Process,[46] and Fundamental Rights[47] tributaries. Yet there are many other influential and competing views of the law—for example, Law and Economics,[48] Critical Legal Studies,[49] and Feminist Jurisprudence.[50] This is a time of engaged and far-ranging debate, an exciting time to be studying and writing about the law.

The germ of a casenote thesis can often be found by analyzing the jurisprudential approach taken by the court in your case and then imagining how taking different approaches would affect the outcome and inform the reasoning. Suppose for example that you are going to write a casenote on *Milligan–Jensen v. Michigan Technological University*,[51] a sex-discrimination case decided by the Sixth Circuit Court of Appeals. The plaintiff in that case, the University's only woman security guard, was consistently assigned the worst work shift, which her supervisor jeeringly called the "lady's job." After unsuccessfully requesting reassignment, the plaintiff filed a complaint with the Equal Employment Opportunity Commission. The University then fired her, and she added a second cause of action, retaliation, to her complaint. During discovery, it was determined that the plaintiff had lied on her initial application, failing to inform the employer of a driving-under-the-influence conviction.

44. Formalists see law as a set of fixed general principles from which conclusions as to specific cases can be deduced. For a Formalist judge, adjudication is largely a matter of deriving the appropriate rule from precedent and applying it without regard to morality or public policy.

45. Legal Realists see law and adjudication in social, political, historical, and economic contexts. Legal Realist judges tend to be willing to consider empirical evidence as well as precedent and often reach conclusions by balancing the equities.

46. Legal Process jurisprudence arose largely from the perception that Legal Realism is not a predictable approach to adjudication. Legal Process judges emphasize rationality, restraint, and fairness—especially fair notice and opportunity to be heard. In essence, Legal Process seeks to reconcile Formalism and Legal Realism.

47. Fundamental Rights theory tends to privilege basic notions of justice and human dignity over concerns for neutrality, judicial restraint, and predictability.

48. Law and Economics jurisprudence uses microeconomics to analyze almost every aspect of the law. The analysis, however, varies according to the writer's particular economic theory. Most early Law and Economics scholars were associated with the conservative "Chicago School," which valued efficiency and maximization of social wealth. More recent scholarship is more eclectic.

49. Critical Legal Studies (CLS) is a descendant of Legal Realism. CLS scholars argue that law is fundamentally indeterminate, and that its purported neutral principles inevitably favor the privileged and fail the underprivileged—in short, that law is politics.

50. As well as seeking fair treatment of women under the law and fair representation within the profession, Feminist Jurisprudence criticizes traditional legal reasoning, hierarchy, and discourse practices.

51. Milligan–Jensen v. Michigan Technological Univ., 975 F.2d 302 (6th Cir. 1992). This example and the analysis that follows are adapted from BAILEY KUKLIN & JEFFREY W. STEMPEL, FOUNDATIONS OF THE LAW 52–57 (1994).

Determining that the plaintiff had been illegally discriminated and retaliated against by her employer, the Sixth Circuit nonetheless granted summary judgment to the University. The court reasoned that the University required a clean record and the plaintiff violated that rule. Therefore, according to the court, she was not a legitimate employee and could not claim damages under a statute enacted to protect employees.

Resolving the issue in these terms, the court took a Formalist approach, dispassionately applying law to fact with no regard to legislative intent, social context, or public policy. A judge practicing conservative Law and Economics would reach the same result as the Sixth Circuit did, but by a very different route, concluding that if the plaintiff prevailed, there would be an unreasonable economic burden placed on employers, who would have to check all statements made on applications.

But a judge following the more liberal Yale School of Law and Economics might find for the plaintiff, reasoning that such an outcome would deter sexually hostile work environments and thus prevent productivity losses attributable to such conditions. A Legal Realist would also be likely to find for the plaintiff, balancing the equities, looking to the intent behind the statute, and calling on "common sense." By these measures, the Legal Realist would conclude that the statute was meant to help mistreated employees like the plaintiff and that her employer's actions were more blameworthy than her omission. Judges practicing Feminist or Critical Legal Studies jurisprudence would without doubt find for the plaintiff, privileging progressive legislation over punitive regulations imposed on the powerless plaintiff. Both would undoubtedly also consider that her victory was small compensation for a life lived in a fundamentally inequitable society. Judges following still other jurisprudential currents would advance still other bases for one or the other outcome.

The point of this simplified sketch of contemporary jurisprudence is that in analyzing a judicial opinion, there is far more to think about than whether a court "correctly" applied or construed the law. Examining the court's understanding of the nature of law, interpretation, and adjudication can take your analysis deeper and help you find something worth saying. You could, for example, balance the approaches and explain why one is the most sensible.

f. Read for Rhetoric and Style

Another way of probing the text is to read for rhetoric and style. Literary critics believe that texts have multiple meanings, meanings beyond those an author intended. Thus, you should not simply take writers "at their word." Instead, examine the undercurrents—the writer's assumptions about and attitude toward reader, self, and subject matter—to gain a greater understanding of the text before deciding whether you agree with it.

In particular, you can learn a lot about a piece by taking a close look at a writer's tone. Some writers are assertive and treat their readers like a herd of sheep that needs to be prodded in the right direction. Others establish a more respectful attitude toward readers by inviting speculation or simply musing out loud. Some pieces exhibit an objective attitude towards the subject. In this type of neutral exposition, writers try to efface themselves by avoiding personal or idiosyncratic comments and by using clear denotative language. Other writers reveal humor, irony, or anger about the subject. These writers may deliberately role-play in their writing, portraying themselves as sardonic or indignant social critics perhaps, as is the case in the following excerpt.

> I learned, much later, that I had "really" been raped. Unlike, say, the woman who claimed she'd been raped by a man she actually knew, and was with voluntarily. Unlike, say, women who are "asking for it," and get what they deserve. I would listen as seemingly intelligent people explained these distinctions to me, and marvel; later I read about them in books, court opinions, and empirical studies. It is bad enough to be a "real" rape victim. How terrible to be—what to call it—a "not real" rape victim.[52]

The hurt and anger that ensues when humiliation is heaped upon injury is effectively conveyed in this paragraph by the artful use of irony, as carefully analyzed by one of its readers in a law review article on feminist legal scholarship.

> The first three sentences set out the distinction about which Estrich wants to make a point. The reader get a subtle clue of the intended irony by the repetition ... of words in the second and third sentences, as well as the colloquial "say" interjected into the sentences. However, Estrich leaves no doubt about her feelings by combining the quotation marks around the "really" in the first sentence and the "not real" in the last, the reference to "seemingly intelligent people" and the author's reaction ("marvel"), and the interjected, somewhat derisive, "what to call it." In this short, highly effective paragraph, Estrich makes her point clearly and persuasively....[53]

It is also informative to pay attention to an author's use of words. For example, a writer who refers to "the disabled" rather than to "persons with disabilities" equates the person to the disability, an attitude distressing to that community.[54] The use of language in *Board of Education v. Dowell*[55] proved especially revealing. In that case, the

52. Susan Estrich, *Rape*, 95 YALE L.J. 1087 (1986). We are grateful to Kathryn Stanchi for bringing this article to our attention.

53. Kathryn Stanchi, *Feminist Legal Writing*, 39 SAN DIEGO L. REV. 387, 414 (2002).

54. *See* Lorraine Bannai & Anne Enquist, *(Un)examined Assumptions and (Un)intended Messages: Teaching Students to Recognize Bias in Legal Analysis and Language*, 27 SEATTLE U. L. REV. 1, 20–21 (2003).

55. Board of Educ. v. Dowell, 498 U.S. 237 (1991).

Supreme Court held that an injunction in a school desegregation case may be dissolved upon a sufficient showing that the school board "complied in good faith with the desegregation decree since it was entered ... [if] the vestiges of past *de jure* segregation ha[ve] been eliminated to the extent practicable." In its opinion, the majority analogized the Oklahoma City Board of Education to a poor student "condemned" to the foreign "tutelage" of the District Court "for the indefinite future." Thus, through a simple metaphor likening judicial supervision to harsh schooling, the former wrong-doer takes on the innocence of the victim: the School Board, not the African–American student, labors under "draconian" tutelage, and the reader is pushed to regard the Board, the oppressor in *Brown v. Board of Education*,[56] as the oppressed in *Dowell*. This kind of rhetorical pressure may affect our view of the merits of a debate—especially if we are unaware of it. Being aware of it can also point the way to a thesis.

In addition to incidental figures of speech like the *Dowell* example, the law also abounds in figures of speech that have become institutionalized as doctrine. First Amendment law is dominated by such expressions—"chilling effect," "marketplace of ideas," and "public forum." Cautious courts warn of "slippery slopes" and gaping "floodgates" and require legislation to pass "constitutional muster." Recently, scholars have begun to analyze these judicial figures of speech;[57] perhaps critical examination of expressions that you have come to take for granted can help point you in the direction of a thesis. Take, for example, the "open fields" doctrine in Fourth Amendment law. It holds, in essence, that there is no constitutionally protected expectation of privacy in undeveloped land. What is the effect on the reader of calling all undeveloped land, even wooded ravines and junkyards, "open fields"? Does the doctrine seem as incontrovertible when we look at its language up close? Taking a long hard look at language very often generates ideas, and even whole critiques.

3. PROBING CONTEXT

In addition to closely analyzing texts, it is often profitable to examine not only the legal, but also the historical or social context of a case or issue.

a. Examine the Legal Context

When the meaning of a statutory provision is in doubt, it may be may be helpful to examine its relation to the larger statutory context. Thus, as we saw earlier, one article analyzed the phrase "other [discriminatory] practice" in the Lilly Ledbetter Fair Pay Act in terms of the statute's remedial purpose in order to argue that the Act's more generous statute of limitations periods should apply to all Title VII discrimina-

56. Brown v. Board of Educ., 349 U.S. 294 (1955).

57. *See, e.g.*, Haig Bosmajian, Metaphor And Reason In Judicial Opinions (1992).

tory employment practices, not just those involving compensation.[58] Alternatively, it might be helpful to examine a new statute in light of its regulatory framework. For example, the Federal Trademark Dilution Act [FTDA], which protects famous marks from the attempts of others to trade upon their renown, was intended as extension of federal trademark protection under the Lanham Act of 1946. One article argues that the FTDA threatens to supplant traditional trademark doctrine, the primary purpose of which was to balance the competing interests of the trademark holder, the consumer, and competitors. The focus of the FTDA, however, is solely on protection of the trademark holder. The article proposes revisions to the FTDA to prevent the overexpansion and misuse of the dilution doctrine.[59] A third strategy is to examine trends in legislative activity. One student author noted that the increasing amount of federal and state legislation requiring interpretation for deaf criminal defendants had led courts to focus on a deaf defendant's statutory rather than constitutional right to interpretation. She parlayed this observation into an argument that this approach results in less protection for deaf defendants.[60] Other theses may arise from tracing what has been changed or omitted when a law is amended.

Lower court decisions are another important legal context; often there can be no proper assessment of higher court decisions without a close look at the lower court proceedings. In order to justify its decision, for example, a court may describe a controversy quite differently from the court below, though even a trial court opinion molds and condenses the transcript by transforming the original event into a legal incident for judgment.[61] Sometimes a higher court will fasten on facts minimized below. At other times, it will ignore relevant facts. Either tactic can result in simplification, omission, and inaccuracy. For example, earlier in this chapter we saw how the court in *United States v. Dickerson*, 166 F.3d 667 (4th Cir. 1999), ignored the lower court decision detailing significant evidence of guilt in order to bolster its decision to admit confession made before a *Miranda* warning was given. To assess a decision, you should therefore read all the decisions—as well as any available transcripts or other reliable accounts of the facts—since exploring the stories of the parties (especially those of the loser) can help you to better understand and evaluate the equities.

Investigating the history of a rule or doctrine can also lead to a thesis. One student used unpublished materials from the archives of the United States Supreme Court to illuminate one of its most puzzling decisions, *Branzburg v. Hayes,* 408 U.S. 665 (1972), in which the Court abruptly reversed course to hold that the First Amendment provides reporters no privilege against compelled testimony concerning their

58. Sorock, *supra* note 20.

59. Jason R. Edgecombe, Comment, *Off the Mark: Bringing the Federal Trademark Dilution Act in Line with Established Trademark Law*, 51 EMORY L.J. 1247 (2002).

60. *See* Deirdre M. Smith, Comment, *Confronting Silence: The Constitution, Deaf Criminal Defendants, and the Right to Interpretation During Trial*, 46 ME. L. REV. 87 (1994).

61. *See* Carolyn Heilbrun & Judith Resnik, *Convergences: Law, Literature, and Feminism*, 99 YALE L.J. 1913 (1990).

confidential sources.[62] Using the justices' own conference notes, the author was able to make a contribution to legal history by tracing the decision-making process that moved the Court from Justice Hugo Black's stalwartly pro-press stance to Justice Byron White's no-privilege position.

It is often profitable to explore the place a case has within a broader debate or to compare it to cases raising analogous issues in related areas. For example, in the 1960s and 1970s, there was a trend to liberalize standing requirements so that suits could be brought to benefit the environment. This trend led one scholar to propose giving substantive rights to natural objects like forests. Through a guardian, natural objects would have legal standing to bring an action and claim compensation for damage to them.[63] Forty years later, a law student picked up on this proposal and urged giving historic property similar legal rights.[64] Another student models state regulation of culturally significant artwork on current historic preservation legislation.[65]

If you are writing about an evolving area of law it is often helpful to ask whether the problem upon which you are focusing requires you to rethink the prevailing legal theories: is it time for doctrinal reconstruction or a paradigm switch? For example, one author was interested antidiscrimination law and its protection of groups that do not have immutable or visible traits, but that can change or conceal their defining trait (like homosexuals). The author begins

> with the question of why the courts have relied on immutability and visibility. A look at the origins of the factors reveals that they were created to capture the similarities between race-based and sex-based classifications. They were then retained because of their gatekeeping function.... The courts will therefore be reluctant to jettison the factors without developing an alternative gatekeeping mechanism. I suggest that this alternative mechanism should be a refinement of the currently existing inquiry into the group's political powerlessness, which would operate in lieu of the immutability and visibility factors.[66]

Exploring the legal theories relevant to your subject not only alerts you to possible theses, arguments, and counter-arguments, but demonstrates your familiarity with the important theoretical principles and literature underlying your topic. Such familiarity only bolsters the credibility of your paper.

62. *E.g.* Sean W. Kelly, Note, *Black and White and Read All Over: Press Protection After* Branzburg, 57 DUKE L.J. 199 (2007).

63. Christopher D. Stone, Comment, *Should Trees have Standing? Toward Legal Standing for Natural Objects*, 45 S. CAL. L. REV. 450 (1970).

64. Guest, *supra* note 21.

65. Michelle Orloski, Comment, *Preventing Gross Injury to Local Culture Patrimony: A Proposal for State Regulation of Deaccessioning*, 81 TEMP. L. REV. 605 (2008).

66. Kenji Yoshini, *Assimilationist Bias in Equal Protection: The Visibility Presumption and the Case of "Don't Ask Don't Tell,"* 108 YALE L.J. 485, 493 (1998).

Finally, in thinking about context, think seriously about ramifications and consequences of your proposals. As one eminent legal scholar cautions, "doctrinal articles seem startlingly schizophrenic when they move from diagnosis to prescription."[67] They offer "touchingly naïve strategies for change"[68] that have little chance of implementation or success because they lack the data needed to connect solutions "to the real world consequences of analytic frameworks."[69] An article's proposal therefore needs the same kind of detailed analysis as the discussion of the problem. For example, the expanded role of magistrates in the federal judicial system was the basis of one article's analysis of the threat this presents to separation of powers principles.[70] Nonetheless, the author concedes that a wider variety of tasks could appropriately be delegated to magistrates if the courts apply a test that weighs "the interests of litigants and the judicial system in rapid and effective adjudication against the threat to the integrity of Article III courts."[71] Left there, the solution is so general as to be only minimally helpful. That solution would need to be supported and tested: What factors should be considered and how will their balancing guard against the perceived dangers? Would the balancing of these factors work in a variety of situations? (See Part D on testing a thesis.)

b. Probe the Broader Context

Some decisions are not fully understandable without looking at the historical context in which they arose. For example, in *Minersville School District v. Gobitis*,[72] for example, the Supreme Court held that a pupil, a Jehovah's Witness, was not deprived of due process or religious liberty by a requirement that all students salute the flag in public school. Yet, only three years later, *Gobitis* was overruled in *West Virginia State Board of Education v. Barnette*.[73] To understand *Gobitis* and *Barnette*, you must look into their social and historical context.[74] *Gobitis* was decided in 1940, when Nazi Germany was at its strongest, and America's response was, in part, to increase displays of patriotic behavior like flag salutes. In rejecting the petition of Jehovah's Witnesses in *Gobitis*, the Court unintentionally but tragically branded that sect as unpatriotic. As a result, in the early 1940s, Witnesses were discriminated against and physically brutalized, and the Court soon found itself and its decision criticized by Congress, the ABA, the press, and the lower federal courts.[75] Thus, when *Barnette* overruled *Gobitis* just three years later, the Justices were responding at least in part to political and social unrest. Of course,

67. Rhode, *supra* note 9, at 1342.

68. *Id.*

69. *Id.* at 1340.

70. *See* Brendan Lineham Shannon, Note, *The Federal Magistrates Act: A New Article III Analysis for a New Breed of Judicial Officer*, 33 WM. & MARY L. REV. 253 (1991).

71. *Id.* at 290.

72. Minersville Sch. Dist. v. Gobitis, 310 U.S. 586 (1940).

73. West Virginia State Bd. of Educ. v. Barnette, 319 U.S. 624 (1943).

74. For an interesting analysis of these cases, *see* Robert A. Ferguson, *The Judicial Opinion as Literary Genre*, 2 YALE J.L. & HUMAN. 201 (1990).

75. Heilbrun & Resnik, *supra* note 61, at 1939.

the Court in *Barnette* did not refer to this rampant disapproval, and a reader of only the decision itself would be unaware of the widespread distress that *Gobitis* engendered[76] and mystified by its rapid overruling.

A seminar paper examining the evolution of the collateral consequences of a juvenile offender conviction also provided an historical explanation of developments in the juvenile justice system. Initially, youth were tried as adult offenders, but during the Progressive Era (1900–1918), a period characterized by social reforms like women's suffrage and prohibition, the public demanded a change in juvenile proceedings. The welfare and rehabilitation of the child became as important as the juvenile's guilt or innocence. This attitude began to shift again in the 1980s with the rise of youth gangs, drug wars, and school shootings. "Get tough" measures were enacted, sentences became harsher, and many youth offenders were again tried as adults. As a result, many of the consequences that flow from an adult conviction began to be experienced by juvenile offenders, even though recent research on child development illustrates clear distinctions between youths and adults that justify reducing the impact of the collateral consequences of youth offender convictions and thereby hopefully reducing juvenile recidivism rates.[77] As these two illustrations demonstrate, putting the law in context can clarify ambiguous or anomalous developments and give you something important to write about.

Evolving social mores and ethical norms can also provide essential context out of which a thesis may arise. For example, the Dog and Cat Protection Act [DCPA] of 2000, which makes it illegal to import dog or cat fur products into the U.S., was enacted against the background of a burgeoning animal rights movement. Noting the role of extensive lobbying by that movement, one student comment argues that the DCPA is a poorly conceived statute because a universalist morality like that of the U.S. animal welfare movement is an improper premise for restrictive trade laws in that it results in "coercive economic punishment based on a powerful nation's subjective (and largely hypocritical) disapproval of a weaker nation's [economic needs and moral] norms."[78]

Besides history, sociology, economics, or psychology also illuminate the law and inform its development. For example, behavioral science and criminology studies have explained and documented pedophiles' recidivism rates, and these studies have been used to justify sex offender registration and chemical castration measures. Game theory supported one writer's analysis of the consequences of the proliferation of corporate leniency programs, which grant amnesty to the first cartel conspirator to reveal and confess an antitrust violation. Using the game theory of the prisoner's dilemma, the author demonstrated that the differences be-

76. *Id.* at 1940.

77. *The Evolution of Collateral Consequences for Juvenile Offenders* was written by Jesse Beier, J.D. candidate at St. Thomas School of Law, and is on file with the authors.

78. Gary Miller, Note, *Exporting Morality with Trade Restrictions: The Wrong Path to Animal Rights*, 34 Brook. J. Int'l L. 999, 1043 (2009).

tween countries' leniency programs has increased a conspirator's uncertainty he would secure complete immunity and has thereby undermined the program's deterrent effect by making confession a less attractive option. The author proposed harmonizing programs to avoid this.[79]

Moreover, insights from other disciplines not only have an effect on the substance of law, but there is an increasing body of literature that demonstrates social norms have an impact on compliance and enforcement.[80] For instance, widespread use of marijuana in the 1960s made drug enforcement both difficult and unpopular. In fact, there were events (like Woodstock) where law enforcement turned a blind eye toward drug enforcement. In contrast, widespread disapproval of cigarette smoking in the last decades has led to voluntary compliance with public smoking bans. You may be able to find a thesis by exploring the impact social norms have on compliance and enforcement.

4. EXPERIMENTING WITH FREEWRITING

"The habit of writing thus for my eye only is good practice. It loosens the ligaments.... The main requisite ... is not to play the part of censor, but to write as the mood comes or of anything whatever...."

-Virginia Woolf

"I write to find out what I think."

-John Ashbery

Original theses and arguments are hard to come by. Most of us have to work to achieve them. We have to explore, to experiment, to play with content—often for extended periods of time—before we come up with workable and creative ideas for a paper. Freewriting is a good way to ward off "premature closure"[81] of the brainstorming process.

Freewriting asks you to focus on a topic and to write down, in a stream-of-consciousness mode, whatever comes to mind. In freewriting, you do not worry about how you appear to your reader—you are your only reader. You forget about grammar, style, and spelling. Digressions are fine—sometimes they are even fruitful. Because in the early stages of a project, you freewrite to generate ideas, not final drafts, you should expect these early musings to be wide-ranging and unfocused. Do not worry about this. Released from the distracting habit of editing and amending the text as it is being written, your creative juices may flow.

79. Jason D. Medinger, Comment, *Antitrust Leniency Programs: A Call for Increased Harmonization as Proliferating Programs Undermine Deterrence*, 52 EMORY L.J. 1439 (2003).

80. *See* Benjamin Crouse, Comment, *Worksite Raids and Immigration Norms: A "Sticky" Problem*, 92 MARQ. L. REV. 591 (2009).

81. *See* Lynn Hammond, *Using Focused Freewriting to Promote Critical Thinking*, in NOTHING BEGINS WITH N: NEW INVESTIGATIONS OF FREEWRITING 72 (Pat Belanoff *et al.*, eds. 1991).

That is why it is often helpful to separate the process of generating ideas from the process of perfecting text. So pick up a pen or sit down at the computer, focus on your topic, and begin to write.[82] If you cannot think of anything to say, write that—over and over until another thought comes into your mind. Continue this process for fifteen to forty-five minutes. Usually the simple mandate that you keep on writing regardless of productivity or progress eventually propels you into focusing your thoughts. After several minutes or several pages, valuable comparisons and specific ideas emerge.

Once this has happened, stop writing, reread, and think about your work.[83] Write down any important idea that has emerged. Make guesses about what your first musings were trying to add up to. Note contradictions, implications, questions. Write down any new thoughts you have in response to what you wrote. Then write a sentence or two that summarizes the focus of your first freewriting—whether it be an assertion, a mood, a question. Once you have summed up your first exercise, start writing again. Your second freewriting exercise should take off from the summing up sentence of your first exercise. You can repeat this process until you are satisfied that some profitable ideas have emerged.[84]

Once some ideas and themes have emerged, you may want to undertake more focused types of freewriting. If you are writing a casenote, you could try brainstorming one of the theses listed in Chapter One, Part B(2). Or you could freewrite on specific knotty problems you are confronting. Make lists of every aspect of an issue. Examine these aspects by freewriting from varying points of view. Work up first impressions. Write about the problems you are having writing. Play with words and punning. Encourage analogies and metaphors: a fresh analogy can turn into a thesis. A student who was freewriting on a decision discussed earlier in this chapter, *Board of Education v. Dowell*, began to muse about how *Dowell* would "wipe out" *Brown v. Board of Education*, the landmark school desegregation decision. "Or more accurately," he punned, "*Dowell*—if not a 'black out'—seems to be a *Brown*-out." Eventually his paper come to focus on this power-failure analogy, *Dowell* as the weakening, the dimming, the *Browning*-out, of the earlier decision.

Freewriting can be part of your reading journal. After finishing a text, spend a few minutes freewriting about it. When rereading your journal entries, freewrite about possible connections or disparities between the texts. These raw reactions, these observations, are grist for the mill. For an example of freewriting, see Chapter Four, Part A(1).

82. Invisible writing is a variation on freewriting that you might try if you use a computer for your writing. All it requires is for you to turn off your computer screen so that self-editing becomes impossible. *See* Sheridan Blau, *Thinking and the Liberation of Attention: The Uses of Free and Invisible Writing*, in NOTHING BEGINS WITH N: NEW INVESTIGATIONS OF FREEWRITING 72 (Pat Belanoff *et al*, eds. 1991).

83. *See* PETER ELBOW, WRITING WITHOUT TEACHERS (2nd ed. 1998) (germinal work on freewriting).

84. *Id.* at 19–22.

5. STILL FISHING? FURTHER THOUGHTS

If you have tried all these techniques and you still do not have a thesis, try to figure out why. Perhaps your subject is not really a good fit for you. If so, do not cling to it stubbornly: try again.

Perhaps you feel too much has already been written on the topic. Try listing other authors' theses on the topic and then search for a niche between the previous papers,[85] that is, search for an issue raised but not dwelt upon. One student article on software copyright infringement cases is a good example of "niche" finding. The author realized that copyright law lacked a workable system of definitions of software program parts, although some commentators had noted that a test proposed by Learned Hand in a different context seemed relevant to computer programming. The student author's "niche" was to propose computer program definitions that developed that test to make it useful in software infringement cases.[86] In addition to finding theses in the gaps between articles, as this author did, you might also find issues in the conclusions and the textual footnotes of law review articles. One writer suggests a clever search technique to use in a full-text law review article database to retrieve ideas that writers mention in passing but dismiss as beyond the scope of their articles. For example, if your basic topic was disability law, you might try a query like the following: *interesting or open or intriguing /s issue or question or topic /p "beyond the scope" or "another day" & "americans with disabilities act."*[87]

There is nothing wrong with developing another writer's idea, or putting it in a new context, as long as you give credit to the source of your inspiration. Indeed, some of the most distinguished works of scholarship had just such a beginning. For example, James Boyd White, a well-known law-and-literature scholar, begins an important article by explaining that it was inspired in part by a colleague's lecture.[88]

D. REFINING AND TESTING YOUR THESIS

"The only sure way to avoid making mistakes is to have no new ideas."

-Albert Einstein

Once you have chosen a topic, narrowed it, and found a promising thesis, the next step is to test your thesis—being prepared to modify it, or even discard it. Often when you write—either in stream-of-conscious-

85. *See* Mary B. Ray & Barbara J. Cox, Beyond The Basics: A Text For Advanced Legal Writing 407 (2nd ed. 2003).

86. John W.L. Ogilvie, Comment, *Defining Computer Program Parts Under Learned Hand's Abstractions Test in Software Copyright Infringement Cases*, 91 Mich. L. Rev. 526 (1992).

87. Mary Whisner, *Seeking Inspiration*, 100 Law Libr. J. 773, 777 (2008).

88. James B. White, *Judicial Criticism*, 20 Ga. L. Rev. 835 (1986).

ness mode or in more formal drafts—you experience conceptual breakthroughs like those below, which may commit you to major rethinking.

- In trying to argue X, you become convinced Y is right. It took working through X to appreciate Y.
- In struggling to evaluate the merits of X and Y, you come up with Z, an even better idea.
- In rereading your work, a digression or subpoint takes on sudden significance. You decide this could be the focus of your paper rather than a peripheral point.
- In the middle of writing, you suddenly see what you have been trying to get at.
- In looking over your work, you see your good idea is not good. Some time later, you realize parts of that idea can be salvaged.[89]

Remember that when these conceptual breakthroughs occur, the shortcomings you discover do not mean you necessarily have to abandon your thesis. You may only need to modify it, acknowledging that it may only work in some situations or with some parties. Thus you might amend your first thesis (that bans on non-misleading commercial advertising should be unconstitutional) after you realize that there are appropriate exceptions: when, for example, minors constitute the audience and the product is harmful even if the speech is not misleading—like some fast food advertising. So you refine your thesis: bans on non-misleading commercial advertising should be unconstitutional except when minors are the audience and the product is harmful. Often this kind of refinement renders your thesis more realistic, more practical, and indeed more sophisticated.

Rather than relying on a conceptual light bulb to go on spontaneously, however, it is essential to submit your thesis to a rigorous testing process. One important way to test is to bombard it with hypotheticals, to see whether the solution works in all its likely applications or whether it produces anomalous results or unintended consequences. You should use the facts of decided cases for this trouble-shooting, but be sure to use your imagination as well, inventing a wide range of scenarios. Be thorough; subjecting your thesis to "test suites," as Professor Eugene Volokh calls these hypotheticals, is likely to result in a more nuanced and useful solution.[90] If your initial thesis is the result of the close reading and critical thinking techniques recommended earlier in this chapter, only rarely will you have to throw it out and start over.

Yet surviving even the toughest "test suites" is just one measure of the worth of a solution, because such testing often tells us only how it would fare in an appellate court. Sometimes that will be sufficient, but in

89. Elbow, *supra* note 52, at 36–37.

90. Eugene Volokh, Academic Legal Writing: Law Review Articles, Student Notes, Seminar Papers, and Getting on Law Review, 40–46 (4th ed. 2010). Professor Volokh specifies that test cases should be plausible but challenging, include famous precedents, differ from each other, yield different results, and appeal to different political perspectives. *Id.* at 43–46.

many cases, we can only arrive at a reasoned and useful thesis by going outside of the box, outside of the courtroom, and subjecting our provisional solution to more wide-ranging interrogation. Turn the tables and use the critical-thinking techniques that you used while reading your sources to test your own ideas.[91] One important line of investigation involves identifying the unarticulated assumptions underlying your thesis and testing their soundness. Another good test is to place your thesis in a variety of contexts—to look at it from the point of view of other disciplines within and outside the law and from the perspective of individuals and groups with varying and conflicting interests. You may find that your thesis needs still further modification in light of this testing; you will almost certainly find objections that need answering.

For example, imagine that you have chosen as the subject of your paper a statute that requires leases in low-income housing to include a provision permitting public housing authorities to evict a tenant if "a member of the tenant's household, guest, or other person to whom the tenant has provided access to the premises engages in any drug-related criminal activity on the premises."[92] This statute has been publicized as the "zero-tolerance" "no-fault eviction" law. Your basic thesis is that the strict liability imposed by the statute is unnecessarily harsh. Under its terms, a tenant, Ms. A., was evicted because her grandson sold drugs from her apartment, even though she was unconscious in the hospital at the time and had no way of knowing about his activities. Your solution to the manifest unfairness of such a result is to suggest an amendment to the statute that would provide an exception for a tenant who could show lack of knowledge. This solution would avoid the inequitable result in cases like that of Ms. A., who could certainly have demonstrated lack of knowledge, yet retain the rigor of the original statute by not requiring the landlord to prove lack of knowledge.

Now, you need to trouble-shoot your thesis by using hypotheticals. What if a tenant, Mr. B., suspected that his sister was using drugs, but he let her stay with him, warning her to keep out of the house when he was home from work? Mr. B. would stand a good chance of fitting within the exemption for tenants who can show lack of knowledge. On the other hand, what if a tenant, Ms. C., knew that her son was using and selling drugs in the apartment and she repeatedly confronted him and asked him to stop, to go into treatment, or to get out of her house, but to no avail? Even if she sought help from social service agencies and feared for her safety, she would not fit within the proposed exception for tenants lacking knowledge. From these two hypotheticals alone, it is evident that your thesis is problematic. Mr. B. will avoid eviction because he chooses to turn a blind eye to the problem, while Ms. C. will be evicted despite

91. The questions suggested in sections C(2)(a) above provide some starting points for questioning your thesis.

92. This example is based on the Public and Assisted Housing Drug Elimination Act, 42 U.S.C. § 1101–1195 (2003). The analysis that follows is adapted from a student law review article. *See* Peter Saghir, Note, *Home is Where the No-Fault Eviction Is: The Impact of the Drug War on Families in Public Housing*, 12 J.L. & Pol'y 369 (2003).

good faith efforts to deal with the problem; your effort to remedy unfairness of one sort seems to result in unfairness of another sort. Yet the thesis can be modified to exclude tenants who didn't know but should have, and to include tenants who knew and did what they could to remedy the problem. You revise your proposed statutory exception so that it applies to tenants who "did not know of the criminal drug activity, could not reasonably have known about it, or who knew but took all reasonable steps to prevent it."

At this point, you have devised an equitable statutory solution, an "innocent tenant" defense to an eviction action. Yet there is still more testing needed. What unspoken assumptions underlie this thesis? For one, it assumes that the tenant will litigate rather than simply submit to eviction. For another, it assumes that the tenant will have counsel who will explain the statute and put on a defense, and that if the tenant loses in trial court, the tenant will appeal, represented by appellate counsel. For yet another, it assumes that the legislature will be open to an amendment that will appear to many to signal a retreat in the "war on drugs," and that the affected tenants have the political savvy and clout to lobby for such a change successfully. The doubtfulness of all of these assumptions means that your thesis, sound as far as it goes, needs to be qualified, modified, defended, and supplemented. One useful addition would be to provide counsel for tenants facing eviction under the statute—yet this modification itself assumes that funding can be found.

Examining our thesis from other perspectives and in light of other disciplines can also help to refine it. For example, it is illuminating to get beyond the fundamental-fairness due process perspective that has informed our thinking about the problem so far and look at the strict-liability eviction provision from the perspective of contract law. Since tenants in public housing have no bargaining power, their choice is usually between signing a lease with the "no-fault" eviction clause or homelessness; under these circumstances, the provision is arguably part of a contract of adhesion, and thus, an unconscionable provision in an unconscionable lease. Further, from the criminologist's perspective, you might ask whether the eviction of even the most acquiescent tenant is an effective way to fight the drug war, although from the law-abiding tenant's perspective, it would clearly improve the quality of life in public housing. You might also consider the insights of psychologists and sociologists on the effect on families of the eviction provision, with or without an "innocent tenant" exception.

Now, after scrutinizing your thesis from many angles, you are close to finding a nuanced and realistic proposal for a complicated problem. You decide to argue as follows. "The 'no-fault' eviction statute is of doubtful usefulness and conscionability, but because of political considerations, it is unlikely to go away anytime soon. The worst effects of the eviction provision could be somewhat mitigated by amending the statute to create an 'innocent tenant' exception and automatic access to legal assistance for tenants threatened with eviction under the statute. Such an amendment would require community organizing and energetic lobbying by tenants and their advocates, who could base their arguments on the findings of criminologists and psychologists with respect to the minimal efficacy and deleterious effects of the current statute."

Finally, if you have a provisional thesis but are just not satisfied that it works (or even if you think it does work), there is one last strategy, perhaps the most agreeable of all: take a rest.[93] When writers take time away from an intellectual problem, even as little as half an hour, a process of "incubation" takes place and they often come back to the problem with a stronger solution. The explanation for this phenomenon seems to be that writers tend to formulate a thesis and then try to fit all subsequently learned information into it. When this does not work, progress seems blocked. But if they take some time off (but not so much that the problem goes stale), they forget or abandon the ineffective parts of their thesis and are able to revise it to fit the new information.[94] One practical reason for starting your paper early, then, is that instead of panicky wheel-spinning when you are stuck in the mud, you can take a relaxing break by the side of the road while your car gets itself out of the rut.

FURTHER READING

PETER ELBOW, WRITING WITHOUT TEACHERS (Oxford University Press, 2nd ed. 1998); WRITING WITH POWER: TECHNIQUES FOR MASTERING THE WRITING PROCESS (Oxford University Press, 2nd ed. 1998).

ELIZABETH FAJANS & MARY R. FALK, *Comments Worth Making: Supervising Scholarly Writing in Law School*, 46 J. LEGAL EDUC. 342 (1996).

ROBERT L. FERGUSON, *The Judicial Opinion As Literary Genre*, 2 YALE J.L. & HUMAN. 201 (1990).

CAROLYN HEILBRUN, & JUDITH RESNIK, *Convergences: Law, Literature, & Feminism*, 99 YALE L.J. 1913 (1990).

BAILEY KUKLIN & JEFFREY W. STEMPEL, FOUNDATIONS OF THE LAW: AN INTERDISCIPLINARY AND JURISPRUDENTIAL PRIMER (West 1994).

ROBERT A. LEFLAR, *Honest Judicial Opinions*, 74 NW. U. L. REV. 721 (1979).

EUGENE VOLOKH, ACADEMIC LEGAL WRITING: LAW REVIEW ARTICLES, STUDENT NOTES, SEMINAR PAPERS, AND GETTING ON LAW REVIEW (Foundation Press, 4th ed. 2010).

JAMES BOYD WHITE, *Judicial Criticism*, 20 GA. L. REV. 835 (1986).

93. On January 22, 2004, the BBC reported a study showing that "because the brain appears to restructure information from the previous day during sleep hours, a period of sleep may produce insights into problems...." *at* http://news.bbc.co.uk/go/pr/fr/-/hi/health/3418017.stm.

94. *See* FLOWER, *supra* note 17, at 77–78.

Chapter Three

THE MOSTLY RESEARCH STAGE

"[R]esearch requires the poetic quality of the imagination that sees significance and relation where others are indifferent or find unrelatedness; the synthetic quality of fusing items theretofore in isolation; above all, the prophetic quality of piercing the future by knowing what questions to put and what directions to give to inquiry."

-Felix Frankfurter

At the heart of the research process there is a chicken-or-the-egg problem: you need a thesis to focus your research, but you cannot focus your thesis without doing research. Yet the problem is only insoluble if we consider inspiration, research, and writing as separable stages of the critical writing process. In fact, the three do not follow in order like the chapters of this book. Rather, the process of critical writing is complex, more like an upward spiral than a straight line. The sequence research-reading-reflection-writing may repeat itself again and again before you have finished your paper.

Yet we can say that there is a part of the process that involves *more* brainstorming than researching and writing, and call that the inspiration stage. Similarly, we can identify a stage that is mostly research, and one that is mostly writing. Thus, it is to the "mostly research" stage that this chapter is addressed, just as the preceding chapter is addressed to the "mostly inspiration" stage and the succeeding chapters address the "mostly writing" stages.

The mostly research stage itself has two major components: gathering information and then making it your own through close reading and meticulous note-taking. In general, the process starts with the acquisition of a general overview, often achieved by browsing and skimming, then moves to a compilation of relevant materials, and culminates in critical reading and note-taking. However, it is unrealistic to expect that you can gather all your materials and later work your way through the stack of books, photocopies, and printouts. If you confine your reading in the early stages of research to browsing and skimming, you cannot adequately focus your thesis and direct your subsequent research. Even the first stages must include some close reading and critical reflection.

Thus, although the two following sections of this chapter deal separately with gathering and assimilating information, you should bear in mind that the two are not truly discrete stages. You should also note that the section on gathering information assumes that you have a general familiarity with the methods and materials of legal research. It also assumes basic knowledge of Internet resources and search techniques.

A. GATHERING INFORMATION

Just as there is no one infallible strategy for retrieving the case law and statutory authorities that govern a client's problem, so there is no one surefire way to research your seminar paper or law review article. An effective strategy is always the function of two variables: your subject matter and your own personal style. There are, however, some sound general principles: ask someone, start with secondary authority, be a savvy user of the Internet, and stay current throughout the process of writing your paper or article. In addition, there is one absolute rule: be thorough.[1]

1. BE THOROUGH

The goal of your scholarly research is to develop, document, and support a new and plausible thesis about some aspect of the law. Thus, your "mostly research" stage is not complete until you are *certain* that no one has said precisely what you want to say, and until you can demonstrate your thesis convincingly against a carefully documented background. Until you reach this stage, you should not begin your first full draft, though this shouldn't stop you from sketching out your ideas as soon as you sense you have read the most important pieces—the ones that seem to be framing the issue. Of course, it may also happen that in the course of writing this draft, ideas will surface that send you back to the library, but this writing stage of supplemental research will usually be brief.

It is easy to urge thoroughness, but difficult to explain how a writer knows how much research is enough. Of course, so long as you continue to find new and relevant material, you must continue. When you find the same materials no matter where you look, however, it is time to wind down your search. For instance, when full-text searches, citators, *American Law Reports* (A.L.R.) annotations, and key-number searches on Westlaw have retrieved the same cases, it is respectable to quit; when

1. The authors wish to thank their Brooklyn Law School colleagues Victoria Szymczak, Library Director; and Kathy Darvil, Reference Librarian, for their help with this section on "Gathering Information."

more and more effort yields less and less result, the research stage is complete.

You should remember, however, that as with practice-oriented research, a search of just one source, no matter how vast, or a search that uses just one method is never sufficient, no matter how successful in itself. Internet searches can be particularly treacherous in this respect. Although a well-formulated Boolean or natural language search may retrieve *only* materials on point, this type of search or query can never be guaranteed to find *all* of the relevant documents. By the same token, topical searches, whether in print or online, are also fallible because the indexers' categorization of sources may be erroneous or the categories themselves may be archaic. Thus, word searching should always be supplemented by topical searching, and vice versa.

A careful search of legal periodicals is of course crucial to any scholarly enterprise, not least of all to ensure that your thesis has not been "pre-empted" by another writer's work. One good way to gauge the thoroughness of your search of legal periodicals is to browse through the footnotes of the articles you have found. When you no longer find relevant new articles cited and are confident your ideas are original, you may be ready to move on, especially if you have found some very recent articles.

One good way to identify relevant articles is to use an index. An index is preferred to a full-text database of articles because it is more up-to-date and covers a wider range of titles. The main indexes to legal periodical literature are the *Current Law Index* and the *Index to Legal Periodicals and Books*. Both exist in print and online, but neither includes the most recent eight weeks of legal publications. To search the most current two months you can access the *Current Index to Legal Periodicals,* an online subscription service available at most law schools. Also recommended is the free Washington and Lee *Current Law Journal Content* database at http://lawlib.wlu.edu/CLJC. The *Current Law Journal Content* database has the widest coverage of the indexes and is the most current, but does not include articles published prior to 2005.

An index may not link you to the full text of an article, however. There are full-text article databases where you can retrieve an article found through an index. You can also try using a keyword search in a full text database if your index searches were unsuccessful. Although Lexis and Westlaw have full-text journal databases that are quite current, they are incomplete and not in PDF form. Many scholars prefer to download their articles in PDF format from the Hein Online database, which contains most law journals published in the United States since 1789; however, Hein Online does not contain the most current issues. You can retrieve these issues in print or from the journals' web sites.

Another good resource is Google Scholar (http://scholar.google.com), which allows you to search scholarly literature across multiple disciplines, including legal periodicals. It indexes most journals produced by American law schools since their publication began, and also indexes articles posted on the Legal Scholarship Network at the Social Science Research Network (http://www.ssrn.com), a database where scholars from many disciplines post their working papers and pre-publication versions of their published articles. Although Google Scholar is a convenient and effective tool to find articles, it is not comprehensive and often excludes law journals published during the current year.

You should bear in mind, however, that a thorough search of legal periodicals is not only one of the most crucial, but also one of the most tedious and time-consuming of research tasks. If you attempt to do all of your periodical research in one sitting, or even in one day, you may well burn out, and compromise the thoroughness of your research. As suggested above, it is always a good idea to vary your research tasks—but when consulting indexes, variety is a real necessity. For instance, when you find a reference to an article that interests you, note down where you left off your index search, find the article, and read it. Besides relieving the tedium, alternating pure search with serious reading can suggest new directions for the search itself.

Finally, in order to be thorough, you must be patient. The literature of the law is vast; reported decisions number in the many millions. If you bog down, just take a break, ask for help, and persevere.

2. ASK SOMEONE

The best way to find that leading case or article is often just to ask. The experienced researcher's first question is "Who would have reason to know about this?" Professors are a good source of start-up information, and so are practitioners. Most reported decisions include the name of the attorneys who litigated the case. A telephone call to one or both attorneys can be a very fruitful first step, especially if you are writing a casenote. Since most people respond favorably to sincere expressions of interest in their work, you may well find yourself rewarded by a discussion of the case and copies of the briefs. You can also find contacts by monitoring the blogosphere as described below. Authors on the blogs include their email contact information.

Librarians are also great sources of information. In this information age, the methods and materials of legal research are constantly evolving. Librarians are in touch with the latest technology and know what is available to you on your library shelves or online and how to obtain materials from other sources. If you are stumped, and your research text does not help, ask a librarian, nicely. Finally, both LEXIS and WESTLAW have "800" numbers staffed by experts in online research.

3. START WITH SECONDARY SOURCES

An experienced researcher's first step is always to see whether someone else has already compiled and summarized the information. When personal contacts do not find that expert, the next logical step is to consult secondary sources. Using digests or online full-text searches in a quest for primary sources is normally the last resort.

In the first year of law school, legal research instruction often focuses on finding case law and statutes in reporters and codes, using digests, citators, and the online services. This focus is appropriate to the first year, first of all because it recognizes that reporters and codes are indeed where the law lives. The first-year emphasis on unmediated access to primary sources is also a practical necessity, because researching through digests, citators, and full-text searches is a complex process unique to the law. In contrast, access to secondary sources—traditionally through indexes—is relatively simple once you gain some familiarity with the language of the law.

Yet the emphasis on primary sources has an unfortunate result: approaching their first scholarly paper, students often waste precious time and enthusiasm by logging onto Lexis or Westlaw and doing natural-language searches in caselaw databases, retrieving huge numbers of cases—off-point, on-point, and everywhere in between—that must be browsed and synthesized. The easier and better way is to start with secondary sources, which will provide helpful overviews of the subject, a range of ideas about it, and compilations of primary sources. *Which* secondary source you begin with will depend on your subject, and also on your own preference. Some researchers look first to a looseleaf service for an up-to-the-minute capsule report; others look to treatises or to A.L.R. for objective overviews and up-dated case compilations; still others look to law reviews for the intellectual stimulation provided by a broad spectrum of opinion. Law review articles are also a good source of case compilations—but since law reviews are not updated, you may have to find the most recent cases yourself.

In general, periodicals are a good place to start when identifying trends in the law or tracking policy issues. In addition, there are two other major sources of information about virtually every aspect of our society: the state and federal governments and various trade, professional, and other special interest organizations. Consulting these resources gives you access to reports, statistics, and other types of publications written by experts in the field. Among the many useful government resources, GPOAccess (http://www.gpoaccess.gov) is highly recommended. At this website, you can find the United States Government Manual (http://www.gpoaccess.gov/gmanual/index.html), which helps you identify relevant federal agencies that produce publications on their area of specialty; reports issued by the Government Accountability Office, which monitors and reports on government activities (http://www.gpoaccess.gov/gaoreports/index.html); and the catalog of government publications, which allows you to search for publications from every sector of the federal government (http://catalog.gpo.gov/F).

You would also be well served to review Congressional Research Reports, which are prepared by the research division of the Library of Congress for Congressional members. A single collection of these reports does not exist, but a large collection of them can be searched and downloaded for free at the Open CRS Network (http://www.opencrs.com) and the Thurgood Marshall Law Library, University of Maryland (http://

www.law.umaryland.edu/marshall/crsreports/index.html) Finally, the U.S. government compiles copious amounts of data and makes it available via the Statistical Abstract of the United States (http://www.fedstats.gov).

In addition to government publications, reports and surveys are produced by trade associations, think tanks, advocacy, nongovernmental and not-for-profit organizations. You can identify them by using resources such as the Encyclopedia of Associations, or by using one of the web-based directories indexed by the University of Michigan Political Science department at http://staff.lib.msu.edu/harris23/govdocs/ttanks.htm.

Since most topics concern new trends in the law, one good place to start your secondary source research may well be with law-related blogs hosted by legal experts. The Law Professor Blog site (http://www.lawprofessorblogs.com), Blawg.com (http://www.blawg.com) and Lex Monitor (http://www.lexmonitor.com) are good resources to identify blogs by practice area. By the same token, some sources are inappropriate starting places if your topic is new or timely. In general, digests and encyclopedias are bad places to begin, because their indexes were formulated a long time ago and do not always adequately describe the current shape of the law.

For most topics, whether purely legal or interdisciplinary, it is a good idea to consult your library's catalogue of books; you may well find valuable material that is not available online. Indeed, you should look even beyond your own library. WorldCat (http://www.worldcat.org) is an excellent resource in this respect, providing not only information about sources that may be of value to you, but also inter-library loan capability. You should, however, be aware that inter-library loans are not instantaneous: books often are sent great distances. So don't wait until the last minute!

Although secondary sources are almost always the best places to gain an overview of a subject and begin the compilation of other sources, you must always read and evaluate those other sources for yourself. Always resist the temptation to go along with a commentator's analysis rather than forming your own views from a careful consideration of the evidence since the writers and compilers of secondary sources are human too, and thus biased and fallible. Thus, you should maintain your independence of judgment, and always test compilations of primary sources to be sure that no relevant document escaped the compiler.[2]

There is just one general exception to the rule that secondary sources are the best place to begin: if you are writing a casenote or a seminar paper that focuses on one case, you should begin by reading it and any lower court opinions and then finding and reading critically

2. Of course, if you decide to borrow an idea from a secondary source, or if you use a body of caselaw compiled by another writer, you must acknowledge your source in an attribution footnote. For more on the ethical use of borrowed materials, see Chapter Six.

every authority cited in your case, whether binding or persuasive, primary or secondary. The direction of your research will inevitably become clear from close study of your case and all of the authority cited by the court—indeed, the court's use of precedent may well provide you with a thesis. Moreover, by starting this way, and recording your own reactions as you read, you may be better able to resist easy acquiescence to the views of other writers.

4. BE A SAVVY INTERNET USER

As part of the research process, you will almost certainly take your Internet research beyond the major subscription research tools like Lexis and Westlaw. There is an ever-expanding universe of information available on almost every conceivable subject. In addition to the types of resources already described in this chapter, Google Books (http://books.google.com) and the Internet Archive (http://www.archive.org) offer access to full text books across multiple disciplines. But in order to make the best use of the Internet, you need to be an educated consumer. You will not always find the best analysis or commentary on a free website. As a scholar, you want to use only information that is relevant, reliable, and current. Before you rely on a source, keep the following tips in mind.

First, try to identify the web resource by searching your library's catalog or visiting on one of the large, law school gateways to the law such as Cornell University's Legal Information Institute (http://www.law.cornell.edu), Washlaw Web at the Washburn School of Law (http://www.washlaw.edu), or the Georgetown Law Library Research Guides at http://www.ll.georgetown.edu. The benefit of using one these types of tools is that the resources have already been evaluated by the professional librarians and professors at these institutions.

If you are not going to a recommended website, you will need to make your own evaluation regarding the information presented. Some questions to ask yourself include: Is the author a known expert on the topic? Does the author have a biased position on the topic? When was it published? Can you verify the information in other sources? When you find information that seems relevant and credible, be sure that you print out every page to which you intend to refer: even the most stable, reliable website is ultimately ephemeral. You should provide copies of printouts for all electronic sources when you submit your draft to your editor or professor.

Try to resist the temptation to do absolutely all of your research on the Internet. Legal scholarship still favors citation to print sources—because websites are ephemeral and because, as noted above, their content is subject to little or no review. Moreover, there is still reliable and authoritative information that is only available in print. Finally, conducting all of your research on the Internet has another real disadvantage if you concentrate too heavily on Boolean searching, because this research process restricts the terms of the debate, and thus, your thinking. Browsing library bookshelves or a book of essays is often more congenial to the lateral thinking that produces "aha!" moments.[3]

5. STAY CURRENT

But beware: all of your hard work may be in vain unless you keep your research current not just in this "mostly research stage," but during the entire process of writing your article or paper—as you assimilate information, during the drafting and revising stages, and right down to the final proofing and polishing stage. If you stay aware of the most recent developments—judicial decisions, legislation, executive action, new articles—affecting your topic, you will almost always be able to avoid mootness or preemption by altering your focus. Keep up to date on law review articles with the resources mentioned above in "Be Thorough." Keep up to date on cases, statutes, and regulations by using an online tracking service like Lexis Alerts or West's Alert Center. Read specialized blogs to stay current on the scholarly conversation in your area of interest. Finally, still other good tracking tools are legal news sources like Jurist (http://jurist.law.pitt.edu), and reporting services from publishers such as BNA (whether United States Law Week or BNA's more specialized services like the Criminal Law Reporter or Products Liability Reporter).

B. ASSIMILATING INFORMATION

Research, no matter how exhaustive, is useless unless you make it your own by critical reading, careful note-taking, and logical organization of your notes. Chapter Two discusses techniques of close and critical reading as an aid to the process of inspiration. Yet once you have found and researched your thesis, those same techniques will help you make intelligent and original use of the fruits of the research stage. Although material that is tangential or duplicative may be skimmed or browsed, any text with a real bearing on your thesis, or which provides essential background, must be read with a critical eye and more than once.

By now, you have developed your own style of note-taking and case-briefing. Yet your topic may well require you to read complex material concerning new areas and new concepts, and to that extent, you will need some new strategies. Because we use what we already know about a topic or discipline to learn more about it, starting in new areas is always difficult.[4] One guide to scholarly writing suggests some strategies for reading dense and unfamiliar material such as law review articles. First, begin by "pre-reading"—read the first paragraph, table of contents or headings, and the last paragraph. Then read the whole text twice or even

3. *See* Colin P.A. Jones, *Unusual Citings: Some Thoughts on Legal Scholarship*, 11 J. Legal Writing 377 (2005) ("Because what we know is infinitely less than what we do not, serendipity is a highly underrated force ... in expanding that knowledge.... Yet by reliance on technology that works primarily through ... searches using specific search terms, we limit ourselves to the knowledge from which such keywords are derived.").

4. Andrew P. Johnson, A Short Guide to Academic Writing 9 (2003).

three times. The first time, make yourself read quickly, despite comprehension difficulties, to try to catch the flow of ideas. Put a dot in the margin next to what seem the most important ideas. On the second reading, go more slowly, using a highlighter on the key passages,[5] being careful not to end up with whole pages of highlighted text. Finally, read the text again, taking detailed notes, using headings to retain the logical structure.[6] As you proceed, evaluate the writer's reasoning: don't just paraphrase and summarize. Apply critical thinking precepts in your note-taking by

- focusing on the author's *purpose*;
- focusing on the key *question* which the written piece answers;
- focusing on the most important *information* presented by the author;
- focusing on the most fundamental *concepts* which are at the heart of the authors' reasoning;
- focusing on the author's *assumptions*;
- focusing on the most important *inferences* or conclusions in the written piece;
- focusing on the author's *point of view*; and
- focusing on *implications*.[7]

In addition to being informed by critical thinking, your notes on important sources should ideally be so complete, and quoted so accurately, that you can write your first draft without recourse to the originals. In particular, you can save yourself last-minute frenzy by including complete citation and bibliographical information in correct Bluebook or ALWD form in your notes. (Of course, checking for accuracy is an important part of the polishing process and essential to ensuring proper acknowledgment of borrowed material.) If, being human, you fall down on the job, you can safely admit it to your notes: "skimmed pp. 125–183, need better notes."

Finding the best note-taking format is essential, too. Because good notes of important sources are not just paraphrase, but include generous portions of quotation and reflection, index cards are not very helpful: even the large ones may be too small for comprehensive note-taking. Notebooks or yellow pads perforated at top or sides are useful: you can take notes on a variety of sources, then tear off the pages and file them. Three-ring binders are very helpful here. You might begin by filing your notes according to the *type* of source: e.g. judicial opinions, law review articles, treatises. As you begin to see patterns and basic ideas emerging, you could put stick-on notes on the pages to make retrieval easier. You

5. If the book doesn't belong to you, copy the key passages verbatim instead.

6. *See* JOHNSON, *supra* note 4, at 10.

7. RICHARD PAUL & LINDA ELDER, A MINIATURE GUIDE FOR STUDENTS ON HOW TO STUDY & LEARN A NEW DISCIPLINE USING CRITICAL THINKING CONCEPTS & TOOLS 32 (2001). For a more detailed description of these critical thinking precepts, see Chapter Two, Part B(1)(a).

could also then refile your notes by issue. Finally, as your ideas become still more focused, you could use stick-ons again and refile again.

Good notes not only include your own reactions to the text, but also distinguish between your own ideas and what you have read. You might adopt the reading-journal style described in Chapter Two, Part C(1), using one side of the page for the author's ideas or the court's reasoning and one side for your own assessment of the text and your own ideas on the subject matter, or using a different font or color for your ideas. Or you might simply preface your own reflections by your initials. In any event, distinction between self and text will ensure that the ideas put forward as your own are indeed your own and that sources are properly credited.

However, your comprehensive and carefully attributed notes will be of limited use unless you organize them. The best organization tracks your thesis. You should develop your own categories from the moment your thesis begins to take shape—assigning primary and secondary sources to issues, noting where you might want to use that source. When your research is nearly complete, it may be helpful to spread out your notes so that you can see them all at a glance. If you have taken notes on your computer, print them all up. Then start moving your notes into the appropriate categories. If one source is useful in more than one category, make sure you have a sheet in each pile referring you to that source. Of course, you may need to revise or fine-tune as your ideas take a more definite shape.

There is one final, simple strategy for effectively assimilating your reading, though it may be the most difficult to implement: relax. We absorb information and use it most creatively when we are relaxed. Anxiety and stress interfere with the ''frictionless flow'' of knowledge in our heads.[8] The best way to cut down on anxiety is to start well before the paper is due. Try to read and take notes in a pleasant, quiet place with few distractions. Working in a study room full of stressed-out law students, even your best friends, may not be a good idea. If you feel yourself tensing up, try some deep breathing.[9]

FURTHER READING

J.D.S. Armstrong & Christopher A. Knott, Where the Law Is: An Introduction to Advanced Legal Research (West, 3rd ed. 2009).

Robert C. Berring & Elizabeth A. Edinger, Finding The Law (West, 12th ed. 2005).

Christina L. Kunz et al., The Process Of Legal Research (Aspen, 7th ed. 2008).

8. Johnson, *supra* note 4, at 11.

9. *Id.*

Chapter Four

THE WRITING PROCESS: GETTING IT DOWN ON PAPER

"Those who plan to relax until their creative inspiration seizes them may have a long uninterrupted rest."

-John R. Hayes

After choosing a subject and developing a thesis, the hardest part of any writing project is beginning it. Red Smith, a well-known sports writer, reportedly said: "Writing? Nothing to it. Just sit down at your typewriter and open a vein." Although many can appreciate this sentiment, such dire strategies have an untoward finality.

Beginning is hard because, even if we have some idea of what we want to say before we start, our thoughts are often in rich disarray. The order in which information is retrieved and ideas occur is all too often not a logical order. Somehow we must wrest an outline out of our research and brainstorming activities and impose order on what is anarchy. Sometimes this order does not come until we have meandered through several drafts, during which process we find out what we actually know and think about a subject.

Some writers, however, are made anxious by this freewheeling process and find they cannot write at all without some kind of outline. These writers may panic if their research and prewriting thinking do not crystalize into an organizational scheme. Still other writers have such high standards that they discard any draft that is not logically organized, thoroughly and creatively argued, and fluidly written. But because the details—the "nitty gritty"—of most arguments emerge only in the writing of them, because many points need refining as we realize logic or evidence does not fully bear them out, such perfectionists are likely to feel doomed early on.

Nonetheless, the early stages of writing become a lot more bearable if we lower our expectations for rough drafts—if we accept that writing is a time-consuming process and that papers, like people, mature slowly. The thing to keep in mind is that your first task is to get your ideas out on the table, that is to say, down on paper. Your second task, fleshing out those ideas and putting them in an order and prose your reader will find logical and compelling, is something you can work toward. Organization and readability can be achieved in stages and through a variety of tactics and techniques. This chapter and the next will describe some of those tactics and techniques.

A. WORKING TOWARD AN OUTLINE

If you have a good grasp on your thesis and the types of arguments you plan to make, you may find it easy and profitable to play with the traditional organizational structure of casenotes and comments and with classic organizational paradigms. (See Part B.) Simple adaptation of organizational schemes will not work for you, however, if you are at an earlier stage—still forging new concepts, synthesizing material, or weeding primary ideas from secondary ideas. Instead you may need to build slowly to an outline, by writing a statement of purpose or a "dump" or "zero" draft, making lists, or drawing diagrams. Sometimes it is helpful to use all four techniques.

1. WORKING ON A STATEMENT OF PURPOSE

Once you have chosen a topic, gathered information, and found a thesis, you are ready—or almost ready—to write. Before you begin, it may be helpful to draft a statement of purpose in order to focus your mind. This is a paragraph that articulates what you aim to do in the paper and that explores how you intend to do it, that is, explores what your organizational options are. A statement of purpose, like freewriting or the zero drafts discussed below, is often written almost as if the writer is thinking out loud.

> The statute permitting public housing authorities to evict a tenant who has provided access to a person who engages in

drug-related criminal activity on the premises is too harsh. A better solution is an "innocent tenant" exception. But how should I organize this discussion? I guess I should first explain the problems of the current statute and then the virtues of the proposed solution. But what about the limitations of the proposed solution? And I need a section on how to overcome the limitations. Okay, so I'll start by arguing that the "no-fault" eviction statute is unfair but because of political considerations is here to stay (this seems like a 2 part discussion). Then I'll explain how the innocent tenant exception mitigates the worst effects of the statute, but that it will be hard to pass for x, y, and z reasons (again 2 parts). Then I'll move on to argue that the feasibility of the solution depends on a, b, and c being done. Yes, that seems like an okay bare-bones structure.

2. FREEWRITING "DUMP" OR "ZERO" DRAFTS

In Chapter Two, we recommended freewriting as a method for generating theses through uncensored but sustained free-association on a topic. Many writers also regard freewriting as a good way to generate an outline and first draft. This kind of freewriting is often called a "dump" draft[1] or "zero" draft[2] (as opposed to a first draft) because it remains that kind of private, exploratory, expressive writing that we would be reluctant to submit to another's scrutiny.

Dump or zero drafts require you to dump on the page every thought you have about your thesis and topic without regard for order, grammar, or brilliance. You can free-associate, summarize material, quote phrases you remember, make lists. Your freewriting might look something like the one that follows, a student's meditations on *Doe v. Taylor*,[3] a case in which the Fifth Circuit Court of Appeals ruled that the state had an affirmative duty to protect a fifteen-year-old public-school student from sexual molestation by her teacher because compulsory school attendance laws create a special relationship by giving the school functional custody of the student.

1. MARY B. RAY & BARBARA J. COX, BEYOND THE BASICS: A TEXT FOR ADVANCED LEGAL WRITING 12 (2nd ed. 2003).

2. Jill N. Burkland & Bruce T. Petersen, *An Integrative Approach to Research: Theory and Practice*, in CONVERGENCES: TRANSACTIONS IN READING AND WRITING 199 (Bruce T. Petersen ed., 1986).

3. Doe v. Taylor Indep. Sch. Dist., 975 F.2d 137 (5th Cir. 1992).

Freewriting

Case is important because it departs from DeShaney [State has no constitutional duty to protect child from abuse by father after it received reports of abuse when child not in its custody] and embraces a custody analysis.

To a feminist, important because imposes liability for sexual abuse and harassment in schools. What are the implications given the plaintiff is a young woman, a high school student...not a child?

Has social pressure dictated the decision? Outrage over DeShaney. Also sexual harassment is a hot topic...Anita Hill. Plus backlash over reproductive rights for the less empowered. Or is Doe premised on statutory rape assumptions? The chastity & innocence of young women. Or just of a child, not a young woman. In an attempt to right the wrong of DeShaney, does Doe fail because it is a pervasive intrusion into the lives of H.S. students? Was this an affair or an assault?

What is interesting to me in Doe is the concept of the state protecting those incapable of protecting themselves b/c a custodial relationship exists. This is a 15-year-old young woman. Is she incapable? Is the situation out of her control? What are we protecting her from? sex? sexual harassment? Consequences of rejecting a teacher? The denial of a sound educational environment? Bodily integrity? The imagery in Doe conjures up five-year-olds and the mentally retarded being tied up in chairs and fondled. It seems different here, given that Jane snuck out of the house to meet her "molester" and lied to protect him—but the result is the same, being that the school has a duty to protect five-year-olds, as well as the fifteen-year-olds having sex with the biology teacher. (cont.)

One law review article says that a student's consent to a sexual relationship with a teacher is inherently suspect and legally ineffective because of the coercive power imbalance. Thus age or maturity of a student is not determinative. Do I believe this? Believe in the presumption of coercion? Is this better than the custody analysis?

The helplessness analysis has backfired in women's law before.

- battered women and learned helplessness
- rape : but women are sexual actors, not only victims
- pornography :

Here too the helplessness analysis has pitfalls...women have to show helplessness, a brassy adolescent should not be denied protection from sexual harassment because sexually active.

Court didn't discuss power imbalance. What are the harmful effects? To education? To emotional welfare? To relations with peers? Taboo topics...both the young and their sexuality and student/teacher affairs.

I need to find a way to grant relief, despite a young woman's brazen behavior, and not b/c parents don't want kids to have sex until marriage, or b/c she is unable to help herself or is in school custody. Need grounds that link the problems of fourteen-year-olds to women experiencing gender subordination in daily life. Is Meritor's test [whether the defendant's sexual conduct toward the plaintiff created a "hostile environment"] relevant to Doe's situation? Is it a more empowering analysis?

When your freewriting is finished, you can try to pull an outline out of the draft, or if you prefer, you can undertake the more focused types of freewriting discussed in Chapter Two in an effort to produce actual text for the first draft.

To pull an outline out of a dump draft, you must first comb through the draft spotting and relating points: highlight all ideas that seem profitable, delete the ideas that appear irrelevant, and cross-reference recurring and related themes. When we examine the freewriting we have provided above, for example, we notice that it opens with a misleadingly upbeat initial reaction to the *Doe* decision based on the writer's approval of the result. Yet closer scrutiny makes it clear that the dump draft contains several criticisms of the decision and even a criticism of the writer's own criticism.

- Liability based on functional custody may be appropriate for a grade school child, but a high school student can, at least up to a point, protect herself...a distinction may be needed.
- High school students may well be sexually active...not necessarily passive, not always victims.
- Feminist legal thinking is turning against legal theories based on helplessness.
- Functional custody seems posited on helplessness.
- Student and teacher might be having a love affair...Or is the power imbalance inherently coercive?

Having listed these thoughts, the writer's next step is to try some provisional orderings. Group related points; articulate headings, categories, or unifying principles that encompass details; separate primary and secondary ideas; play with hierarchical orders. In the end, make sure that each division is based on a single principle, that the sum of the parts equals a whole, and that each part is mutually exclusive. Such an exercise resulted in the following tentative outline.

I. Functional custody provides inappropriate grounds for holding school districts liable for sexual molestation under the due process clause because courts must create law that is responsive to women's true experiences.

A. Functional custody is a bright line test. Liability is posited on characterization of young women as passive and dependent.

B. The sexuality of high school students is too complex for a bright line rule.

C. Moreover, the functional custody standard limits understanding of the nature and impact of sexual harassment of students on teachers.

1. It focuses on sexual contact alone.

2. It is insensitive to how the imbalance of power affects other aspects of a teenager's life—like her education and social welfare.

As seen here, freewriting can help you generate an outline. It is also a way to produce actual text. Sometimes, simply by deleting digressions and looping together related points, actual paragraphs emerge. More often, text is generated through freewriting focused on a particular topic. Begin by summarizing in a couple of sentences one of the main ideas in your initial freewriting. Then examine that idea by embarking on further free association. You may, in the end, be able to work these more focused meditations into your first draft with only minor revision. In fact, these passages may have great immediacy and vividness.

3. USING CHARTS AND DIAGRAMS

Some writers find it hard to move directly from dump drafts to outlines. They find graphic representations helpful in gaining perspective on a body of material. Case charts, cluster diagrams[4] and issue trees[5] are three such aids.

a. Case Charts

Sometimes it is hard to get on top of your case law. You have read so much that it is hard to see patterns and trends. To get an overview, try diagramming your cases. The chart that follows organizes the case law on a state's affirmative duty to protect students.

4. *See* LAUREL C. OATES, ANNE ENQUIST & KELLY KUNSCH, THE LEGAL WRITING HANDBOOK 564–565 (4th ed. 2006).

5. *See* LINDA FLOWER, PROBLEM-SOLVING STRATEGIES FOR WRITING, 87–94 (1981).

Cases	Court	Due Process Violation Based On Breach of Affirmative Duty to Protect?	State Deprivation of Liberty to Act Own Behalf?	Abuse by Private or State Actor?	State Knew of Danger?
DeShaney v. Winnebago (1989)	U.S. Sup. Ct.	No	No	Private (father)	Yes
Stoneking v. Bradford (1990)	3rd Cir.	Yes	Yes functional custody [FC] based on Compulsory Attendance Law [CAL]	State (Teacher)	?
Doe v. Taylor (1992)	5th Cir.	Yes	Yes FC = CAL	State (Teacher)	Yes
Yvonne L. v. New Mexico (1992)	10th Cir.	Yes	Yes state ordered foster care	Private	?
Pagana v. Massapequa (1989)	2nd Cir.	Yes	Yes FC = CAL	Private (Other student)	?

b. *Cluster Diagrams*

At times, you may have trouble relating facts to legal issues. Try creating a cluster diagram. Write down some ideas and details and draw lines attaching details to main ideas.

She actively protects teacher by lying, sneaks out to see him

↑

Functional custody test requires students to be dependent →

But Jane is a H.S. student - a teenager, not passive child

↓

But is power imbalance inherently coercive?

↙

Thus court describes Jane as a passive child

c. *Issue Trees*

Once you have a sense of how points relate to each other, you can try drawing an issue tree. Put a primary idea—a broad, inclusive point—at the top of your tree and work down to subpoints. You may find you need to create subheadings that relate and encompass specific details. You may also find some subpoints are actually new issues, separate branches requiring separate discussions.

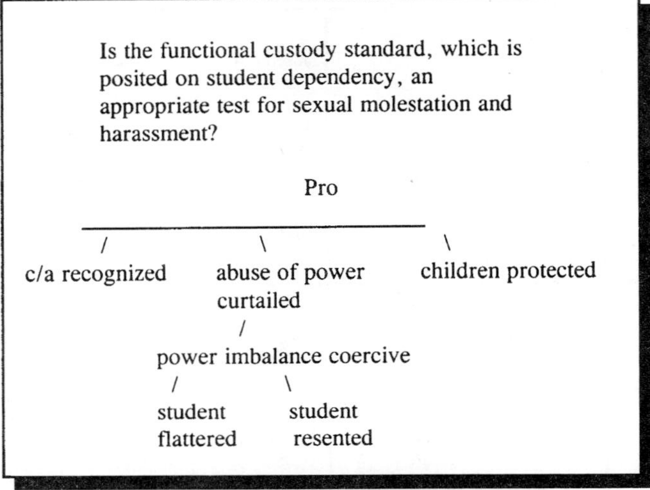

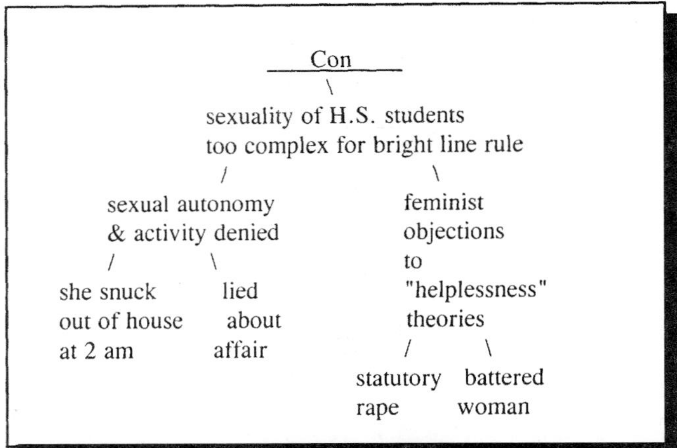

This working tree can then be revised into a hierarchical outline.

I. The result in Doe v. Taylor is correct, but the functional custody test is inappropriate.

A. The decision will have some positive effects on sexual harassment and sexual molestation claims.

1. Cause of action for harassment in schools recognized for the first time.

2. School children are protected.

3. Abuse of power is curtailed.

B. But the decision may have unforeseen negative effects on women's law.

1. The sexual autonomy of high school students is denied.

2. The myth of women's passivity and victimization is continued.

3. The standard is objectionable for the same reasons some feminists reject statutory rape statutes or "learned helplessness" in the Battered Woman's Syndrome defense.

B. CREATING AN OUTLINE

1. ADAPTING THE TRADITIONAL CASENOTE OR COMMENT OUTLINE

The structure of a casenote, a comment, or a seminar paper is essentially the same. At a minimum, all three move from an introduction through background and analysis sections to a conclusion. Only the section called "Statement of the Case" is peculiar to the casenote. Thus, with some modification, law review articles and seminar papers tend to be modeled on the following outline.

Introduction

The introduction establishes context, articulates your thesis, and provides a roadmap.

1. Introduce and note why the topic is important
2. Briefly summarize necessary background information
3. Narrow the topic and state your thesis, typically a problem and solution
4. Convey your organization of the paper

Background

The background section provides a thorough, but focused summary of any material the reader needs to understand the analysis. Often it begins with the genesis of the issue, moves through developments, and ends with the status quo—the current approach or approaches to your topic. You may need several subsections here. We list some typical ones below, but structures differ depending upon the type of article being written.

1. Provide the history of an issue
   a. Provide necessary facts
   b. For each domestic law issue, provide a chronological summary of relevant authorities: constitutional provisions, statutory provisions, common law rules, and decisions construing them
   c. For international law topics, provide a summary of relevant treaties, conventions, and customary international law
   d. For a comparative law topic, provide a discussion of relevant jurisdictional approaches
   e. Provide, as needed, historical, sociological, economic, psychological, or scientific background
2. Summarize policy considerations
3. Summarize relevant secondary sources
4. Report on the status quo: Current state of the issue

Statement of the Case (casenote)

The statement of the case provides a thorough discussion of the court's analysis of the issues relevant to your thesis.

1. Include the relevant facts
2. Include the procedural history
3. Include the court's holding and reasoning at each level, as well as the reasoning of dissenting or concurring opinions

Analysis

Like that of the background section, the structure of the analysis is also dependent on the nature of the topic. In a traditional doctrinal article, you would analyze the legal issue, pose the problem, propose a remedy, and explain why this remedy resolves the problem more effectively than other remedies.

A. For a Problem/Solution Thesis

1. Analyze the problem
   - Explain the advantages and disadvantages of the current approach
   - Explains the reasons for change
2. State your proposal
3. Explain its efficacy
4. Explain the weaknesses of alternative proposals
5. Conclude

B. For an Empirical Research Paper

1. State the purpose of study
2. Outline your methodology
3. Report your findings
4. Analyze your findings
5. Make recommendations (if appropriate)
6. Conclude

Conclusion

1. Summarize problem
2. Summarize proposal
3. Summarize your discussion of the viability and ramifications of the solution
4. Restate conclusion

Although the outline provided above is a step toward a concise and logical exposition, you need not follow it rigorously if your topic or case calls for a different approach. In the end, the issues raised by a particular case or topic should shape not only your analysis, but also your structure. Nonetheless, you may come up with a useful provisional outline if you try plugging the specific content of your topic into a structure like the one above. (See Chapter 5, Part D(1) for an example of an introduction that follows the structure outlined here.) Because an outline consisting of words and phrases is less helpful than one that clearly identifies each point, make sure that your outline is substantive. (See Chapter 5, Part D(3)(a) for examples.)

2. USING PARADIGMS

In shaping your analysis, you may want to borrow from established organizational paradigms when your arguments correspond naturally with them. You may find it helpful to use a general outline in conjunction with basic paradigms.

a. The Problem/Solution Pattern

As seen in the traditional outline of a law review article, the paradigm most common in legal scholarship is the *problem-solution pattern*. This paradigm is useful if, for example, you have identified a problem that you think could be solved by a new rule, exception, or modification.

—Identify and explain the problem

—Announce and explain your solution

—Explain how and why your solution solves problem more effectively than others

To see how this paradigm works in practice, look at the following outline of a student casenote criticizing the Federal Communications Commission's approval of the merger of the only two providers of satellite radio.[6]

Introduction
I. Background and the FCC's Approval
  A. The Applicants
  B. The FCC's Involvement in Satellite Radio
  C. FCC's Review of the Proposed Merger
II. The Mistake of Relying on a Voluntary Price Cap [***PROBLEM***]
  A. Ineffectiveness of the Price Cap
    i. Not All Pricing Elements Were Taken into Account
    ii. Decrease in the Quality of Programming Is a Likely Result
  B. Price Caps are Anti-competitive
  C. The Uncertainty Problem
    1. Definition of an Uncertainty Problem and How It Can Be Remedied
    2. The Price Cap Will Not Resolve the Uncertainty Problem
  D. Conclusion
III. Proposed Policy for Mergers Plagued by Uncertainty
  A. The Flaw of Outright Approval and Rejection Solutions ***[WEAKNESS OF ALTERNATE SOLUTION]***
  B. Proposal: Merger Approval Conditioned Upon Subsequent Ex Post Monitoring & Evaluation [***SOLUTION***]
    1. Rationale
    2. Implementation ***[EFFICACY OF SOLUTION]***
IV. Conclusion

b. Comparative Paradigms

Comparative paradigms arise when you need to justify one choice among competing alternatives and interests, or reject them all in favor of a new approach. A topic that involves, for example, balancing litigants' competing interests or choosing among different policies or jurisdictional approaches lends itself to one of two comparative paradigms.

The *alternating pattern* examines each point in terms of the alternatives.

Thesis Statement

  Point One

    Alternative A

    Alternative B

6. Samuel Gordon, *Are You Sirius? The Mistake of Conditioning Approval of the Sirius–XM Merger on a Price Cap*, BROOK. J. CORP. FIN. & COM. L. 513 (2007).

Point Two

Alternative A

Alternative B

Point Three

Alternative A

Alternative B

Comparison and Evaluation of the Alternatives

The *divided pattern* is organized around the alternatives rather than the points.

Thesis Statement

Alternative A

Point One

Point Two

Point Three

Alternative B

Point One

Point Two

Point Three

Comparison and Evaluation of Alternatives

A divided pattern similar to the one above was used in a law review article on the results of two surveys on workable definitions of pornography.[7]

I. The First Survey on Three Definitions of Pornography
- A. Vagueness
- B. Overbreadth and Underbreadth
- C. Demographic Breakdown of Responses

II. The Second Survey on Three Definitions of Pornography
- A. Vagueness
- B. Overbreadth and Underbreadth
- C. Demographic Breakdown of Responses

7. Adapted from James Lindgren, *Defining Pornography*, 141 U. Pa. L. Rev. 1153, 1154 (1993).

Had the author wished, he could have used the alternating pattern, as follows.

I. Vagueness
  A. The First Survey
  B. The Second Survey
II. Overbreadth and Underbreadth
  A. The First Survey
  B. The Second Survey
III. Demographic Breakdown
  A. The First Survey
  B. The Second Survey

In deciding whether to use a divided or alternating pattern, you should be aware that each of these patterns has its own advantages and disadvantages. The alternating pattern provides for a clear point-by-point assessment of the alternatives, but the larger picture may recede into the background. Thus the alternating pattern often begins or ends with an overview. The divided pattern provides the reader with a good grasp of each alternative but a point-by-point assessment is harder. Thus, the writer using the divided pattern would be wise either to refer back to the first discussion when she gets to the second, or to provide a comparative overview after the alternatives have been discussed. This is what the writer of an article comparing British and American approaches to compelled decryption did, as the outline below shows.[8] Notice also that sometimes one type of organizational paradigm becomes embedded in or follows another and, as they do, your outline grows more complex. For example, in the outline below, a problem/solution paradigm follows a comparative paradigm because the writer wants to show that the current approaches are less satisfactory than the one proposed.

Introduction
I. History & Technical Background of Encryption
  A. History and Background of Encryption
  B. Technical Background
II. The American Approach to Compelled Key Disclosure ***[FIRST APPROACH]***
  A. Fifth Amendment Analysis
  B. *In re Boucher*
III. The British Approach to Compelled Key Disclosure ***[SECOND APPROACH]***
  A. Background of the Regulation of Investigatory Powers Act
  B. RIPA
    1. Section 49
    2. Schedule 2
    3. Section 50
    4. Section 51
    5. Section 53
    6. Section 54

8. Brendan M. Palfreyman, *Lessons from the British and American Approaches to Compelled Decryption*, 75 Brook. L. Rev. 345 (2009),

IV. Criticisms & a Middle Ground
  A. Criticisms of the American & British Approaches ***[COMPARISON AND CRITICISM OF THE TWO APPROACHES—THE PROBLEM]***
  B. Middle Ground ***[THE SOLUTION]***

Conclusion

c. Cause and Effect Pattern

Sometimes you will need to use a *cause and effect pattern*. You may wish to use this pattern to explain the evolution of law, as in the background section, or to predict developments, as in the analysis section.

—Effect [status quo or result] is announced

—Possible causes are suggested

—Evidence is provided showing how causes led to the effect

This paradigm was used in an empirical research article studying the effect of a decision by the Supreme Court widely believed to have tightened the traditionally very liberal federal pleading requirements under Rule 8 of the Rules of Civil Procedure.[9] The author looked to see whether, in the wake of the Court's decision, more complaints were dismissed for failure to state a claim.

Introduction

I. The Historical and Scholarly Context
  A. Prior Supreme Court Precedent
  B. *Twombly*'s Interpretation
  C. The Response in the Literature

II. Methodology

III. Findings ***[EFFECT OF TWOMBLY]***

IV. Explaining the Results
  A. Hypothesis One: *Twombly*'s Hidden Effect ***[HOW CAUSES LED TO EFFECTS]***
  B. Hypothesis Two: Institutional Inertia

Conclusion

C. WRITING THE DRAFT

"The last thing one discovers in writing a book is what to put first."

-Blaise Pascal

The techniques we have described so far are primarily directed to helping you outline your paper. Although some writers never outline, most would probably admit that it is easier to write with an outline than

9. Kendall W. Hannon, *Much Ado About* Twombly*? A Study on the Impact of* Bell Atlantic Corp. v. Twombly *on 12(b)(6) Motions,* 3 NOTRE DAME L. REV. 1811 (2008).

without one. If you have already worked out the large-scale organization of your piece, you do not have to worry about where to go next. This frees you to concentrate more fully on the particulars of the moment, on documenting and wording your contentions.

Once you are ready to sit down and write a full draft, here is another piece of advice: Begin anywhere. Many people labor under the misconception that the right way to write is to begin at the beginning, with the introduction, and to move sequentially through to the conclusion. But there is no real reason to write a document in the order you must eventually present it. In fact, introductions are notoriously difficult to write cold. A moment's reflection makes it obvious that a clear statement of your thesis and organization may be easier to write after the fact than before. Indeed, the habit of writing a draft straight through, without rewriting the introduction, may explain why the theses of so many articles are more clearly stated in the conclusion than in the introduction. Indeed, you may want to make the conclusion of your first draft the introduction to your second.

It is often helpful to write in the order of ease. Is summarizing a decision the easiest thing to do? Write it first. Are you clearer about one point than another? Start there. Not only does your confidence build as your document grows, but a lot of subliminal thinking—a lot of sorting, discarding, and combining—may be occurring as you work on other sections. When you finally get to the thorniest argument, you may find yourself better prepared to handle it. In fact, you may get ideas for that thorny section as you are working on something else. If you do, take the time to scribble them down; otherwise you may lose them. Once you have written enough to jog your memory, return to the section you have been working on.

One problem with "order of ease" writing is that it tends to suffer from poor transitions. When you write out of order, or if you write without an outline, you must take special care to review your work with an eye to organization and smooth, logical connections. Outline your draft after it is done and examine its structure for logical development. Be ruthless about deleting material that appears to be digressive or irrelevant. This may be hard to do—writers often find it wrenching to discard material they have worked long and hard to create. To overcome this impediment, one writer recommends a psychological trick he calls the bone pile.[10] He cuts out all the material he think interferes with the argument and moves it to the end of the paper. The thoughts sit there—a bone pile of discarded ideas—but they can also be easily retrieved if a proper section for the material is found.

Regardless of whether you work straight through from introduction to conclusion or work in order of ease, try to schedule your work so that you can work without interruptions of more than a day or two. Picking up the cold trail of your ideas can be a lengthy and anxiety-inducing process. Luckily, there are a couple of good techniques for re-engaging

10. ANDREW P. JOHNSON, A SHORT GUIDE TO Academic Writing 26–27 (2003).

with material after a break. The most common method is to reread the work both to regain perspective on the whole and to remind you of your direction. Some writers retype their last page as a way of re-engaging with the material. By the time they retype a page, they are able to pick up the threads of their thoughts. One good tip, usually attributed to Ernest Hemingway, is to stop writing when you know what you are going to say next, not when you have hit an impasse. This will make it easier to begin the next session. But before you stop, jot down your thoughts about what to do next, or you may lose them.

Finally, if you become bent on perfecting a particular passage and time is running out, try "invisible" writing. When rewriting is an evasion blocking your progress, turn off your computer screen and forge ahead. Once your head is full of new ideas for the next section, you can turn the screen back on. Polishing your prose is a necessary *last* step in the writing process. Do not let it inhibit the drafting stage.

All the techniques we have discussed in this chapter are meant to produce a first full draft. A first full draft differs from a zero draft, dump draft, or rough draft in its greater organization, development, and clarity of purpose. A first full draft has all the requisite parts of a paper, including footnotes, and all the main arguments. It is a document that needs to be revised and perfected, not a document that needs to be created. First full drafts are often shorter than your finished paper—or longer. If the draft is short, it may be because it needs further documentation and explication. You may also need to add introductions and conclusions to each section, as well as transitions. If the draft is very long, it may be because it is repetitive or wordy. There may be confusing digressions. Nonetheless, in some form, all your ideas have been articulated. The paper contains enough information and enough structure that, after a break, both you and an outside reader can see what work remains to be done.

Chapter Five

THE WRITING PROCESS: REVISING AND POLISHING

"The essence of editing [your own work] is easy come easy go. Unless you can really say to yourself, 'What the hell. There's plenty more where that came from, let's throw it away,' you can't really edit. You have to be a big spender."

-Peter Elbow

"What is written without effort is in general read without pleasure."

-Samuel Johnson

A. REVISION AND THE READER

When you have gone beyond the stage of outlines, charts, and zero drafts and completed your first full draft, the next step is to read your work with a critical eye, to decide what revisions[1] are needed, and to make them. How extensively you revise and how many drafts you do will depend on your purpose, the complexity of your subject-matter, and the level of skill and experience you bring to the project.

At no stage of the process is revision merely a matter of trying to say the same thing "better," however. Rather, revision is writing for the reader's eye, just as the "getting-it-down-on-paper" stage is writing for yourself, the discovery and memorialization of what you think. The goal of all revision is to convince your readers to see your subject as you do. It is to that end that you will supplement or streamline your background

1. We use "revision" generally to refer to any changes and improvements in a text. We also use it more specifically to refer to large-scale changes—content and overall organization. We use "polishing" to refer to smaller-scale revisions—the restructuring of individual paragraphs and sentences.

material, reorganize your ideas in a more logical sequence, create or omit headings, add transitions, recast paragraphs to give them unity and cohesion, and polish your prose until it gleams.

Put another way, the revision process is governed by what composition theory calls the "rhetorical situation." Broadly defined, a rhetorical situation is the conjunction of three elements: *purpose*, *audience*, and various *constraints*, including the conventions of the genre and the skills of the persuader.[2] Sizing up the rhetorical situation—consciously or automatically—is a crucial moment in every writing project, even in the brainstorming stages. But it is above all when you revise that your particular rhetorical situation should inform all your efforts.

In order to convince your audience to see as you see, to accept the thesis that is the purpose of your paper, you must of course know your audience. The audience for legal scholarship is at once unitary and multiple: although it is drawn almost exclusively from the legal profession, the profession itself is diverse and becoming more so daily—composed as it is of litigators, state and federal judges and their clerks, legislators, prosecutors, public defenders, corporate counsel, mediators, arbitrators, law professors. Although your subject and thesis may tempt you to write exclusively for one of the micro audiences within the profession, this temptation should be resisted, unless you are writing for a specialized publication. The basic rhetorical situation of legal scholarship is idiosyncratic in that, although scholarly articles are largely read by specialists (contracts professors read articles on contracts and prosecutors read about criminal law), they are usually written for an audience of generalists that has in common only a law school education.

The specifics of revision discussed in the rest of this chapter are determined by the needs and expectations of an audience of law-school-educated readers and the conventions of scholarly writing. But *how much* revision is appropriate before submission of your draft will depend in part on how much you take your audience automatically into account in your first drafts. (Some experienced writers seem able to do this without sacrificing spontaneity or creativity.) The amount of revision you do before submission will also depend on the preference of your professor or editor. Some professors and editors believe that they can be most helpful to the writer if they read very early drafts because those versions track the writer's thought processes and often include significant insights that novice scholarly writers tend to censor when they revise. Other teachers and editors want a polished draft that takes their needs and expectations fully into account. For such readers, a first submitted draft means the most polished work that you can do on your own. Before you submit, be certain that you know which kind of draft your own particular first audience expects.

2. For a more detailed discussion, see Lloyd F. Bitzer, *The Rhetorical Situation*, *in* PHILOSOPHY AND RHETORIC, Jan. 1968, at 1.

No matter how much or how little you do, you should try to revise in the order of sections C–G of this chapter. Resist the temptation to tinker with wording before you have checked the content and organization of your draft. Polishing material that you may eventually discard or extensively reorganize can be a waste of precious time. Yet, like all of the guidelines in our book, this is a signpost, not a hitching-post. There are times when rewriting just one sentence clarifies a writer's thinking so effectively that a better organization of the paper becomes immediately apparent. In the end, only you can decide what is the best way for *you* to proceed.

B. GAINING PERSPECTIVE

The central difficulty of revision is that it requires you to be yourself and your reader at the same time, requires you both to know and not know what you know. When we read what we have written, we tend automatically to supply missing information and missing transitions. Ambiguity, vagueness, and over-generality often go unnoticed, because we know what we meant to say. Taking some time off between writing and revision is helpful, because what we wanted to say no longer interposes itself so solidly between ourselves and what we actually wrote. On the other hand, if we take too much time between writing and revision, the friendly ghost of our intentions may vanish entirely, leaving us wondering what on earth we were trying to say.

Formatting your draft to look like a work in progress can also help you gain critical perspective. Word-processed first drafts can look dangerously like finished work, and it takes much determination on the writer's part to read them with a critical eye. Triple-spacing or even quadruple-spacing your draft and using a large font may help overcome such inhibitions.

For most writers, some combination of on-screen and hard-copy revision is usually most effective. Of course, some experienced writers do their revisions entirely, and successfully, on-screen. One great advantage to on-screen revision is that you are never limited to what you can write between the lines; unsatisfactory text can be easily discarded and replaced, not just tweaked. On the other hand, it is often easier to check content and organization on hard copy because you can more easily see the relation of the parts to the whole. Moreover, on-screen revision tends to encourage browsing and skimming, not close and critical reading. Words on a screen tend to seem impersonal, immutable somehow, even though we know we wrote them ourselves. But a scrawled on, crossed out, coffee-stained draft is *personal*—imperfect but full of possibility.

C. REVISING: CONTENT

The obvious first step in the revision of scholarly writing is to be certain that you have provided your reader sufficient (but not suffocating) background material and that your analyses are appropriate and sufficiently developed (but not soporific). Early drafts often assume too much knowledge on the part of your audience. They are too specifically geared to a particular professor or editor, rather than for the audience identified earlier in this chapter—a law school graduate largely unfamiliar with your subject matter.

How much information that audience needs is difficult to gauge. In general, however, all but the very basics need to be supplied. You can assume, for instance, that your reader is familiar with fundamental structural concepts like judicial review and stare decisis. But, whether in footnote or in text, the substance of the law—no matter how obvious it seems—almost always needs to be articulated and documented. In requiring comprehensive documentation, legal scholarship is like scholarly writing in general. However, legal scholarship is much more densely documented than most scholarly writing in the humanities; this is one of its most frequently criticized aspects. (In connection with this discussion, you may want to read Part A of Chapter Six, on authority footnotes.)

For example, if you are writing a casenote about a recent state court decision concerning the propriety of warrantless searches of undeveloped land, you should note, however briefly, that the United States Constitution forbids unreasonable government searches of our houses and effects, and cite the Fourth Amendment in a footnote. Yet you would not ordinarily need to explain in your casenote that the Fourth Amendment was made applicable to the states by judicial "incorporation" into the Fourteenth Amendment, because this is an assumption fundamental to the contemporary legal culture.

Of course, the need for meticulous documentation does not mean that you should include irrelevant information. Nor does the existence of certain basic assumptions mean that there are no occasions for articulating and examining those assumptions. For instance, your casenote on warrantless searches of undeveloped land would not discuss the prerequisites for a valid warrant, nor would it discuss the exclusionary rule. But if your thesis is that the state court should have disagreed with the United States Supreme Court's interpretation of the Fourth Amendment and prohibited such searches, a discussion of the "incorporation" of the Fourth into the Fourteenth Amendment—ordinarily an unstated assumption—would be relevant because your thesis puts the relationship between the state and federal courts in issue.

Your descriptions of caselaw should also be tailored to your subject and thesis—they should not be case briefs. In the example given in Chapter Four, our student decided to write about a decision of the Fifth Circuit Court of Appeals holding that the state had a duty to protect a teenager from sexual molestation by her teacher because a compulsory education law gave the state "functional custody" of her and thus created a "special relationship." Our student's thesis was that although the result was proper, the court's "functional custody" rationale actually demeaned the victim. The paper would obviously have to include a discussion of the Supreme Court decision upon which the Fifth Circuit relied, *DeShaney v. Winnebago*.[3] There, the Supreme Court held that a state social services agency investigating a charge of child abuse was not responsible for the child's death at his father's hands because, absent a "special relationship" created by custody, the Due Process Clause does not create an affirmative duty to protect. The majority's opinion provoked a passionate dissent. Yet neither the horrific facts of *DeShaney* nor the reasoning of the dissent would be relevant to the student's paper: the Court's notion of a "special relationship" should be the only focus of her discussion of it, and any other aspects of *DeShaney* would be appropriate only in a textual footnote, if at all.

Although your thesis should largely dictate the amount and type of background information that you provide, you must be certain to provide enough information so that the reader can disagree as well as agree with you. For instance, if, like the author of one student note, you were writing about the proper role of *Miranda* warnings in prison, you would of course need to provide some background on *Miranda v. Arizona*—even though it is common knowledge among laypersons as well as lawyers that suspects in government custody must ordinarily be informed of their constitutional rights before being questioned.[4] If, like the writer, your thesis was that despite their undoubted custodial status, prison inmates do not invariably need to be "Mirandized" before questioning, your background section would obviously focus more on the Burger and Rehnquist Courts' pragmatic limitations on *Miranda* than on the policies that underlie *Miranda* itself. Yet if you ignored those policies, you would not be dealing candidly with your audience, one of a scholar's first responsibilities. By the same token, if your thesis was that *Miranda* warnings are *per se* required in prison, you would be obliged at the very least to document the practical arguments against such a rule.

Of course, checking the content of your draft requires you to take a long, hard look at your analysis, as well as the more objective and factual sections. Be sure that your position is consistent throughout: our ideas sometimes change in the course of writing a first draft. Be sure, too, that you are not begging the question—arguing from a debatable, but unargued premise—or generalizing from too little evidence. Finally, try to imagine *all* the arguments against your thesis. Then be certain you have dealt candidly with them. You cannot convince a reader to see as you see by sheer insistence that yours is the only true view.

When in doubt, it is better to provide too much background or too many examples rather than too little or too few, and better to flesh out your argument too solidly than too meagerly. As well as better serving the reader's needs, this rule of "more is more" can save you time and misery in the end. Write more rather than less while the information or reasoning is fresh in your mind, whether in the drafting or first revision stage. Trying to implement your editor's or professor's suggestion "I

3. 489 U.S. 189 (1989).

4. *See* Steve Finzio, Comment, *Prison Cells, Leg Restraints and "Custodial Interrogation": Miranda's Role in Crimes that Occur in Prison*, 59 U. CHI. L. REV. 719 (1992).

think you need some examples here" can be a major undertaking when you have been away from your material for weeks or even months. Editing down does not present the same problem.

Of course, "more is more" is not a license to go over the assigned page limit. If your paper or note starts to grow uncontrollably in revision, you are including irrelevant information and analysis, or your thesis is either not sufficiently focused or too ambitious for your page limit.

Finally, you may find that you can increase the reader-friendliness of your work by relegating information or arguments that are necessary, but not crucial, to footnotes. (You may also find, however, that material in a footnote fills an important gap in the text.)

You may also find it helpful to use the following checklist when you revise for content.

- Have you done a thorough preemption check so that you know the thesis and arguments are original? Are you continuing to check for new developments even as you revise? ("Stay Current" in Chapter Three has some suggestions.)
- Does the paper properly balance how much information readers have against how much they need?
- What is assumed in your paper? Are the assumptions warranted? Do we really need this? Covered by problems with premises?
- What relevant material was ignored? Does it matter? Do we really need this?
- Are there ideas or information that seem peripheral or irrelevant?
- Are there internal inconsistencies? Are the introduction and conclusion consistent with each other?
- Are there logical mistakes—problems with premises or reasoning?
- Is there missing support? Is authority or an example needed? Are types of argument overlooked?
- Do you consider counter-arguments? Are you fair-minded in your evaluation of opposing views?
- Are there missing links in your arguments?
- Are there missing footnotes? Should some footnotes go in text? Should text go into footnotes?

D. REVISING: ORGANIZATION

"I sometimes think that writing is like driving sheep down the road. If there is a gate to the left or right, the readers will most certainly go into it."

-C.S. Lewis

Once you are certain that you have said all that you need to say to your reader and all that your reader needs to hear, the revision process can focus on organization, on connecting ideas and information in ways that make them easily accessible to the reader.

Human beings have very limited short-term memory, and as readers, we avoid total confusion only because we can put complex material into categories as we read and thus reduce the number of specifics to remember. We also put these categories into a hierarchical framework as we read: e.g. major idea, first minor constituent idea, second minor constituent idea, qualification of second minor constituent idea, etc. If the writer does not provide us with an unambiguous context, that is, a logical and clearly signposted hierarchical organization of the writer's material, two things happen to frustrate the writer's connection with us. First, we become confused and unreceptive. Second, we import or create our own context, one which may not be what the writer had in mind.

Thus, if you as the writer want your readers to see as you see, attention must be paid to your organization, both large-scale (the clear division of the sections of your paper and the clear relation of the sections to each other) and small-scale (the relation of ideas within each section to each other). Attention must also be paid to your signposts, that is, to your general introduction, as well as to the headings and introductions that announce the content of sections and sub-sections, and the transitions that make explicit the relationship between ideas.

1. LARGE–SCALE ORGANIZATION

We said in Chapter One that the same basic four-part organization is appropriate to virtually all legal scholarship: introduction, background, analysis, and conclusion. Introductions are traditionally short, rarely more than a few pages, sometimes less than one. But long or short, the introduction should be as clear, polished, professional, and engaging as you can possibly make it. Your reader will form an impression of your paper—and often, of you—based on the introduction. Over-worked law review editors frequently reject submissions to their journals based on a weak, tedious, or confusing introduction. In terms of content, your introduction should state your topic and provide just enough background to make it comprehensible to any law-school-educated reader. It must also narrow the topic and state the thesis you explore in the paper, whether it is a traditional doctrinal problem and solution paper, or an empirical, historical, or other interdisciplinary study. Finally it should include an explicit "roadmap" that provides your reader with a graphic itinerary—e.g., "Part I provides an overview of X doctrine, Part II discusses and evaluates recent decisions on X in state Y, and Part III argues that Z is the better view." The following introduction from a student note[5] makes effective use of this organization. (Footnotes have been omitted.) It is also admirably clear and invites the reader to read about an interesting and consequential issue.

5. Marguerite S. Dougherty, *The Lanham Act: Keeping Pace with Technology*, 7 J.L. & POL'Y 455 (1999).

Background on Topic & Its Import

Electronic commerce has exploded in recent years. As a result of the Internet's astounding growth, intellectual property offenses have been magnified. While patent and copyright issues of infringement and piracy have arisen from Internet activity, trademark piracy dominates the Internet cases in the courts. The proliferation of Internet trademark offenses surprised both government and business.

Internet technology has engendered a variety of new trademark offenses including dilution, infringement, unfair competition and false advertising based upon the appropriation of another's trademark as a domain name. These new offenses also include trademark appropriation based upon metatagging, hyperlinking, framing and keyword triggering. These offenses often present cases of first impression for our courts. The nature of the Internet, and its continually expanding capabilities together with its unregulated nature, will present greater challenges in trademark law for years to come.

Narrowing the Topic

The Lanham Act is the codification of federal trademark law and the primary vehicle for the enforcement of trade mark rights of either registered or unregistered marks. The most significant threshold issue in the enforcement of trademark rights, in controversies arising from electronic contacts in cyberspace, is that of personal jurisdiction. Although the Supreme Court has long recognized that personal jurisdiction exists over a non-resident, the exercise of personal jurisdiction over a non-resident has recently been the cause of extensive litigation. Of the recent personal jurisdiction decisions issued by the federal courts, more than one-third have centered on trademark cases derived from Internet use. As a result, courts have, at least superficially, tried to fit this new electronic medium into the existing personal jurisdiction analysis.

The Problem

Solution: the Thesis

Presence of the Internet is electronic, not physical, making the traditional analysis of contacts inapplicable. The traditional personal jurisdiction analysis applied in Internet trademark cases has resulted in a body of law that lacks clarity, consistency and uniformity. This lack of uniformity undermines the policy of the Lanham Act, which was draft ed to promote national uniformity in trademark law, simplify registration procedures and foster speedy resolution of cases. Congress would best serve these goals by enacting an amendment to the Lanham Act providing for nationwide jurisdiction in controversies arising from electronic use of a mark or trade name on the Internet. Such an amendment would provide clarity, give all Internet users and operators "fair warning," and permit an already over-burdened judicial system to concentrate on the new substantive issues

> presented by trademark piracy, infringement, false advertising and dilution on the Internet.

The Roadmap

Different Background Sections

Analysis in 3 Parts

> This Note posits that analyzing personal jurisdiction in trademark Internet controversies by using a framework founded on physical contacts is inappropriate, because its uneven application to an electronic medium by the courts defeats the national uniformity policy of the Lanham Act. Part I provides an overview of the Internet. Part II examines trademark issues arising from Internet use, Part examines the existing jurisdictional framework and the tests III derived by the Supreme Court and surveys federal court decisions applying those tests to trademark issues and the Internet. Part IV reviews trademark legislative history and the national uniformity policy of trademark law that has been tested by court decisions and amended by Congress. Part V proposes a statutory solution to clarify personal jurisdiction in trademark controversies arising from the Internet and discusses the benefits and arguable disadvantages of a statutory enactment. This Note concludes that the policy of federal trademark law would best be served by an amendment to the Lanham Act expressly authorizing nationwide personal jurisdiction in infringement, dilution, unfair competition and false advertising controversies arising from electronic contacts on the Internet.

In classic fashion, this introduction begins broadly and then narrows the topic in successive paragraphs until the thesis is explained. The concluding roadmap paragraph describes each part, giving the reader an indication of each section's substance as well as the article's organization.

Background and analysis often require more than one section each or may require division into subsections. In determining your sections, you will need to find categorizing principles that organize your material. For example, the necessary background might include both a historical overview and a summary of recent decisions. It might also include a discussion of your methodology. In the trademark paper introduced above, the article had four background sections: one on the internet, one on trademark issues arising from the internet, and two on the law as it has thus evolved. Similarly, your analysis might consist of a critique of existing approaches and your own proposed solution, or, as in the trademark example, it may present a solution to the problem articulated in the background section and then have separate discussions of the benefits and disadvantages of that solution. Once you have conceptualized your sections, spend some time thinking about their order. Should methodology precede or follow the historical overview?

In general, these sections should be of roughly equal length. Very short and very long sections should usually prompt rethinking: a very short section might be just an aspect of the longer section, or it might need fleshing out. A disproportionately long section might more appropriately be two sections, or perhaps on the other hand it just needs trimming. In general, a major (i.e. roman numeral) section of a seminar paper or law review article should not be shorter than ten manuscript pages, and it may be much longer.

Like introductions, most conclusions are short, only a few pages. A traditional conclusion reiterates your thesis and summarizes your analysis. Ideally, it also inspires the reader to take up where you have left off.

Be certain that the major sections of your paper or note are mutually exclusive—that is, that you have the right material, and only the right material, in the right place. Be sure that your background sections contain just that and do not segue imperceptibly into your analysis of that material, unless you decide your topic can best be understood if background is integrated into your analysis, and therefore dispense with background sections altogether. You should also check to see that your analysis does not contain afterthought background material: sometimes, as you draft your analysis, your thinking takes a new turn requiring more background material, and the easiest (but temporary) solution is simply to supply it as you go along. In the event that your particular topic and thesis dictate an organizational pattern in which alternative approaches are described and evaluated in the same section, the mutual-exclusivity principle can still be respected by putting information and opinion in separate *sub-sections*. In no event, however, should the reader be left wondering whether you are describing or evaluating.

In short, your large-scale organization should exhibit the three key principles of organization:

1. the parts should be mutually exclusive,
2. the sum of the parts should equal the whole, and
3. the parts should be in a logical order.

EXERCISE 5.1

Diagnose the problems in the following outline of an analysis section, excerpted from the outline of a paper evaluating a state statute limiting punitive damages. Then suggest how it might be revised. Sample revisions are included in Appendix B.

IV. Constitutional Challenges
A. Plaintiff's Challenge
   1. The Takings Clause
   2. Substantive Due Process
   3. Procedural Due Process
   4. Equal Protection
B. Defendant's Challenge
   1. The Excessive Fines Clause
   2. The Double Jeopardy Clause

C. State Constitutional Challenges
   1. The Right to a Jury Trial
   2. The Remedy Clause
   3. Separation of Powers
   4. The Single Subject Clause

2. SMALL-SCALE ORGANIZATION

Being sure that the right material is in the right place is easier than the next step, checking your small-scale organization to see whether you present your material in clear and logical sequence. By its very nature, background information usually poses fewer organizational problems than does analysis. Much background is simple past-to-present narrative, and when you present a court's reasoning or another commentator's views, you work from a pre-existing organization, whether you choose to adopt, modify, or reject it. But your own thoughts are most difficult of all to organize.

One good way to check the organization of your analysis sections is to make a paragraph-by-paragraph topic outline. Be sure, however, that you are making an outline of what you wrote, not what you intended to write. Making the outline from the content of your topic sentences may avoid this temptation. (It will also ensure that your paragraphs have topic sentences and that the paragraphs don't wander off their topics.) If you find graphical representation more congenial than outlines, try drawing an issue tree using the technique described in Chapter Four, Part A(2)(c), being certain, however, that your representation is realistic.

3. SIGNPOSTS

Like justice, organization must not only be done, but also be seen to be done. Because anticipation is inherent in the reading process, you should give the reader explicit notice of the organization of your paper not only in the roadmap in the introduction, but also through the use of headings, section introductions and conclusions, topic sentences, and transitions. These signposts help get your ideas across by directing the reader's anticipation to your way of thinking. Of course, the number of signposts you use should be proportionate to the difficulty and complexity of your material; the trick is to keep your readers on the right road without insulting their intelligence.

a. Headings

Use headings to divide and subdivide the text of your paper or notes into appetizing and digestible portions. The main difficulties posed by headings are two: how many to use and how much substance to include in them.

With the exception of "Introduction" and "Conclusion," all of your headings should be substantive—and even your introduction and conclusion can have descriptive subtitles. Your headings should form a short substantive outline of your paper; one that alerts your reader to the purpose of each section and its place in your overall argument. Some writers even print these heading-outlines at the beginning of their articles, a strategy you might consider if your subject and thesis are complex. How descriptive your headings should be is a function of personal preference and the complexity or novelty of your material. For instance, a writer urging a new theory of liability—negligent employment discrimination—under Title VII of the Civil Rights Act of 1964 understandably concluded that he needed detailed, didactic headings, and thus headed Part II of his article "The Supreme Court's Analysis of Employment Discrimination Incorporates Negligence Analysis and Invites the Development of an Independent Theory of Negligent Discrimination."[6] On the other hand, more familiar material or less novel proposals would require less detail. For instance, the author of the note on *Miranda* warnings in prison was able to use shorter, but still helpful headings, entitling his Part I, a background section, "*Miranda*, Prison Interrogation, and the Supreme Court."[7] Regardless of how detailed your heading, do not treat a section heading as the first sentence of the opening paragraph. Headings are not part of the text.

How many headings you use, that is, how finely you sub-divide your text, depends on the length and complexity of your work. Although headings help us hold onto our readers by guiding their anticipation, too many headings chop up the text, distracting and alienating the reader. In general, it is unwise to have more than two levels of subdivisions below the roman numeral level, and one level is usually sufficient. If you end up with subsections less than a page long, you are probably using too many headings. A good topic sentence directing your reader to the forthcoming material may be less disruptive and just as informative.

The effective headings of two student articles are reproduced below—the first is from a sixty-page comment, and the second is from a thirty-page casenote.

EXAMPLE A

Retelling the Story of Affirmative Action: Reflections on a Decade of Federal Jurisprudence in the Public Workplace[8]

Introduction
I. The Dominant Narrative of Affirmative Action
  A. Narrative as a Source of Societal Meaning
  B. Enacting the Dominant Affirmative Action Narrative
    1. The Liberal Invocation of the Dominant Narrative
    2. The Conservative Invocation of the Dominant Narrative
II. The Constitutionality of Affirmative Action: Remedial Need as a Compelling State Interest
  A. Setting the Stage: Supreme Court Pronouncements
    1. *Wygant v. Jackson Board of Education*
    2. *City of Richmond v. J.A. Croson Co.*

6. David B. Oppenheimer, *Negligent Discrimination*, 141 U. Pa. L. Rev. 899 (1993).

7. Finzio, *supra* note 4, at 721.

8. John Cocchi Day, Comment, *Retelling the Story of Affirmative Action: Reflections on a Decade of Federal Jurisprudence in the Public Workplace*, 89 Cal. L. Rev. 59 (2001).

B. Defining Remedial Interests as "Compelling" in the Lower Federal Courts
  1. How Much Discrimination is Sufficient to Justify Affirmative Action?
    a. The Standard of Review: Defining a "Strong Basis in Evidence"
    b. The Mechanics of Presenting a "Strong Basis in Evidence"
  2. Can Statistics Alone Evidence Remedial Need?
  3. Which Population is "Relevant" When Measuring Statistical Disparity?

III. The Constitutionality of Affirmative Action: Narrow Tailoring
A. Setting the Stage: Supreme Court Pronouncements in *Paradise* and *Croson*
  1. *United States v. Paradise*
  2. *City of Richmond v. J.A. Croson*
B. Defining "Narrowly Tailored" in the Lower Federal Courts
  1. The Necessity of Relief and the Efficacy of Alternative Remedies
  2. The Flexibility and Duration of Relief
  3. The Relationship of the Numerical Goals to the Relevant Labor Market
  4. The Impact of Relief on the Rights of Third Parties

IV. Revisiting the Dominant Narrative

Conclusion

EXAMPLE B

Drug Testing: Can Privacy Interests Be Protected Under the "Special Needs" Doctrine?[9]

Introduction

I. Background
A. The Fourth Amendment
  1. Steps in Fourth Amendment Analysis
  2. The Rise of Reasonableness and Balancing
B. The Government's War on Drugs

II. The Supreme Court Cases
A. *Skinner v. Railway Labor Executives Association*
  1. Lower Court Proceedings
  2. The Supreme Court Decision
    a. The Majority Opinion
    b. Justice Marshall's Dissent
B. *National Treasury Employees Union v. Von Raab*
  1. Lower Court Proceedings
  2. The Supreme Court Decision

9. Andrea Lewis, Note, *Drug Testing: Can Privacy Interests Be Protected Under the Special Needs Doctrine*, 56 BROOK. L. REV. 1013 (1990).

a. The Majority Opinion
b. Justice Marshall's Dissent
c. Justice Scalia's Dissent

III. Analysis
  A. "Special Needs": The Further Demise of Probable Cause
    1. The Emergence of the "Special Needs" Doctrine
    2. Ramifications and Problems
  B. Tipping the Balance in Favor of Privacy
    1. Random Testing
    2. Reasonable Suspicion Testing

Conclusion

No matter how many or how few headings you use, be certain that each level (*i.e.*, Roman numerals, capital letters, etc.) requires more than one heading. Violation of the "no-A-without-B" rule suggests a flaw in the logic of your small-scale organization. (Note also that the most usual practice is to leave the introduction and conclusion unnumbered, but to use roman numerals for the sections between.)

b. Section Introductions and Conclusions

"First you tell them what you're going to tell them, then you tell them, then you tell them what you told them."

-The Teacher's Credo

Just as important as headings are introductory paragraphs. Each section needs its own introduction, one that foreshadows the particular point or thesis to be made in that section and the arguments supporting the thesis. When a section is short and each point has been explicitly articulated, you may not need a concluding paragraph for that section. Where the section is long, however, readers find a brief recapitulation of the thesis and supporting arguments helpful. The purpose of the concluding paragraph is to draw together your points so that the meaning of that section is unmistakable.

c. Topic Sentences and Transitions

We can get home without reminding ourselves to turn left at the third traffic light or turn right off the elevator, but strangers need directions. In the same way, readers need explicit directions to guide them through our texts, especially when the road is long and twisting. Topic and transition sentences traditionally provide those directions. Topic sentences direct our anticipation and memory. By summarizing the main idea of the paragraph, they save us from the need to deduce the main idea from the material in a paragraph ourselves. Topic sentences also present us with one big idea to remember instead of several component ideas, thus helping us to keep track of the basic argument that is unfolding.

A topic sentence need not necessarily be the first sentence in a paragraph. For example, the first sentence might be a transition summing up preceding text and the second might announce the next topic. Or the topic sentence might be the last sentence, articulating what otherwise must be deduced from the content of the paragraph. And sometimes the "topic sentence" is not in fact a sentence, but a clause embedded in a longer sentence. Occasionally, but rarely, the subject of the paragraph is so obvious that a topic sentence is not necessary.

In addition to announcing topics, it is helpful to announce a change of topic or a change of perspective on that topic through the use of transition words or phrases. Each section, subsection, and often each paragraph of text should display some clear signal of its function, alerting the reader to the imminence of an example, addition, qualification, refutation, or other intellectual change of gear. Although transitions do pose the danger of falling into a ritual incantation of "further, moreover, finally" and "first, second, third," an uninspired "moreover" is still preferable to silence unless the unmarked transition is very obvious indeed.

A worse danger is the use of "crazy glue" transitions that do not usefully describe the relationship between sections or paragraphs, but simply stick them together. For example, although it has a proper use, "additionally" all too often signals that some miscellaneous ideas not inconsistent with the previous idea are being attached. "Conversely" has also gained entirely undeserved popularity among legal writers, who tend to use it as a signal that miscellaneous ideas different from the previous idea will follow. "As such" is another vague connector to avoid. If you are unclear in your own mind how paragraphs or larger chunks of text relate to each other, you have problems that cannot be solved with transition words or phrases—problems with small-scale organization or paragraph structure that your revision needs to address first.

The following passage, the conclusion of an article by Professor Cass Sunstein, makes effective use of topic sentences and transitions, which we highlight here in italics.

> *Analogical reasoning is the conventional method of the lawyer; it plays a large role in everyday thinking as well.* Its distinctive properties are a requirement of principled consistency, a focus on concrete particulars, incompletely theorized judgments, and the creation and testing of principles having a low or intermediate level of generality.
>
> *Because of its comparative lack of ambition, this form of reasoning has some* important *disadvantages*. Compared with the search for reflective equilibrium, it is insufficiently theoretical; it does not account for its own low-level principles in sufficient depth or detail. Compared with economics and empirical social science, it is at best primitive on the important issue of likely social consequences. Law should be more attuned to facts, and on this score analogical thinking may be an obstacle to progress.

But in a world with limited time and capacities, and with sharp disagreements on first principles, analogical reasoning has some beneficial features as well. Most important, this form of reasoning does not require people to develop full theories to account for their convictions; it promotes moral evolution over time; it fits uniquely well with a system based on principles of stare decisis; and it allows people who diverge on abstract principles to converge on particular outcomes. In any case it is unsurprising that analogical reasoning continues to have enormous importance in legal and political discussion.

A notable aspect of analogical thinking is that people engaged in this type of reasoning are peculiarly alert to the inconsistent or abhorrent result, and they take strong convictions about particular cases to provide reasons for reevaluating their views about other cases or even about apparently guiding general principles. The emphasis on particular cases and particular convictions need not be regarded as an embarrassment, or as a violation of the lawyer's commitment to principle. On the contrary, it should be seen as a central part of the exercise of practical reason in law (and elsewhere).

In this light, it seems most unfortunate that analogical reasoning has fallen into ill repute. To abandon this method of reasoning may be to give up, far too quickly, on some of the most useful methods we have for evaluating our practices, and for deciding whether to change them through law.[10]

Here, the first sentence announces a topic ("analogical reasoning") and four major transitions ("because," "but," "a notable aspect," and "in this light") alert the reader that the writer's argument will proceed through an explanation, a qualification, an example, and a conclusion. With a clear itinerary thus in hand, the reader is ready and willing to follow.

EXERCISE 5.2

Focusing on small-scale organization and the use of topic and transition sentences, evaluate the following background discussion from an article on corporate-fraud legislation providing long jail terms. The text describes the potential objections of a group of scholars known as "optimal penalty theorists" to the statute's sentencing provisions for white-collar criminals.[11] *(The footnotes have been omitted.)*

First, read the passage carefully, diagnosing the problems. Then provide guidance for the writer, using marginal comments and a suggested outline. Be sure to note any gaps that need filling as well as any

10. Cass R. Sunstein, *On Analogical Reasoning*, 106 HARV. L. REV. 741, 790–91 (1993).

11. This exercise is adapted from the much better-organized discussion of optimal penalty theory in Jennifer S. Recine, *Examination of the White-Collar Crime Penalty Enhancements in the Sarbanes-Oxley Act*, 39 AM. CRIM. L. REV. 1535, 1559–63 (2002).

information that seems superfluous. A sample critique can be found in Appendix B.

The Objections of Optimal Penalty Theorists

The optimal penalty theorists' approach to sanctioning convicted criminals assumes that it is better to impose fines than jail sentences. This view is based upon the economic rationale that the best option for solving a problem is the one that preserves the most societal resources. From an optimal theorist's perspective, the imposition of optimal fines creates as much deterrence as the imposition of a prison sentence; therefore, it is better to impose a fine, because doing so conserves resources that would have been expended to incarcerate the convicted criminal.

Given the legislative history of the recent legislation, optimal penalty theorists likely will argue that political expediency superceded rationality in the furor to ensure enactment of a package that creates the impression that politicians are tough on corporate fraud. The number of politicians who, in speaking about the new law to the press, focused on the enhanced prison terms for corporate criminals, bolsters their argument. For example, upon signing the bill, the President commented that "there will be no more easy money for corporate fraudsters, just hard time." The Speaker of the House similarly was quoted as warning "If you lie, cheat, or commit some other white collar crime, you'll face the same consequences as a street criminal." Optimal penalty theorists will cite comments like these as an indication that Congress and the President were not motivated by rational judgments, but rather, that they included enhanced penalties for white-collar criminals in the legislation as a way to show their voters that they are opposed to corporate wrongdoing.

While incarceration has the obvious effect of constraining a convict's freedom, optimal penalty theorists argue that the main purpose of incarceration is to protect the public. Optimal penalty theory suggests that this goal is not very important in the context of white-collar crime because white-collar criminals pose no threat of physical harm. They discount the deterrent effect flowing from loss of liberty because white collar criminals are unlikely to serve lengthy sentences. Other psychological effects of incarceration, such as shame or loss of reputation, optimal penalty theorists argue, are ineffective deterrents because they are too costly to achieve—contrary to fines, they do not yield any revenue. Moreover, optimal penalty theorists resist the idea that such stigma effectively attaches as a result of sentencing, maintaining that whatever stigma does attach to a felon does so as a result of conviction, not of sentencing.

Optimal penalty theorists argue that white-collar defendants are more likely than other offenders to make decisions from a cost-benefit point-of-view. Therefore, imposing fines directly deters unde-

> sirable behavior among this group. By contrast, non-monetary sanctions, whether jail sentences or corporate probation, are an indirect method of curbing undesirable behavior and therefore provide a less effective deterrent. Optimal penalty theorists would only impose non-monetary deterrents, such as jail time, when collecting fines is likely to be a problem.
>
> Optimal penalty theorists were hostile to efforts to impose criminal liability on corporations. They argued that corporations convicted of fraudulent business practices should not receive corporate probation. Corporate probation (in which the government monitors a convicted corporation for a specified number of years) was subjected to the criticisms that it 1) wasted societal resources in comparison to fining and 2) did not have a deterrent effect greater than fining. From an economic point of view, punishment of individuals or corporations that is costly to the government can only be produced by irrational motivations like personal political gain.

E. POLISHING: PARAGRAPH STRUCTURE

When you have completed your revisions at the content and organization levels, the business of polishing paragraphs and sentences can begin. This is a satisfying stage of revision when meaning starts to shine through; try to leave ample time for it. Although they are dealt with separately here, the paragraph-and sentence-revision processes are of course inseparable in practice.

Effective paragraphs must exhibit *unity* and *cohesion*, that is, the ideas within each paragraph must not only bear on the idea expressed in the topic sentence (have unity), they must be meaningfully related to each other (show cohesion). Cohesion makes the difference between a satisfactory paper that a reader can struggle through with some profit and first-rate work that fully engages the reader's intellect and sympathies.

Even a unified paragraph with a clear topic sentence may nonetheless alienate your reader if it lacks cohesion. A list is not a paragraph, and strong transition words and phrases are helpful to the reader. Dovetailing is a technique to avoid choppy prose. Dovetailing puts new information at the end of sentences and old information at the beginning. Parallel sentence structure and the repeating of key words and phrases can be used to enhance cohesion.

As you have guessed by now, the previous paragraph fails because it lacks cohesion, although it has unity. Rewritten to take its own poorly expressed advice, it might read as follows.

> Even a unified paragraph with a clear topic sentence will alienate your reader if it lacks cohesion, that is, if it remains a mere list of kindred ideas. One way to promote paragraph cohesion is to use strong and accurate transition words or phrases, remembering, however, that "and" is a very weak transition. Another way to

promote cohesion is to "dovetail" your sentences, fitting them together as neatly as a carpenter joins pieces of wood. In a series of dovetailed sentences, new information appears at the end of sentences and old information begins sentences. This technique does not entail the literal repetition of information. Rather, it uses abstractions and pronouns (like "technique" and "it") when new information becomes old. Finally, in addition to dovetailing your sentences and using strong transitions, you can promote cohesion by repeating key words and phrases and by echoing the structure of one sentence in another.

This rewritten paragraph makes use of explicit transitions. "That is" implies that a definition follows, "one way" and "another way" announce examples, "however" tells us that a further qualification will follow, "rather" signals a correction, and "finally" lets our overextended attention-span know that relief is just a sentence or so away. In addition, the sentences on dovetailing are themselves dovetailed, consistently hooking new information onto old.

Now read the two paragraphs that follow, the first by Professor David Luban and the second by then law student Eric J. Grannis. These two writers have composed paragraphs that have unity and cohesion, texts that carry us along as we read them, whether in the end we agree or disagree with the ideas expressed. As you read, try to identify the techniques that make these strong paragraphs.

Example A

Legal argument is a struggle for the privilege of recounting the past. To the victor goes the right to infuse a constitutional clause, or a statute, or a series of prior decisions with the meaning that it will henceforth bear by recounting its circumstances of origin and assigning its place in history. I shall call such a historical placement of legal materials a *political narrative*. A string of precedents, a legislative history, an examination of framers' intent are all political narratives. To the victor goes also the right to recite what I shall call the *local narrative* constituting "the facts of the case at hand," and, following on these two rights, the additional right to pronounce the correspondence or mirroring of each narrative in the other that renders further argument unnecessary.[12]

Example B

Some commentators have criticized Americans for becoming too thin-skinned, urging that painful controversy is one of the costs of a vigorous First Amendment. However, surely being so thick-skinned as to withstand rhetorical jabs does not entail being so thick-skulled as to withstand violent blows. For groups that have been traditional

12. David Luban, *Difference Made Legal: The Court and Dr. King*, 87 MICH. L. REV. 2152 (1989).

targets of bigotry, the toleration of their fellow citizens' speech advocating certain ideas will be a special burden, but that toleration is demanded by the Constitution. The Constitution does not demand, however, that such groups stoically bear the special burden of being selected for victimization on the basis of their race or other characteristics. Rather, the Constitution permits government to prevent the resulting disproportionate victimization and impediments to the exercise of liberties by imposing more severe penalties on bias-motivated crime. Thus, notwithstanding the decisions of two state supreme courts, statutes that enhance the penalties for bias-motivated crimes are valid under the First Amendment. Such statutes are facially content-neutral, and they advance many interests that are unrelated to the suppression of free expression without restricting First Amendment freedoms any more than is necessary to achieve those interests.[13]

Example A begins with a short, enigmatic topic sentence about the nature of legal argument that the rest of the paragraph artfully expounds. The repetition of the rather formal construction "to the victor goes . . ." structures the paragraph and creates cadence. Example B uses transitions to move the reader swiftly and logically along ("however . . . however . . . rather . . . thus") to the writer's conclusion ("statutes that enhance the penalties for bias-motivated crimes are valid under the First Amendment"). Note that here the topic (the statutes are valid) is not stated at the beginning of the paragraph but is a general statement summarizing at the end what must otherwise be deduced. Note also the effective dovetailing of the first and second and third and fourth sentences.

EXERCISE 5.3

Revise the following paragraph of background information for an article on spousal maintenance. The paragraph has unity, but it needs a topic sentence and it needs cohesion in the form of transitions and dovetailing. A sample revision can be found in Appendix B.

It was in England that the law of spousal maintenance originated. Under English ecclesiastical law, divorce was forbidden, though spouses were permitted to live separately. A husband's duty to support his wife provided judicial awards of maintenance with their rationale. The practice of awarding maintenance was applied to divorce as well as to separation in the United States, and the rationale underpinning maintenance became somewhat shaky. Divorce would appear to negate the existence of a spousal support duty. The rationale for maintenance retained some plausible bases before the advent of no-fault divorce. Punishment and deterrence of wrong-doing could be seen as support for maintenance. No-fault divorce became the norm, undermining those rationales.

13. Eric J. Grannis, Comment, *Fighting Words and Fighting Freestyle: The Constitutionality of Penalty Enhancement for Bias Crimes*, 93 COLUM. L. REV. 178, 230 (1993).

F. POLISHING: SENTENCE–LEVEL REVISION

There are sentence-level problems that *must* be corrected, and those that *should* be corrected. Grammatical errors, missing or misplaced punctuation marks, and diction errors (wrong words) must be corrected. Such flaws distract all readers and offend many. They shake the reader's faith in your ideas. Thus, if you have problems with the mechanics of English, take the time to understand and banish from your writing the common grammatical mistakes detailed in Chapter Seven. Whether you have problems or not, your permanent library should include at least one grammar text. (Several are listed at the end of this chapter.) Similarly, if you cannot articulate the correct uses of the comma or the only two correct uses of the semicolon, you may need to spend time with Chapter Seven, on punctuation. (Do you believe that commas belong where you would pause if you were reading aloud? If so, you definitely need to read Chapter Seven. The "comma-when-you-pause" fallacy is responsible for many errors.)

Chapter Seven also discusses common usage and sentence structure problems—what you *probably should* as opposed to *absolutely must* fix. When we revise the structure of our sentences, we are almost always looking for greater clarity, for a more direct connection to the reader. But before we can cure our prose, we need a vocabulary for diagnosing its ills. Whether we are editing our own or someone else's writing, the epithets "wordy," "confusing," or "vague" are rarely helpful in themselves, no matter how accurate. But if we can see that vagueness can be caused by inappropriate use of the passive voice, wordiness by an overbearing compound subject, and confusion by a lack of parallelism, we are on our way to banishing unintended ambiguity. Chapter Seven aims to help you develop that vocabulary.

There is just one matter of usage discussed in Chapter Seven that is not, in our view, optional: avoiding sexist language. When one prominent judge publicly exhorted lawyers to banish sexist language from their briefs, the subject is no longer controversial.[14] The minimal work of avoiding sexist language is more than compensated by the dignity it confers on our prose.

Finally, when your writing is correct and clear, there is one more step to go. Within the conventions of scholarly writing, you can develop your own style, find your own distinctive voice: it is authenticity that divides good from exceptional writing. Chapter Eight suggests ways to make your writing *more* than professional and effective.

14. Judith S. Kaye, *A Brief for Gender–Neutral Brief–Writing*, N.Y. L.J. Mar. 21, 1991.

G. POLISHING: PROOFREADING

"Nobody is prefect."

-The authors

Proofreading someone else's work is a demanding job that calls on highly specialized skills; proofreading your own work is that and simple misery. The only thing worse, is discovering all those humiliating typographical errors after you have handed in your work. Moreover, even the friendliest reader is turned off by typographical errors and typographical inconsistencies (inconsistent spelling capitalization, or use of hyphens. Fairly or not, he effect of work that is carefully researched, thought out and written can be compromised if you do not allow enough time for an equally careful proofreading.

The first rule of proofreading is more in the nature of a warning: your computer's Spell-check program is just a beginning. Spell-checkers are a congenial time and embarrassment saver for all writers, and a positive blessing for people who simply can not cope with the eccentricities and infidelities of english spelling. But your spell-checker cannot detect wrong words or missing words. For instance, it will not fault you for typing "he" for "the" or "their for "there". In addition, spellcheckers do not speak the language of the law. For example, your computer will be undisturbed by "judgement" (a variant spelling aceptable in Standard American English) although in the American legal culture, "judgment" is the *only* correct spelling.

The second rule is harder to observe: read every word, do not skim. Reader anticipation is the enemy of proofreading: we see the words we expect to see. One of the most useful anti-browsing techniques simply to move a ruler or a sheet of blank paper under each line of text as you read, so that your eye can go no farther than the end of one line. Some writers force themselves to start at the end of their texts and read sentence-by-sentence toward the beginning. Whether you choose to endure this particular from of torture or not, it is a good idea to proofread the latter sections first, because they are more likely to have undetected errors. Be sure to proofread headings and epigrams as well as text. And check specifically to see that quotation marks, parentheses, and brackets all have their partners.

If you are writing for publication you *must* profread for typographical consistency as well as for accuracy; even if you are not writing for publication, you *should* read for consistancy. Foolish consistency may well be the hobgoblin of small minds, as Emerson said, but inconsistency certainly gives your paper an air of carelessness and unprofessionalism that puts off a serious reader and complicates a copy-editor's job. Be sure that all headings of equal weight are treated the same way. Be sure that your use of capitalization is consistent (If you are writing for Law Review, your capitalization must of course follow Bluebook or ALWD style. And be sure that compound terms are consistently, as well as *correctly*, rendered: hyphenated, one word, or two words. When no preferred form can be found, choose one form and stick to it. For instance, westlaw and lexis can be described as "online" or on-line" services and one of their major uses as "fulltext" or "full-text" searches. We use "online" and "full-text," largely because the latter, a newer coinage, looks strange to us as one word. But in any event, you should make a list of recuring difficult words or terms so that you can refer to it as you proofread. (You can also use your computer to search and replace inconsistent usage.)

As you may have noticed, this section on proofreading is plaqued by common typos. As Exercise 5.4, go back and proofread it carefully. Then look at the corrected version in appendix b. If you missed more than one, your proofreading skills need polishing.

PROOFREADERS' MARKS

^	Insert
	Delete
STET	Let original stand
#	Add space
	Close up space
tr.	Transpoes
l.c.	Make Lowercase
caps	Make capital letters
sm caps	Make small capital letters
ital	Set in italics
b.f.	Set in boldface
	Insert comma
	Insert apostrophe
	Insert period
	Insert hyphen
	Insert note number
1/n	Insert en dash
1/m	Insert em dash
sp.	Spell out abbrev.
wf	Wrong font
	Move right
	Move left
	Center
	Move up
	Move down
	New line
	Run-in

FURTHER READING

Style, Usage, & Grammar

THEODORE BERNSTEIN, THE CAREFUL WRITER: A MODERN GUIDE TO ENGLISH USAGE, The Free Press (1998).

CLAIRE COOK, THE MLA'S LINE BY LINE: HOW TO EDIT YOUR WRITING, Houghton, Mifflin (1985); LINE BY LINE: HOW TO IMPROVE YOUR OWN WRITING, Houghton, Mifflin (1986).

WILMA R. EBBITT & DAVID R. EBBITT, INDEX TO ENGLISH, Oxford University Press (8th ed. 1990).

BRYAN GARNER, THE REDBOOK: A MANUAL ON LEGAL STYLE, Thomson/West (2d ed. 2006).

DIANA HACKER, A WRITER'S REFERENCE, Bedford/St. Martin's (6th ed. 2007).

DONALD HALL & Sven Birkerts, Writing Well, LONGMAN CLASSICS (9TH ED. 1997).

JOSEPH M. WILLIAMS & GREGORY G. COLOMB, STYLE: LESSONS IN CLARITY & GRACE, Longman (10th ed. 2010)

JOSEPH M. WILLIAMS, STYLE: THE BASICS OF CLARITY & GRACE, University of Chicago Press (3rd ed. 2010).

Manuscript Preparation

BRYAN A. GARNER, THE REDBOOK: A MANUAL ON LEGAL STYLE, Thomson/West (2d ed. 2006)

THE CHICAGO MANUAL OF STYLE, University of Chicago Press (16th ed. 2010); THE CHICAGO MANUAL OF STYLE ONLINE (htttp://www.chicagomanual of style.org).

TEXAS LAW REVIEW MANUAL ON STYLE, Texas Law Review Association (11th ed. 2008).

Chapter Six

FOOTNOTES[1] AND THE ETHICAL USE OF BORROWED MATERIALS

"Symbolically, of course, the footnote is of minor importance. It is relegated to the bottom of the page ... [and] lives a life of exclusion and marginalization.... Yet simultaneously deconstruction argues that ... the marginalization and exclusion necessary for intellectual conception is never complete. Traces of banished and deemphasized alternatives lurk within the dominant conception, supporting it and at the same time calling its dominance into question. This is the problem of the footnote writ large."

-J.M. Balkin

"Encountering [a footnote] is like going downstairs to answer the doorbell while making love."

-Noel Coward

Footnotes are a rich source of humor in legal academia, the lawyer's lawyer joke. Law review articles with as many as 1,000 footnotes and leviathan mazes of cross-references have prompted lengthy satires on footnote practice. For example, one writer has diagnosed the "Single–Sentence–String–Cite" Syndrome, the "Too–Many–Footnotes–To–Change–Text" Syndrome, and the "Musical Chair" cross-referencing Syndrome.[2] Another has exposed the practices of "footnote trashing"[3]

1. As a rule, textbook authors, unlike scholarly writers, use footnotes mainly to attribute borrowed materials to their sources. However, this chapter will use authority footnotes and textual footnotes, as well as attribution footnotes, in order to provide examples of scholarly practice. At the end of each footnote we will frequently explain the note's function(s) in brackets. [This is a textual footnote.]

2. William R. Slomanson, *The Bottom Line: Footnote Logic in Law Review Writing*, 7 LEGAL Reference Services Q., 47, 56–58 (1987). [This footnote attributes borrowed material to its source.]

and "footnote networking."[4] Still another tries to make up for the scholarly inattention given to the asterisk footnote by charting its remarkable growth and development since its origins forty years ago as the place for "name, rank, and serial number."[5] The author honors one recent article for using the asterisk footnote to acknowledge financial support, "fifty-one named individuals, twenty-three conferences or workshops (in at least three different countries), and thirty-four research assistants."[6]

Yet, although this gleeful self-criticism accurately describes and rightly condemns some pretentious excesses, footnotes also serve important values—accuracy, honesty, and thoughtfulness—and there remains a lot of commonsense information about them that a novice needs to learn. This chapter discusses the theory and practice of footnoting and the related problems of plagiarism and fair use.[7]

As we noted in Chapter One, footnotes have three basic functions: (1) they provide authority for assertions, and in so doing, provide a bibliography for further research; (2) they attribute borrowed materials to their sources, thus meeting the writer's ethical obligation; and (3) they continue a discussion begun in the text, but along lines somewhat peripheral to the logical development of the primary argument. This chapter will discuss each of the three functions, but perhaps a few preliminary examples will make the distinctions clearer.

If we write, for example, that suspects in government custody must be informed of their constitutional rights before they may be questioned, we are stating a very general and settled legal proposition familiar to lawyers and laypersons alike. Yet the conventions of legal scholarship nonetheless require us to document this proposition with an *authority* footnote that cites *Miranda v. Arizona.*[8] If we further state that the lower federal courts have taken different approaches to *Miranda* in the

3. Arthur D. Austin, *Footnotes as Product Differentiation*, 40 VAND. L. REV. 1131, 1153 (1987). [This is an attribution footnote.]

4. "Publishing a stream of names in an author's note can sustain a movement to higher status and reputation. The tacit code assumes reciprocity: if you mention a colleague, he is obligated to use your name." *Id.* at 1146. [This footnote is textual in that it defines a term in the text. It also attributes the term to its author.]

5. Charles A. Sullivan, *The Under–Theorized Asterisk Footnote*, 93 GEO. L.J. 1093, 1100 (2005). [Authority and attribution footnote.]

6. *Id.* at 1104.

7. Beyond the scope of this chapter are the format and typography of footnotes. This complicated matter is set out in THE BLUEBOOK, whose rules must be observed if you are writing a law review article for a journal that follows Bluebook style. The footnotes in this chapter attempt to conform to Bluebook style. With its labyrinth of rules both commonsensical and arbitrary, THE BLUEBOOK itself is increasingly controversial. Indeed, there is now an alternative, the ALWD CITATION MANUAL, which is gaining popularity. It was written because some professionals objected to THE BLUEBOOK'S rigid and tormenting prescriptions. [This textual footnote forestalls a potential criticism that the chapter ignores a competing system of citation.]

8. Miranda v. Arizona, 384 U.S. 436 (1966).

prison context, we make a less obvious factual statement that also and more obviously requires documentation in an authority footnote. If, however, we adopt another writer's conclusion that the best solution to the problem of *Miranda* in prison is to require warnings only for inmates upon whom official suspicion has focused, we need to *attribute* that idea to its source, in this case the author of the article mentioned in Chapter Five.[9] Finally, if we wish to comment on that idea, but the comment is incidental or marginal to the subject under discussion, we might put our comments in a *textual* footnote.[10]

As you can see from these examples, authority and attribution are somewhat similar notions; often, one footnote serves both functions. But the need for authority footnotes is grounded in the conventions of the law and legal scholarship, while attribution is an ethical imperative—an absolute prohibition on the uncredited use of another writer's words or ideas.

A. AUTHORITY

As the examples above and the discussion in Part C of Chapter Five also suggest, legal scholarship is characterized by extensive documentation. Indeed, the genre's devotion to authority sometimes understandably appears (especially to writers) to be more like a mania. It may well be that legal scholarship has unthinkingly adopted the authority conventions of the judicial opinion, and that these rigid requirements need to be reconsidered by scholars. On the other hand, "footnote-itis" serves some valuable purposes.[11] It "instills a drive for perfection" and teaches "the importance of documentation, a critical skill in legal practice."[12] It also helps the writer to keep her argument on track by ensuring that every reference to a source is completely accurate—that no accidental misstatements have crept in and that she hasn't unconsciously distorted the source to better fit her thesis.[13] But whatever the origins and merits of authority footnotes, beginning scholars are well-advised to observe the ground rules, although well-known scholars may on occasion "take greater 'risks' in making statements for which there is presumably little or no authority."[14]

9. Steve Finzio, Comment, *Prison Cells, Leg Restraints and "Custodial Interrogation": Miranda's Role in Crimes that Occur in Prison*, 59 U. Chi. L. Rev. 719 (1992).

10. We might, for instance, use a textual footnote to wonder whether the writer's proposed standard was so vague as to invite abuse from over-zealous prison authorities.

11. Cameron Stracher, *Reading, Writing, and Citing: In Praise of Law Reviews*, 52 N.Y. L. Sch. L. Rev. 349, 361 (2008). [Authority/Attribution footnote.]

12. *Id.*

13. *See id.* at 362–63.

14. Slomanson, *supra* note 2, at 55. [This is a footnote providing both authority for the proposition and attribution to the writer.]

Professor Delgado tells the beginning scholar that authority footnotes must substantiate every proposition in the text, including every assertion of law or fact. The only exceptions, he says, are passages of pure argument, topic sentences, and conclusions.[15] Law review manuals often offer similar advice, requiring documentation of everything but the author's opinions, transitions, and conclusions.[16] In other words, the concept of "common knowledge," which exempts writers in some other disciplines from the duty to document information found in five or more sources, has almost no application to legal scholarship.

This is not to say that your every statement requires encyclopedic documentation. Background sections often need fewer and more general footnotes than analysis sections, particularly where the background information is not highly specialized. "See generally" and "see, e.g." cites can frequently be used in background footnotes. Some information needs to be documented only once. A rule, term of art or other important term or concept, for instance, may need to be cited the first time, but not thereafter.

> **First Reference:** The Supreme Court upheld a statute making it a crime to provide "material support" to a terror group. *Cite authority.*
>
> **Subsequent Reference:** Many may disagree that material support includes intangible advice on human rights law or how to use international law to resolve disputes peacefully. *Needn't put term in quotation marks and cite.*

But authority footnotes pose problems of degree as well as number for the writer, who has to decide not only how many footnotes to use, but also which, if any, "signal" to use in which footnotes. Signals principally let the reader know how strongly the authority in the footnote supports the proposition in the text. Both the *Bluebook* and the *ALWD Citation Manual* contain concise and similar guides to their proper use that you should consult.

15. Richard Delgado, *How to Write a Law Review Article*, 20 U.S.F. L. Rev. 445, 451 (1986). [This is an authority footnote attributing borrowed material to its source.]

16. *See, e.g.,* Terri M. LeClercq, ed., *Plagiarism: Pilfered Paragraphs*, 8 The Second Draft 1 (1993) (citing the Manual of the American University). [This authority footnote uses a "see, e.g." cite to indicate that a number of authorities include a similar rule concerning authority footnotes.]

The most consequential differences distinguish "no signal," "see," and "cf." from each other. "No signal," of course, denotes absolute four-square support of the proposition in the text; it is thus appropriate only for verbatim quotation from or accurate paraphrase of a source.

"See" means that the proposition in the text is an obvious and logical inference from the cited source. Although not required, a parenthetical explanation, sometimes including a quotation from the cited authority, may be helpful for the reader.

"Cf." means that the proposition in the text can be derived by analogy from the cited source. Because "cf." suggests somewhat tenuous support, it must always be accompanied by a parenthetical explanation of the cited case which makes clear its relationship to the proposition in the text. The example below excerpts some texts, then shows their appropriate use in authority footnotes.

Authority

Mass. Const. Art. 15

> In all controversies concerning property, and in all suits between two or more persons, except in cases in which it has heretofore been otherways used and practiced, the parties have a right to a trial by jury; and this method of procedure shall be held sacred....

Dalis v. Buyer Advertising, Inc., 636 N.E.2d 212, 214 (Mass. 1994)

> [A]ccording to the language of Article 15, the "sacred method for resolving all manner of cases and controversies was trial by jury unless the case was one in which a court of equity in either England or Massachusetts would have exercised jurisdiction in 1780."

Nei v. Burley, 446 N.E.2d 674, 678 (Mass. 1983)

> [A]nalogies between common law claims for breach of contract, fraud, or deceit and claims under C.93A [the consumer fraud statute] are inappropriate because C.93A dispenses with the need to prove many of the essential elements of those common law claims.... The court should therefore be hesitant to imply a right to a jury trial for the sui generis [statutory] causes of action for unfair or deceptive practices....

Appropriate Use of Authority

> Article 15 of the Massachusetts Constitution confers the right to a jury trial in suits between two persons except in cases that would have been tried in a court of equity, not a court of law, at the time of the adoption of Article 15 in 1780.**1** Thus, parties in a suit alleging racial discrimination in the workplace are not entitled to a jury trial, because the statutory cause of action for such discrimination**2** does not require the complainant to prove the elements of any cause of action cognizable at common law in 1780.**3**
>
> ---
>
> 1. *Dalis v. Buyer Advertising, Inc.*, 636 N.E.2d 212, 214 (Mass. 1994); [*The text sentence accurately paraphrases* Dalis.]; *see* Mass. Const. Art. 15 (providing jury trial in civil cases "except in cases in which it has heretofore been otherways used and practised") [*The text sentence is a logical inference from the language of Art. 15.*].
> 2. M.G.L. 151B, §§ 5, 9. [*Citation to the statute mentioned in the text.*]
> 3. *Cf. Nei v. Burley*, 446 N.E.2d 674, 678 (Mass. 1983) (holding there is no right to a jury trial under Massachusetts consumer fraud statute, because the statute "dispenses with the need to prove many of the essential elements of...common law claims" for fraud, deceit, or breach of contract). [*The text sentence is derived by analogy from* Nei, *which deals with a different statute.*]

Legal scholarship not only requires the use of authority, it also forbids its misuse, whether in footnotes or text. Some writers misuse authority by using "no-signal" and "see" cites for sources that only tenuously support their viewpoints and therefore need "cf." and an explanatory parenthetical. Others use quotations in a misleading manner. To avoid distorting meaning, do not quote a work out of context where to do so creates a misleading impression of its content, or paste together portions of a text in order to give it a meaning inconsistent with the text taken in its entirety.[17]

As an example of what not to do, consider the story of an attorney who was censured by the Federal Court of Trade for distorting the meaning of a quotation.[18] She had argued in a brief that by filing a motion three weeks after the Court of Trade's order that she file it "forthwith," she had complied with the court's order. Obviously, the outcome turned on the meaning of "forthwith." The attorney's brief contained the following citation.

17. Michael L. Closen & Robert M. Jarvis, *The National Conference of Law Reviews Model Code of Ethics: Final Text and Comments*, 75 Marq. L. Rev. 509, 527 (1992). [Authority footnote.]

18. This example is taken from *Precision Specialty Metals, Inc. v. United States*, 315 F.3d 1346 (Fed. Cir. 2003). [Authority/attribution footnote.]

> *See City of New York v. McAllister Brothers, Inc.*, 278 F.2d 708, 710 (2d Cir.1960) (" 'Forthwith' means immediately, without delay, or as soon as the object may be accomplished by reasonable exertion.").

However, this citation distorted the meaning of the cited authority by omitting very important language. The opinion in *McAllister* actually reads as follows.

> "Forthwith" means immediately, without delay, or a soon as the object may be accomplished by reasonable exertion. The Supreme Court has said of the word that "in matters of practice and pleading it is usually construed, and sometimes defined by rule of court, as within twenty-four hours." *Dickerman v. Northern Trust Co.*,176 U.S. 181, 193 (1900).

The attorney's quotation from *McAllister* left out the reference to *Dickerman*, where the Supreme Court strongly suggested that in situations like the one in which the Court of Trade lawyer found herself, "forthwith" meant "within the next twenty-four hours."

Given that such distortion of authority is improper in appellate advocacy, where some exaggeration is inextricable from zealous representation and where inflated claims are sure to be deflated by one's adversary, it is even more improper in scholarly writing. Exercise 6.1 at the end of this chapter asks you to assess whether authority has been distorted or used candidly.

In addition to providing quantitatively sufficient authority accurately represented, writers need to exercise good judgment in their choice of authority—quality matters. An internet search will provide authority for any proposition—but sometimes not the best authority. For example, Colin P. A. Jones, a lawyer, was surprised to find an article he had written in law school for a seminar on Law and Defense cited in a student law review article for the fact that the Communist Chinese under Mao Tse Tung defeated the forces of Chiang Kai Shek in the 1949 civil war.[19] He hypothesized that the student author, needing authority, had run a search in the law review databases of LEXIS or WESTLAW and, finding Jones' article with its incidental mention of the Chinese civil war, looked no further. A more appropriate source would have been a well-known historian or a respected almanac or encyclopedia—but these sources would have taken more time to find and might even have had to be consulted in print.[20] Be sure that your assertions are not only based on authority, but on truly *authoritative* authority.

Finally, authority footnotes—like all footnotes—should be sketched in as much detail as possible in your first draft. Use full cites in every footnote in your draft—do not use *id.* and *supra* in your drafts because,

19. This anecdote comes from Colin P. A. Jones, *Unusual Citings: Some Thoughts on Legal Scholarship*, 11 J. LEGAL WRITING 377 (2005). [Attribution footnote.]

20. 377 *Id.*

as you cut and paste, you may become confused and accidentally cite material to the wrong source or to none at all—thus unintentionally misattributing or even plagiarizing. Moreover, detailed footnotes in all your drafts means you won't have to comb through your sources a second time or, worse still, like the student writer in the anecdote above, conduct a desperate midnight Internet search for something—*anything*—that supports your assertions.

B. ATTRIBUTION, PLAGIARISM, AND FAIR USE

An understanding of attribution begins with the recognition that credit is more than an academic convention.[21] Like new law, which is constantly being fashioned out of existing rules, scholarly papers commonly build upon and advance ongoing intellectual debates. Thus reliance on the ideas of others is intrinsic to scholarly pursuits and is something to parade, not bury. Indeed, acknowledgment of our intellectual ancestors both establishes the quality of our research and provides useful references for readers who wish to delve into the subject matter.

But acknowledgment is also an ethical imperative, an obligation to give credit where credit is due. When we fail to give credit to scholars whose ideas or language we have borrowed, we commit at least two ethical breaches. First, we are implicitly lying, claiming someone else's work as our own. Second, we are treating the writer disrespectfully by appropriating his work, even when no financial gain is involved. The self-evident wrongness of putting forward someone else's work as our own is underscored by a survey indicating that 90 percent of college students "strongly" view it as unethical.[22]

The failure to properly acknowledge the work of another, whether in footnote or text, lays a writer open to charges of plagiarism, most commonly and clearly defined as the representation of the words or ideas of another as one's own. Moreover, and despite dissension on the issue, the legal and academic communities do not routinely regard an intent to deceive as a necessary element of plagiarism. Although lack of intent is often a mitigating factor in determining sanctions, many regard the

21. The discussion of attribution that follows is specifically geared to issues facing student scholarly writers. Much more could be said about proper attribution (or its lack) in law firms and about judges' unattributed use of their clerks' drafts and law professors' use of student assistants' research and summaries. *See generally*, RICHARD A. POSNER, LITTLE BOOK OF PLAGIARISM (Pantheon Books 2007); Lisa G. Lerman, *Misattribution in Legal Scholarship: Plagiarism, Ghost-writing, and Authorship*, 42 SO. TEX. L. REV. 467 (2001). Of course, the fact that some members of the legal profession are in breach of the ethical duty of proper attribution doesn't give permission to emulate them. [Textual/authority footnote.]

22. *Combating Plagiarism: The Issues*, 13 No. 32 CQ RESEARCHER 776 (2003) (quoting Patrick M. Scanlon & David R. Neumann, *Internet Plagiarism Among College Students*, J. OF COLLEGE STUDENT DEVELOPMENT, May/June 2002). [Authority/attribution footnote.]

negligent or reckless appropriation of another's work as plagiarism, even when it is the inadvertent product of careless research and note-taking.[23]

The Internet undoubtedly tempts writers to plagiarize from those billions of websites providing text on every conceivable subject, ready for copying and pasting into our documents with a few mouse clicks. Moreover, some experts on plagiarism think that students feel that "materials found online are free, or somehow inherently different from something you ... get out of a book or magazine," and that this inevitably means more students will plagiarize.[24] Other experts disagree, finding fears of a plagiarism explosion inflated,[25] and indeed, studies, largely based on "self-reporting" by students, seem to suggest that the Internet has not created an increase in plagiarism.[26]

What is not in doubt, however, is that in the academic context, proper acknowledgment of your sources, whether print or Internet, requires you to do the following.

1. Provide a footnote for any borrowed language, facts or ideas whether quoted or paraphrased in your text, whether the source is audio-visual, print or electronic, published or unpublished. If you cite ideas that come from personal communication, be sure to get permission. Letters and emails are private, unpublished material, and it is unethical to use them without the writer's permission.
2. In addition to providing an attribution footnote for paraphrases, introduce the borrowed material with some reference to its source. For example, "One recent commentator points out that...." This way the reader knows where the paraphrased material begins as well as where it ends.
3. Acknowledge the source of a fact that you think is common knowledge if it was unknown to you until you encountered it in that source.[27]
4. Whenever you cite a source ("source B") that you found in another source ("source A"), you must indicate that source B is cited in source A. (Of course, as a matter of good scholarship,

23. *See generally*, Terri LeClercq, *Intent to Deceive*, 8 THE SECOND DRAFT 3 (1993). [This footnote provides authority for the proposition made in the text.]

24. 13 No. 32 CQ RESEARCHER, *supra* note 22, at 775–76 (2003) (quoting John Barrie, president of a firm that produces plagiarism-detection software). [Authority/attribution footnote.]

25. *Id.* at 778 (quoting Jim Purdy, assistant director of the Center for Writing Studies at the University of Illinois, Champaign–Urbana). [Authority/attribution footnote.]

26. *Id.* at 778. [Authority/attribution footnote] It is, however, the case that the Internet has facilitated plagiarism detection, at least Internet plagiarism detection. Several specialized software packages are available to educational institutions. Even without such tools, internet plagiarism can often be diagnosed simply by using a search engine to search a suspect string of words. [Textual footnote.]

27. Of course, you would almost always need an *authority* footnote for such a fact since, as suggested earlier in this chapter, the "common knowledge" rule has very limited application to legal scholarship. [This is a textual footnote.]

you won't cite source B without reading it to be certain it stands for the proposition for which it is cited in source A.)

5. Provide attribution when you copy string cites or parenthetical descriptions of authority. It is unethical to "lift" without attribution a footnote that compiles sources or one that uses sources—even a single source—in an original fashion.

6. Use quotation marks when you borrow five words or more. However, whenever language is used distinctively, use quotation marks for fewer than five words, even for a single word.[28] (The text at footnotes 2–4 above provides examples of this situation.)

7. Don't confuse a paraphrase with an altered quotation. Changing a few words does not transform a direct quotation into a paraphrase. It is an altered quotation that requires the differences to be signaled by the use of brackets for changed language, ellipsis for omissions, and quotation marks. For a quotation to become a paraphrase, the language and syntax must be significantly different.

In addition you should format quoted material carefully. Quotations of fewer than 50 words should be run into your text and surrounded by quotation marks. Quotations of 50 words or more should be indented and single spaced. In this "block quote" format, no quotation marks are required.

Following these rules will insure against plagiarizing your sources. In addition, you should also avoid any appearance of plagiarism by conducting frequent preemption searches to be certain that no recent articles on your topic go unacknowledged, especially articles that raise points similar to those in your text. Finally, like authority footnotes, attribution footnotes should always be included in your very first draft: if you wait until the revision stage, paraphrased material may escape attribution altogether, causing inadvertent (but inexcusable) plagiarism.

The examples that follow will help you to distinguish between plagiarism and appropriately attributed use. In addition, you should work through the exercises at the end of this chapter.

28. The publication for which you write or edit may have a rule requiring quotation marks around more or even fewer than five words. Or the rule may not specify any number at all. The vital (and difficult) determination, of course, is whether language is distinctive, the writer's particular creation. And this is ultimately a case-by-case determination for which no bright-line rule can ever be adequate. Of course, it is still plagiarism to copy longer chunks of even the most workaday, boilerplate prose without attribution and quotation marks. [This is a textual footnote.]

Original Material

The Crisis of Modern Jurisprudence:
Casey v. Planned Parenthood
Paul M. Zimmerman
20 Fictional L. Rev. 1, 13 (1993)

The most promising aspect of the joint opinion in *Casey v. Planned Parenthood*1 was its sensitivity to critical race and critical feminist studies, specifically to their techniques of "looking to the bottom."2 The *Casey* court listened to the stories of women who stood to suffer most when it struck down the spousal notification requirement of the Pennsylvania abortion regulation and affirmed that women have the right to abort pre-viability fetuses. Such a jurisprudential development may restore the court's institutional legitimacy by providing a normative basis for legal analysis.

---

1. Casey, 505 U.S. 833 (1992).
2. Mari J. Matsuda, *Looking to the Bottom: Critical Legal Studies and Reparations*, 22 HARV. C.R. - C.L. L.

Overt Plagiarism

The court's acceptance of legal storytelling techniques in *Casey v. Planned Parenthood*1 was an interesting development. The *Casey* court listened to the stories of women who stood to suffer most when it struck down the spousal notification requirement of the Pennsylvania abortion regulation and affirmed that women have the right to abort pre-viability fetuses. This approach may allow for the reconstruction of a coherent jurisprudence that restores the court's institutional legitimacy.

---

1. Casey, 505 U.S. 833 (1992).

This example overtly plagiarizes the original article. The writer usurps the comment's thesis without acknowledgment. The first and third sentences of the passage are paraphrases that require a footnote attributing the content to the source. In addition, the writer retains the exact wording of the original in the second sentence but fails to surround the language with quotation marks.

Covert Plagiarism

The *Casey* court's acceptance of legal storytelling techniques, its decision to "look to the bottom,"**1** was an interesting development. "The *Casey* court listened to the stories of women who stood to suffer most when it struck down the spousal notification requirement of the Pennsylvania abortion regulation and affirmed that women have the right to abort pre-viability fetuses."**2** This approach may allow for the reconstruction of a coherent jurisprudence that restores the court's institutional legitimacy.

---

1. Mari J. Matsuda, *Looking to the Bottom: Critical Legal Studies and Reparations*, 22 HARV. C.R-C.L. L. REV. 323 (1987).

2. Paul M. Zimmerman, Note, *The Crisis of Modern Jurisprudence:* Casey v. Planned Parenthood, 20 FICT. L. REV. 1, 13 (1993).

This version covertly plagiarizes the original article. First, by citing to Professor Matsuda instead of to the casenote, the writer suggests she has read the cited source, although this may not be the case. Moreover, even if she had read Professor Matsuda, she must also cite the casenote because it was that author who had the idea to use Professor Matsuda in this context. Second, although the writer correctly places quotation marks around the language directly borrowed from the casenote, and also provides the appropriate footnote, the citation gives the erroneous impression that the quoted sentence is the only borrowed material in the paragraph. In fact, the ideas in the first and third sentences are also borrowed. To avoid a charge of plagiarism, the writer needs to acknowledge the author of the casenote at the outset [''As one commentator argues . . .''] and to add a footnote at the conclusion of her summary of the borrowed material, as in the example that follows.

Proper Attribution

As one commentator argues, the *Casey* court's acceptance of legal storytelling techniques, its decision to "look to the bottom," was an interesting development.**1** "The *Casey* court listened to the stories of women who stood to suffer most when it struck down the spousal notification requirement of the Pennsylvania abortion regulation and affirmed that women have the right to abort pre-viability fetuses."**2** This approach may allow for the reconstruction of a coherent jurisprudence that restores the Court's institutional legitimacy.**3**

---

1. Paul M. Zimmerman, Note, *The Crisis of Modern Jurisprudence:* Casey v. Planned Parenthood, 20 FICT. L. REV. 1, 13 (1993), (quoting Mari J. Matsuda, *Looking to the Bottom: Critical Legal Studies and Reparations*, 22 HARV. C.R-C.L. L. REV. 323 (1987)).
2. *Id.*
3. *Id.*

Note that in this passage the author's attribution footnote correctly credits both the original and citing sources.

Finally, above and beyond proper attribution, writers and editors—especially those preparing a manuscript for publication—must be familiar with the concept of fair use in order to avoid copyright infringement. Fair use has to do with the extent to which you may use another's work, whether published or unpublished, without permission from the copyright holder. It balances copyright protection—which provides authors with an incentive for creating work that enriches society—against the public's need to use the work of others to promote knowledge and culture.[29] When courts determine whether the use of a work is fair, they consider four statutory factors:

1. the purpose and character of the use, including whether such use is of commercial nature or is for nonprofit educational purposes;
2. the nature of the copyrighted work;
3. the amount and substantiality of the portion used in relation to the copyrighted work as a whole; and
4. the effect of the use upon the potential market for or value of the copyrighted work.[30]

29. KENNETH D. CREWS, COPYRIGHT, FAIR USE AND THE CHALLENGE FOR UNIVERSITIES: PROMOTING THE PROGRESS OF HIGHER EDUCATION 22–23 (1993). [Authority and attribution footnote.]

30. 17 U.S.C. § 107 (1988). [Authority footnote.]

Because law reviews have an educational rather than commercial purpose, the first prong of the fair use doctrine does not present many obstacles to legal scholars. Since legal writers tend to borrow from copyrighted work of a scholarly nature, the second factor is also not especially problematic. With respect to the third factor, courts consider the proportion of quoted material in relation to the length of the source. You will almost certainly be safe if you stay within a 5% limit. Finally, note that the Court in *Harper & Row Publishers, Inc. v. The Nation Enterprises stated that the fourth factor "is undoubtably the single most important element of fair use."*[31] However, it is unlikely that scholarly use of copyrighted material will affect the source material's potential market or value. In general, therefore, fair use is given special deference when copyrighted material is used for a nonprofit educational purpose.[32] Nonetheless, when in doubt, seek permission.

C. TEXTUAL FOOTNOTES

Textual footnotes provide discursive commentary supplementing the text. They serve many purposes. Often they provide the reader with an example or illustration of a point made in the text, or they offer a needed definition.[33] Frequently they clarify or qualify an assertion made in the text.[34] Sometimes they raise a potential criticism or complication . . . and then proceed to address it or defer it to another day.[35] Increasingly, they are used for musing or for sharing with the reader an amusing anecdote or insight. Authors of this latter type of "personal" notes welcome the footnote as an opportunity to break with an objective, formal tone.[36]

The phenomenon of the "personal" footnote crystallizes the larger debate over the value of textual footnotes. Many readers, especially practitioners and judges, find textual footnotes distracting—fit only for a reader with multiple personalities or split consciousness. The length and complexity of some textual footnotes make it difficult to resume reading the text without backtracking to pick up the threads of the argument.

31. Harper & Row Publishers, Inc. v. Nation Enterprises, 471 U.S. 539, 566 (1985). [Authority footnote.]

32. Crews, *supra* note 29, at 23. [Authority and attribution footnote.]

33. Thus, for example, footnote 4 in this chapter defined a term used in the text. Note, by the way, that footnotes 26–28 in this chapter all serve an illustrative purpose. [Textual footnote.]

34. For example, one writer added a qualifying footnote to the following sentence in the text: "The Supreme Court concluded that both *Smith* and *Jones* have defied consistent application by the lower courts." The footnote observed: "However, in support of the argument that *Smith* and *Jones* have defied consistent application, the Court could only muster the authority of a concurring opinion of one lower court judge." [Textual footnote.]

35. *See, e.g., supra* note 10 and accompanying text. [Does it bother you to turn back? If so, curb your cross-references.]

36. Indeed, adventurous authors like ourselves have been known to shift in footnotes from the conventional use of the third person to the first person. For an example of "personal" notes, see John Hart Ely, *Another Such Victory: Constitutional Theory and Practice in a World Where Courts Are No Different from Legislatures*, 77 Va. L. Rev. 833 (1991). [Textual footnote/authority.]

One prominent commentator remarked that "[i]f footnotes were a rational form of communication, Darwinian selection would have resulted in the eyes being set vertically rather than on an inefficient horizontal plane."[37] Thus, critics of textual footnotes prefer a "minimalist" style, in which footnotes are "devoid of interpretation or discursive commentary"[38] and exist only to provide authority and attribution.[39]

As a writer, you will need to develop your own footnote style and discover whether you fall into the minimalist, centrist, or expansionist camp. But whether you use only a few textual footnotes or a great many, your decision whether to footnote or not to footnote should depend upon whether a textual footnote would be helpful to your reader. The point is not to prove you have thought of every conceivable tangential issue. The point is to provide textual footnotes that further enrich the paper's theme.

In making this determination, you will—as an editor of your own work or as a law review editor of another's work—occasionally find that you have put material into a footnote that is really central to the text, or, conversely, that you could tighten the text by relegating some peripheral matter in the text to a footnote.[40] Computers make it easy to move material between text and footnotes and thus aid us in deciding which position works best in each case.

EXERCISE 6.1

Read the excerpts of authority that follow. Then evaluate the use of authority and attribution in the excerpt from a draft of a law review article that follows. Are citation signals used appropriately and candidly? Do the quotations and paraphrases accurately reflect the meaning of the cited authorities, or do they distort meaning? Are quotations appropriately attributed to their sources? The answers to this exercise are in Appendix B.

37. Abner J. Mikva, *Goodbye to Footnotes*, 56 U. Colo. L. Rev. 647, 648 (1985). [Attribution footnote.]

38. Austin, *supra* note 3, at 1143. [Attribution footnote.]

39. However, the quotation by J.M. Balkin that prefaces this chapter is representative of the opposite position. Richard A. Matasar also regards alternative perspectives as an intellectual and ethical imperative: "The language of neutral principles, rationales, and holdings may be perceived as a cover for actual reasoning, the influence of culture, and the hold of ideology. Thus, today many legal scholars are searching for a new rhetoric that more candidly reveals the myriad ways that law is a reflection of very personal matters." Richard A. Matasar, *Storytelling and Legal Scholarship*, 68 Chi.-Kent L. Rev. 353, 355 (1992). [Authority and textual footnote.]

40. For instance, should we have put the discussion of The Bluebook in note 7 or the discussion in note 28 into the text instead?

Authority

Mass. Const. Art. 15

In all controversies concerning property and in all suits between two or more persons, except in cases in which it has heretofore otherways been practised, the parties have a right to a trial by jury; and this method of procedure shall be held sacred. . . .

Dalis v. Buyer Advertising, 636 N.E.2d 212, 214 (Mass. 1994)

The jury system, as the "sacred" method for resolving factual disputes, is the most important means by which laypersons can participate in and understand the legal system. *Commonwealth v. Canon*, 368 N.E.2d 1181, 1193 (Mass. 1977) (Abrams, J. dissenting). It brings the "rules of law to the touchstone of contemporary common sense." *Id.*, quoting 1 W. Holdsworth, A History of English Law, 348–349 (3d ed. 1922). "Jurors bring to a case their common sense and community values; their 'very inexperience is an asset because it secures a fresh perception of each trial, avoiding the stereotypes said to infect the judicial eye.' " *Parklane Hosiery Co. v. Shore*, 439 U.S. 322, 355 (1979) (Rehnquist J., dissenting), quoting H. Kalven & H. Zeisel, The American Jury 8 (1966).

Stonehill College v. Massachusetts Commission Against Discrimination, 808 N.E.2d 205, 233 (Mass. 2004) (Sosman, J. concurring)

Laws prohibiting workplace discrimination against racial and ethnic minorities, women, and homosexuals were enacted precisely because prejudices against, or stereotypical assumptions concerning, those persons were so widespread and deeply held. When the legislature first authorized private suits to redress discrimination in 1974, the Legislature could reasonably have been of the view that plaintiffs asserting their rights under [the anti-discrimination statute] would face reluctance or even downright hostility from jurors. . . . (By way of historical reference to illustrate the point, 1974 was the first year of court-ordered busing to desegregate the Boston public schools, a time terrible racial strife within the city.) That discrimination claims were to be handled either by [an administrative agency] . . . or by the court . . . reflected the practical reality of the times. . . .

Draft

The right to a jury trial in civil cases is "sacred" in Massachusetts.**1** It provides laypersons with an opportunity to participate in the legal system and, in the words of Holdsworth, brings the "rules of law to the touchstone of contemporary common sense."**2** But though the right may be sacred, juries themselves are not always pure. Discrimination in many forms—racism, ethnic hatred, sexism, homophobia—pervades our society,**3** and when jurors "bring to a case their...community values," those values are not uniformly positive.**4** Thus, in drafting Massachusetts' anti-discrimination statute in 1974, a year of terrible racial strife in Boston, the Legislature deliberately did not provide for trial by jury, fearing that "plaintiffs asserting their rights under [the statute] would face reluctance or even downright hostility from jurors."**5**

---

1. Mass. Const. Art. 15.
2. 1 W. Holdsworth, A History of English Law 348-49 (3d ed. 1922).
3. *Stonehill College v. Massachusetts Commission Against Discrimination,* 808 N.E.2d 205, 233 (Mass. 2004) (Sosman, J., concurring).
4. *Parklane Hosiery Co. v. Shore,* 439 U.S. 322, 325 (1979) (Rehnquist, J., dissenting).
5. *Stonehill College*, 808 N.E.2d at 233 (Sosman, J., concurring).

EXERCISE 6.2

On the following page, you will find an excerpt from an article by Professor Welsh S. White, "False Confessions and the Constitution: Safeguards Against Untrustworthy Confessions," published in the Harvard Civil Rights—Civil Liberties Law Review in 1997. You will also find two sample texts, both of which "borrow" from Professor White's article. Evaluate the acknowledgments of sources in Samples A and B. Are the conventions for proper, ethical acknowledgment followed? Refer to the list of attribution conventions in Part B of this chapter. (You may find it helpful to photocopy Sample B in order to compare all three texts side-by-side.) The answers to this exercise are in Appendix B.

Original Material

Over the past two decades, a significant number of suspects have claimed that standard interrogation techniques have led them to give false confessions.**26** Modern psychological studies indicate that when standard interrogation techniques are used on suspects who are especially vulnerable to the pressures generated by these techniques, one of two types of false confessions may result: "coerced-compliant" false confessions in which a suspect knows he is confessing falsely but confesses in order to obtain some goal or to "escape from a stressful or an intolerable situation,"**27** or "coerced internalized" false confessions in which a "suspect comes to believe in his own guilt."**28**

In considering the empirical data, it is useful to provide definitions of both false and untrustworthy confessions. A false confession may be defined as one in which the facts admitted in the confession appear to be either totally incorrect or materially inaccurate. An untrustworthy confession, on the other hand, should be defined as one that is obtained under circumstances that provide significant doubt as to its accuracy. If there is a significant likelihood that the circumstances under which a confession was produced would lead to a false confession, then a confession produced under those circumstances should be viewed as untrustworthy....

---

26. *See, e.g.*, CONVICTING THE INNOCENT, (Donald S. Connery, ed., 1996) (claiming that Richard Lapointe, a brain-damaged defendant who was convicted of the murder of his wife's grandmother, falsely confessed to the murder following several hours of intensive police interrogation); Sharon Cohen, *"Ringmasters" Unlock Truth, Free Man who Confessed to Murder*, L.A. TIMES, Mar. 31, 1996, at A2 (recounting case of Johnny Lee Wilson, a retarded defendant who was convicted of murder after falsely confessing to a crime that subsequent evidence showed he did not commit). See generally GISLI H. GUDJONSSON, THE PSYCHOLOGY OF INTERROGATIONS, CONFESSIONS AND TESTIMONY 235-40, 260-73 (1992) (analyzing several British cases and one American case in which defendants were charged or convicted on the basis of confessions later shown to be false)....

27. GUDJONSSON, *supra* note 26, at 228.

28. *Id.*

Sample Borrowing A

In the last twenty years or so, defendants have asserted that routine police questioning has forced them to make false confessions.**1** Psychological studies have demonstrated that when routine questioning techniques are used on people who are especially vulnerable to the pressures generated by these techniques, the result may be a coerced-compliant or a coerced-internalized false confession.**2** In a coerced-compliant confession, the suspect confesses to stop the questioning or gain some other benefit. Coerced-internalized confessions occur when the suspect actually comes to believe in his own guilt.**3**

Whenever there is a real possibility that the circumstances of interrogation will produce a false confession, a confession so obtained should be deemed untrustworthy. "A false confession may be defined as one in which the facts admitted in the confession appear to be either totally incorrect or materially inaccurate. An untrustworthy confession, on the other hand, should be defined as one that is obtained under circumstances that provide significant doubt as to its accuracy."**4**

---

1. *See, e.g.*, CONVICTING THE INNOCENT, (Donald S. Connery, ed., 1996) (claiming that Richard Lapointe, a brain-damaged defendant who was convicted of the murder of his wife's grandmother, falsely confessed to the murder following several hours of intensive police interrogation); Sharon Cohen, *"Ringmasters" Unlock Truth, Free Man who Confessed to Murder*, L.A. TIMES, Mar. 31, 1996, at A2 (recounting case of Johnny Lee Wilson, a retarded defendant who was convicted of murder after falsely confessing to a crime that subsequent evidence showed he did not commit). See generally GISLI H. GUDJONSSON, THE PSYCHOLOGY OF INTERROGATIONS, CONFESSIONS AND TESTIMONY 235-40, 260-73 (1992) (analyzing several British cases and one American case in which defendants were charged or convicted on the basis of confessions later shown to be false)....
2. GUDJONSSON, *supra* note 26, at 228.
3. *Id.*
4. Welsh S. White, *False Confessions and the Constitution: Safeguards against Untrustworthy Confessions*, 32 HARV. C.R.-C.L.L. REV. 105, 109 (1997).

Sample Borrowing B

The last quarter century has seen a good number of criminal defendants assert that their confessions were false, induced by the vices inherent in the most routine custodial interrogation.**1** Such assertions are supported by psychological studies, which differentiate between two types of false confession–"coerced compliant" (where a vulnerable suspect confesses simply to stop the interrogation, or for some other perceived benefit)**2** and "coerced internalized" (where vulnerable suspects become convinced that they have committed the crime.)**3**

Professor Welsh S. White argues that whenever there is a "significant likelihood that the circumstances under which a confession was produced would lead to a false confession, then a confession produced under those circumstances should be viewed as untrustworthy...."**4** He distinguishes between "false" and "untrustworthy" confessions as follows.

> A false confession may be defined as one in which the facts admitted in the confession appear to be either totally incorrect or materially inaccurate. An untrustworthy confession, on the other hand, should be defined as one that is obtained under circumstances that provide significant doubt as to its accuracy.

---

1. *See* examples collected in Welsh S. White, *False Confessions and the Constitution: Safeguards against Untrustworthy Confessions*, 32 HARV. C.R-C.L. L. Rev 105, note 26 (1997) [Hereinafter White].
2. GISLI H. GUDJONSSON, THE PSYCHOLOGY OF INTERROGATIONS, CONFESSIONS, AND TESTIMONY 228 (1992), cited in White, *supra* note 1, at note 26.
3. *Id.*
4. White, *supra* note, at 109.

EXERCISE 6.3

Do the following involve instances of plagiarism or other types of academic dishonesty? Answers are in Appendix B.

1. May a writer take the factual description of a case from a case or from a commentary on a case and use it verbatim and without attribution, reasoning that facts belong to no one, and therefore, it is not plagiarism to repeat them? Assume the analysis is original. Is this reasoning valid, or is this plagiarism?
2. May you include in a law review article or seminar paper work done in a different class or different article? Is this ever permissible? Under what conditions?

3. Sometimes writers cite all material taken from external sources, but do not indicate when they were using the exact language of that source by putting it within quotation marks or block quotation form. Is this plagiarism?
4. Writers often read an author who has relied upon and cited the work of another writer. Is it permissible to cite the second author when they haven't read the second author?
5. In some other cultures, the unattributed use of another person's work is accepted practice. Do you think foreign students in American law schools should be sanctioned if their written work doesn't cite sources?
6. Assume a writer downloads material from the internet and incorporates it into the first draft of a memo or seminar paper without attribution. When the writer returns to the website to retrieve the citation information, the material has disappeared from the database. Is it permissible to use the material without attribution in this situation?
7. If a writer has an original idea and later learns of its publication in an earlier source, does she need to acknowledge that source?

EXERCISE 6.4

Does the student paper on warrantless searches use the source, the Supreme Court's opinion in Georgia v. Randolph, 547 U.S. 103, 122–123 (2006), *correctly? Are citations necessary? Is there language that should be in quotes? Answer is in Appendix B.*

Source:

This case invites a straightforward application of the rule that a physically present inhabitant's express refusal of consent to a police search is dispositive as to him, regardless of the consent of a fellow occupant. Scott Randolph's refusal is clear, and nothing in the record justifies the search on grounds independent of Janet Randolph's consent. The State does not argue that she gave any indication to the police of a need for protection inside the house that might have justified entry into the portion of the premises where the police found the powdery straw (which, if lawfully seized, could have been used when attempting to establish probable cause for the warrant issued later). Nor does the State claim that the entry and search should be upheld under the rubric of exigent circumstances, owing to some apprehension by the police officers that Scott Randolph would destroy evidence of drug use before any warrant could be obtained.

Student Paper:

To determine the validity of a warrantless search, a court must regard as dispositive a physically present co-inhabitant's clear refusal to permit a search. Moreover, here, as in *Georgia v. Randolph,* the state does not claim that the entry and search should be upheld because of exigent circumstances, owing to apprehension that defendant would destroy evidence of drug use before any warrant could be obtained.

Chapter Seven

WRITING WITH CARE

"I will not go down to posterity talking bad grammar."

-Benjamin Disraeli

A. GRAMMAR AND USAGE

This section reviews some of the basic principles and prescriptions of standard written American English that careful writers observe. This review is not intended as a substitute for a good basic text or reference book, however. Every writer's permanent library should include at least one grammar and one usage book like those on the reading list at the end of Chapter Five.

A few of the topics in this section are "musts": to violate them is to do serious injustice to your ideas. Sentences must have a subject and a predicate, subject and verb must "agree" in person and number, nouns and pronouns must "agree," verb tenses must be appropriate, and modifiers and modified must be rationally related. We also consider the use of inclusive rather than sexist language an imperative. For the rest, though, as you will see, we prefer sensible flexibility to rigid rules. Our aim here is to provide you with a vocabulary for articulating your own and your editees' writing problems. Once you have a diagnosis, revision is easier. The last entry in this section, Editors' Abbreviations, provides a useful shorthand for indicating errors and problems.

We have included short exercises where we thought they would be helpful. The answers are in Appendix B.

1. AGREEMENT: SUBJECT/VERB AND PRONOUN/ANTECEDENT

Subjects and verbs must agree in number—that is, singular subjects go with singular verbs and plural subjects go with plural verbs.

Ex: The fifth amendment guarantees due process of law.

Ex: The fifth and fourteenth amendments guarantee due process of law.

Most of the time, compliance with this basic rule is automatic. Writers nonetheless get into trouble in a few situations. For example, when a sentence becomes complex and the subject is far from the verb, it is easy to lose track of the subject, as did the writer in the example below.

Not: Some commentators have argued that *the venerable history and principled rationale* supporting the exercise of peremptory challenges by the defense in a criminal prosecution, particularly in view of the heterogeneous nature of our society, *outweighs* the individual juror's right to serve on a given case.

Confusion also occurs when a singular subject is followed by prepositional phrases like "together with," and "in addition to." Remember that unlike conjunctions, these phrases do not make a plural verb form necessary.

Ex: Its venerable history *and* principled rationale *outweigh* other considerations. (Conjunction; plural verb form.)

Ex: Its venerable history, *together with* its principled rationale, *outweighs* other considerations. (Prepositional phrase; singular verb form.)

Other problems arise with collective nouns like "government," "corporation," or "jury" used as subjects. Traditional legal usage treats most of these as singular.

Ex: The jury deliberates in secret.

Ex: The government has fewer peremptory challenges.

Pronouns and their "antecedents"—the words they replace—must agree in gender and number. Agreement is basic and automatic—and also the occasion of many errors. As with subject/verb agreement, collective nouns are troublesome. In general, they need the singular neuter pronoun "it."

Ex: The jury rendered *its* verdict and the court *its* judgment.

But the most frequent error is the use of the third-person plural pronouns "they," "them," and "their" with singular antecedents—for example, "A person is responsible for the foreseeable consequences of their actions." This usage arises from the commendable attempt to avoid both sexism ("his") and awkwardness ("his or her"), but despite its growing acceptance in speech and very informal writing, this use of plural pronouns is inappropriate in scholarly writing. (See "Avoiding Sexist Language," below.)

2. AVOIDING SEXIST LANGUAGE

Perhaps the hardest part of writing sexist language out of our prose is avoiding the "generic" use of the pronouns "he," "him," and "his."[1]

1. The problem is that "he," like "man," is never really gender-neutral. This is why we find "irredeemably odd" the sentence "Each applicant is to list the name of

Not: A judge must try to put *his* personal biases aside.

Some common solutions follow.

- Make the *noun* plural. (Using a plural pronoun with a singular noun is not appropriate in scholarly writing.)

Ex: Judges must try to set their personal biases aside.

Not: A judge must try to set their personal biases aside.

- Omit the pronoun.

Ex: A judge must try to set personal biases aside.

- Use "a," "an," "the," "any."

Ex: A judge must set any personal biases aside.

- Use "who."

Ex: A judge who has personal biases must set them aside.

- Use "one," "you," or "we."

Ex: As judges, we must set our personal biases aside.

When all else fails, and only when all else fails, rewrite in the passive voice or resort to "he or she," "his or her," etc.

When writing a long document where the pronoun problem is endemic, some writers choose to alternate "he" and "she" or use "she" alone to heighten the reader's awareness of the issue. These are more controversial solutions, however.

EXERCISE 7(A)(2)

Propose four rewrites for the following sentence.

Common sense suggests that when a patient is injured in the hospital, he should promptly notify his attorney.

3. BEGINNING SENTENCES WITH CONJUNCTIONS

Some writers and editors believe that it is incorrect to start a sentence with "and," "but," or "because." Although they may perhaps strike a too casual note in contracts or wills, we believe that "and," "but," and "because" are entirely acceptable sentence openers in scholarly writing. Indeed, they sound less stilted than their fancy equivalents "additionally," "however," and "since."

4. COMPLEX SUBJECTS

Long, abstract subjects make sentences difficult to understand.

his husband or wife." Moreover, empirical evidence suggests that the generic "he" is in fact perceived by readers as male; thus footnotes to the effect that the writers use "he" to refer to both males and females are futile gestures despite the best of intentions. *See* Virginia L. Warren, *Guidelines for Non–Sexist Use of Language*, 59 Am. Phil. Ass'n. Proc. 471 (1986).

Not: *The government's use of sophisticated technology to reconstruct evidence of criminal activity found in trash discarded in a publicly accessible place* does not violate the fourth amendment.

In the example above, the reader trudges through a complicated and depopulated twenty-one-word subject—composed of one main noun ("use") and its modifiers—in order to reach the verb. The message in this sentence can be conveyed more effectively by using a short subject that is the agent of the action.

Ex: *The government* does not violate the fourth amendment when it uses sophisticated technology to reconstruct evidence of criminal activity found in trash that has been discarded in a publicly accessible place.

EXERCISE 7(A)(4)

Rewrite the following sentence to eliminate the complex subject.

The arrest and subsequent conviction of a suspect for failing to identify himself during a lawful Terry stop are reasonable within the meaning of the fourth amendment.

5. INTERRUPTING CLAUSES AND PHRASES

Long or habitual interruptions between subject and verb most often confuse and frustrate the reader, so keep the subject near the verb and move interruptions to the beginning or end of the sentence.

Not: *The Supreme Court,* which had earlier held in *Engel* and subsequently in *Lee* that state-sponsored prayer in public schools has an inescapably coercive effect on children who do not wish, for whatever reason, to participate, nonetheless *denied* certiorari.

Yet interruption can sometimes be used to good effect for emphasis or cadence. In the following passage from his dissent in an affirmative action case, Justice Blackmun uses interruptions to make his point.

> I never thought that I would live to see the day when the city of Richmond, Virginia, the cradle of the Old Confederacy, sought on its own, within a narrow confine, to lessen the stark impact of persistent discrimination. But Richmond, to its great credit, acted. Yet this Court, the supposed bastion of equality, strikes down Richmond's efforts. . . .

6. MODIFIERS: MISPLACED AND DANGLING

Misplaced and dangling modifiers are inevitable in first drafts. If they are not fixed at the revision stage, however, they make our prose look slipshod. Always keep modifiers close to what they modify. When modifiers stray, confusion and incongruity follow, as in the example below, where the writer unwittingly gives new meaning to the term "contempt of court."

Not: *Even when they are mechanically shredded*, the federal courts will not find a reasonable expectation of privacy in *discarded documents*.

Ex: The federal courts will not find a reasonable expectation of privacy in *discarded documents, even when they are mechanically shredded*.

More difficult to diagnose and fix than misplaced modifiers are "dangling" modifiers. They "dangle" because there is in fact nothing for them to modify, nothing in the sentence to which they can properly attach themselves.

Not: *Citing the first amendment*, the injunction was dismissed. (The injunction did not cite the first amendment, a court did.)

The simplest way to correct the example above would be to insert the word being modified—"the court."

Ex: Citing the first amendment, the court dismissed the injunction.

EXERCISE 7(A)(6)

Identify the modifier error in each of the following sentences and correct.

1. Applying this test to the facts of the case, the defendant's interest was considered minimal.

2. The defendant had a scar on his left cheek that resembled a crescent moon.

3. We accept statutes as legitimate in part because our legislators are democratically elected.

7. NOMINALIZATIONS

"Nominalizations" are nouns formed from verbs. For example, "reversal" comes from the verb "to reverse" and "collision" from "to collide." Your prose will be stronger and more direct if you habitually use verbs, and not their nominalizations.

Not: The planes were involved in a mid-air collision.

Ex: The planes collided in mid-air.

You should note, however, that nominalizations are not always inappropriate. They can lend formality to your prose and they can be useful in parallel construction (see below) and in dovetailing sentences (see Chapter 5, Part E).

EXERCISE 7(A)(7)

Rewrite to eliminate the nominalizations in the following sentence.

The Supreme Court has given no indication that an identification requirement is constitutional.

8. PARALLEL CONSTRUCTION

When items in pairs or series are "parallel"—all in the same grammatical category (e.g., nouns, clauses, past participles)—sentences are balanced and readable. Verb tenses should be consistent, and if the conjunction "that" begins one element in a series, each element of the series should begin with "that." However, if "that" precedes the enumeration, one is enough.

> Ex: Plaintiff challenges the Pledge-recitation statute, arguing 1) that its plain meaning violates the free speech clause, 2) that recitation of the phrase "under God" violates the establishment clause, and 3) that recitation by teachers and willing pupils unconstitutionally coerces children who do not wish to pledge.
>
> Ex: Plaintiff challenges the Pledge-recitation statute, arguing that 1) its plain meaning violates the free speech clause, 2) recitation of the phrase "under God" violates the establishment clause, and 3) recitation by teachers and willing pupils unconstitutionally coerces children who do not wish to pledge.
>
> Not: Plaintiff challenges the Pledge-recitation statute, arguing 1) that the free speech clause was violated, 2) reciting the phrase "under God" violates the establishment clause, and 3) children who do not wish to pledge are unconstitutionally coerced by recitation by teachers and willing pupils.

Faulty parallelism makes the third example hard to read. The writer uses "that" in only one of three items, uses both passive and active voice, uses past and present tenses, and uses the noun "recitation" and the participle "reciting."

EXERCISE 7(A)(8)

Correct the faulty parallelism in the following sentences.

1. Reasonable efforts to maintain secrecy include putting the recipe in a locked office, storing parts of the recipe in separate locations, or a continuing course of conduct that creates a confidential relationship.

2. Part II of this note will discuss the historical background of agreements leading up to the TRIPS agreement, the scope of other agreements, and lay out the reasons for limiting geographical protection.

9. PASSIVE v. ACTIVE VOICE

Prose in which the active voice predominates is generally clearer and stronger than prose that relies on the passive voice. In the active voice, the grammatical subject of the sentence is the agent of the action.

> Ex: The defendant breached his duty of care.

In the passive voice, however, the grammatical subject of the sentence is not the agent of the action, but rather, the person or thing acted upon. Indeed, the agent of the action need not appear in the sentence at all.

Ex: The duty of care was breached.

The passive voice is most appropriate when the agent of the action is understood, or when the agent is unknown.

Ex: The judgment was reversed.

Ex: The building was vandalized.

The passive voice is also useful in dovetailing your sentences into a cohesive paragraph. (See Chapter 5, Part E.)

10. SENTENCES AS NARRATIVE

As readers, we expect sentences to tell stories. We expect grammatical subjects to be characters in a story, and we expect verbs to express the characters' actions. Thus, as writers, we express ourselves most clearly when we follow this pattern, living up to reader expectation.

In the examples below, subjects are in italics, and verbs are underlined. Note that the subjects are characters and the verbs describe their actions.

Ex: The *special agent* detained and arrested the suspect as the *plane* landed.

Ex: The *government* must obtain a search warrant before eavesdropping on telephone conversations.

Sentences are clearest when the character is a person, of course, but abstractions resemble characters in a story if those abstract concepts "do" things.

Ex: The *Constitution* forbids only searches and seizures that are unreasonable.

The basic rule is simple, then: in the clearest sentences, syntax follows plot. Yet too many writers consistently ignore this principle, with the result that much professional prose is harder to understand than it needs to be. Writers too often complicate the reader's job by hiding the characters in prepositional phrases (most often in phrases beginning with "of"), in adjectives, or in pronouns and by hiding the actions of the characters in nominalizations, nouns formed from verbs.

Not: The detention and arrest of the suspect by the special agent occurred during the landing of the plane.

In the sentence above, all the characters in the story—the agent, the suspect, the plane—are hiding in prepositional phrases—"of the suspect," "by the special agent, "of the plane." All the actions are hiding in nouns—"detention," "arrest," "landing." Although this sentence is certainly decipherable, chronology is clearer when the subject of the sentence is the actor who does things. When many of the subjects are abstractions, syntax and plot sequence are often divorced; this taxes the reader's powers of comprehension.

Not: An opportunity to escape was never presented to Clemente, who had been threatened at gunpoint with being shot by Frost. Moreover, a refusal to participate in the offense was articulated by Clemente when he said "no way" would he rob Sheldon. Imminence of threat can therefore be established.

Not: When the anti-discrimination statute was enacted in 1974, there were reasons for the belief that suits under the statute would be inappropriate for jury decision. The redress of workplace discrimination against racial minorities, women, and homosexuals based on widespread prejudice and stereotyping was the aim of the statute. Thus, the belief that jurors' hostility to the protected groups would result in frustration of rights asserted under the statute was reasonable.

EXERCISE 7(A)(10)

Rewrite the two bad examples above. Pull out the characters and make them subjects. Express the actions as verbs.

11. SENTENCE COHERENCE: USING THE RIGHT WORD

When writers are in a hurry to get their ideas down on paper, they often write incoherent sentences. They yoke inappropriate verbs to their subjects and create apples-and-oranges comparisons. Enhancing sentence coherence is an important goal of the revising and editing processes.

Not: The Court also felt that gender-based challenges to jurors could be used as a pretext for racist challenges.

Not: Like *Barnette*, the court held that no one should be compelled to recite the Pledge of Allegiance.

Note how in the first example above, the use of the vague, "grab-bag" verb "felt" blurs meaning. (Was the Court reasoning? Expressing apprehension? Expressing approval?) In the second sentence, a decision is inappropriately compared to a court.

EXERCISE 7(A)(11)

Correct the incoherence in the following sentence.

A violation of a federal statute grants jurisdiction if the statute authorizes a private right of action.

12. SPLIT INFINITIVES

Although opinions differ, most careful writers still apply a presumption against splitting infinitives (putting an adverb after the "to").

Not: It is the court's task to judiciously balance the equities.

In the example above, the adverb can easily be moved.

Ex: It is the court's task to balance the equities judiciously.

But always begin by asking yourself whether you really need the offending adverb. In the example above, "judiciously" is redundant. How else should a court balance equities?

The presumption against splitting infinitives is overcome when placement of the adverb elsewhere in the sentence creates ambiguity or the adverb and verb are frequent companions.

> Ex: The failure to properly acknowledge sources exposes a writer to charges of plagiarism.

In the example above, "properly" cannot follow "sources" without creating ambiguity ("properly exposes"). Moreover, when "to properly acknowledge" is translated into an adjective-noun pair, the result is "proper acknowledgment," a common expression.

EXERCISE 7(A)(12)

The following sentence has one split infinitive that a careful stylist would avoid and another that is acceptable. Which is which?

> To properly assess the situation, you have to carefully weigh planned improvements against anticipated results.

13. THAT OR WHICH?

The relative pronouns "that" and "which" are the subject of confusion among writers and controversy among editors. "That" is used only to introduce restrictive clauses—clauses intrinsic to a sentence's message—and does not properly begin a non-restrictive, incidental clause. Only "which" properly introduces a non-restrictive clause. (Remember that non-restrictive clauses are set off by commas, as though between parentheses.)

> Ex: The issue *that* divided the court most bitterly was capital punishment. (restrictive)

> Ex: The issue, *which* divided the court most bitterly, was whether execution constitutes cruel and unusual punishment. (non-restrictive)

Many writers use "which" interchangeably with "that" in restrictive clauses.

> Ex: The issue *which* divided the court most bitterly was capital punishment.

Others, known to the less zealous as "which-hunters," insist that only "that" is correct in restrictive clauses. We believe both are acceptable in scholarly writing. However, where the confusion of restrictive with non-restrictive language would be consequential, use "that" to introduce restrictive clauses. "That" and "which" introduce modifiers describing a concept or thing. Use "who" to introduce a modifier describing a person. (See Part B (3), Commas, below.)

EXERCISE 7(A)(13)

Determine whether the "who" modifier below should be restrictive or non-restrictive.

Children who do not wish to pledge should not be coerced into recitation.

14. VERB TENSES

Always use the past tense to relate the facts of a case.

Ex: The suspect fled from the scene, but was arrested two months later. Charged with murder, he pled guilty.

Always use the past perfect to describe the earlier of two past actions.

Ex: The suspect *had* disappeared by the time the police arrived at the scene.

The "historical present" is not ordinarily appropriate in scholarly writing. And it is never appropriate to combine the historical present and the past.

Not: The suspect flees from the scene, but is arrested two months later. Charged with murder, he subsequently pled guilty.

The present tense may be appropriate when you are describing a court's reasoning, although the past tense may also be used.

Ex: The majority analogizes gender-based discrimination to race-based discrimination. The dissent, however, finds them distinguishable.

Ex: The majority analogized gender-based discrimination to race-based discrimination. The dissent, however, found them distinguishable.

15. WHO OR WHOM?

The rules governing the use of this fiendish pair of pronouns are easy to state, but difficult to apply. Careful writers use "whom" when the pronoun is 1) the object of a preposition, 2) the object of a verb, or 3) the subject of an infinitive. "Who" is appropriate when the pronoun is 1) the subject of any verb form except an infinitive, or 2) the subject of a subjective complement. Problems arise because it is not always easy to tell whether the pronoun functions as subject or object. It helps to take the troublesome clause out of its context, rearrange it in normal subject-verb-object order, and substitute a personal pronoun for who/m. If a subject pronoun—"I," "we," "he," "she," or "they"—seems appropriate, use "who." If an object pronoun—"me," "us," "him," "her," "them"—sounds more natural, use "whom."

Ex: Justice Holmes is a jurist *about whom much has already been written*. (object of the preposition "about") (much has already been written about *him*)

Ex: The suspects *whom the police arrested* were questioned. (object of the verb "arrested") (the police arrested *them*)

Ex: *Whom do we want to interpret* our Constitution? (subject of the infinitive "to interpret") (we want *them* to interpret)

Ex: Police officers may not arrest just anyone *who they think committed a crime*. (subject of the verb "committed") (they think *she* committed a crime)

Ex: The perpetrator was not the man *who they thought he was*. (subject of a subjective complement) (they thought it *was he*)

Finally, if nothing seems to help, do what experienced writers do: rewrite the sentence to eliminate the problem whom.

EXERCISE 7(A)(15)

In each of the following sentences, determine whether "who" or "whom" is correct.

1. Rhetorical analysis asks, "For ____ is this document intended"
2. The Committee decides ____ should be nominated for a judgeship.
3. The defendant, ____ they knew, was convicted of fraud.
4. She asked him ____ he thought had gone.
5. Is there no one ____ we can trust?
6. ____ should we permit to alter our civil liberties?

16. WORDINESS: DIAGNOSIS AND CURE[2]

Wordiness is something we all know when we see it. But the simple marginal comment "wordy" rarely serves writer or editor well; it is a general description of a writing problem, not a precise diagnosis. A line-edit may solve the immediate problem, but it will not help the writer. Take, for example, the sentence below.

> In general, the end result of the correction of any and all errors of substance, organization, grammar, usage, spelling, and punctuation that may have been made by the author will be an article, note, or comment that is excellent with respect to quality and an author who, it is fair to say, is desirous of implementing a homicidal design upon the person of the editor.

We can all agree that this sentence is unacceptably "wordy." But what makes it that way?

Wordiness is really a constellation of bad writing habits, the most common of which are the following.

- The use of complex subjects. (See above, "Complex Subjects.")

2. The discussion that follows is inspired in part by Joseph M. Williams and Gregory G. Colomb's excellent section on the causes and cures of wordiness in Style: Lessons in Clarity & Grace, Longman (10th ed. 2010).

- The use of compound prepositions—for example, "with respect to."
- The use of nominalizations instead of verbs. (See above, "Nominalizations.")
- The utilization of jargon and pompous legalese.
- The use of redundant pairs. English has these in abundance—for example, "one and only," "basic and fundamental," "any and all."
- The use of unnecessary categories—for example, "green in color," "the crime of homicide."
- Redundant or meaningless modifiers—for example, "personal belongings," "past history."
- "Meaningless "throat-clearing" phrases—for example, "on the whole."
- Elaborating on the obvious.
- Piling on unnecessary detail.
- Using "of" to express possession—for example, "the extent of the responsibility of appellate counsel."
- Over-use of writing about writing, called "metadiscourse"—for example, "This paper will now discuss in turn each prong of the three-prong test."

With this in mind, we can diagnose the example above.

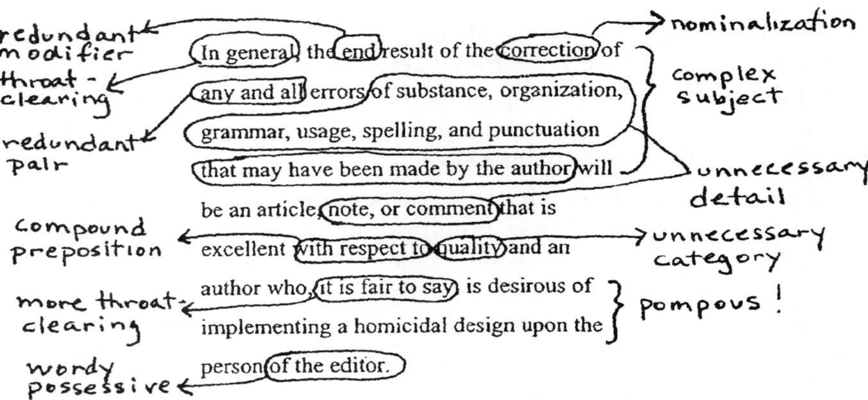

With all of the various kinds of wordiness removed, this sentence might read:

> The correction of all of the author's errors will result in an excellent article and a homicidal author.

Finally, we could improve our rewrite further by making an "actor" in the story the subject of the sentence and using the verb "to correct" instead of the nominalization "correction."

If you correct all your author's mistakes, you will have an excellent article and a homicidal author.

EDITORS' ABBREVIATIONS

sp	Spelling error	r-o	Run-on sentence
w.w	Wrong word	n/pro	Noun-pronoun agreement
m.m.	Misplaced Modifier	s/v	Subject-verb agreement
d.m.	Dangling modifier	ref?	Pronoun reference unclear
frag.	Sentence fragment	coh	Coherence
A.V.	Use active voice	llism	Use parallel Construction

B. PUNCTUATION

1. PUNCTUATION STYLES

This section is not a complete guide to punctuation; it focuses on the most basic rules and those most often broken.

Preliminarily, though, a few words about rules and styles are in order. There are two basic styles of punctuation, "tight" and "loose." Tight punctuation follows all of the rules all of the time. Loose punctuation distinguishes between optional and mandatory rules and even condones occasional violations of mandatory rules in the service of personal style. Tight punctuation is a tool of precision, and is therefore required in instrumental legal writing, especially in private and public rule-making prose: statutes, regulations, wills, contracts, and leases. Loose punctuation is often used in informal letters, in fiction or personal essays, and in journalism. What style of punctuation is appropriate for scholarly legal writing? A casenote or seminar paper is at once more personal than a contract and more formal than a short story. It is our view that as a scholarly writer, you can never go wrong by following all of the rules of punctuation all of the time. We also believe, however, that as an editor, you can be *too* zealous. Where an author has punctuated loosely, and that style does not compromise clarity, we would require only consistency. Of course, your journal may have a strict house style that leaves editors no choice. Where the choice is yours, however, we urge respect for the writer's own style. The discussion that follows will indicate which rules are optional in a loose punctuation style. Tight punctuation style requires you to observe all of the rules below.

2. PERIODS

Put a period at the end of a sentence—and nowhere else. In other words, avoid both run-on sentences and sentence fragments. At a minimum, a sentence consists of a subject and a predicate and expresses a complete thought. For example, the simple sentence "The witness testified" is composed of a subject (the witness) and a predicate (testified) and expresses a complete thought. Most sentences also need a complement to finish the thought begun by the subject and predicate: "The discovery rule *is an equitable doctrine*."

Two complete sentences incorrectly joined by a comma create a variety of run-on sentence sometimes called a "comma-splice."

> Not: The discovery rule is an equitable doctrine, its purpose is to do justice between the parties.

There are three ways to correct this comma-splice: by replacing the comma with a period, by replacing it with a semicolon, or by adding a coordinating conjunction after the comma (here "and" is the obvious choice).

Although run-on sentences should always be avoided, good writers sometimes deliberately use sentence fragments, for emphasis or to surprise the reader.

> Ex: Perhaps these proposals, so contrary to the established approach, come too early. Or too late.

3. COMMAS

a. Put a comma after an introductory word, phrase, or dependent clause.

> Ex: During the past several terms, the Court has had ample opportunities to revisit the issue.

> Ex: If the jury had been properly instructed, it would have acquitted the defendant.

However, when the introduction consists of a word or very short phrase, loose punctuation omits this comma.

> Ex: Today the courts approach the issue differently.

b. Put a comma, called the "serial comma," between all items in a series of three or more. Loose punctuation omits the comma that precedes the "and," but the better practice is to use it, because it can resolve ambiguities. Note that without the final comma, it would be unclear in the example below whether "the latter" refers to "services" or "goods and services."

Ex: Real property, securities, and goods and services were all involved, particularly the latter.

c. Put a comma between two independent clauses joined by a coordinating conjunction (and, but, or, nor, for, so, yet). An independent clause has a subject and predicate and could stand alone as a sentence. When the clauses are short, loose punctuation omits this comma.

Ex: No arrests or prosecutions under the statute occurred, and the union and the employer eventually resolved their dispute.

Ex: Negotiations broke down and the union struck.

You should note that "however" and "therefore" are *not* coordinating conjunctions and cannot be used with a comma to join two independent clauses. Only a semicolon is correct in that situation.

Not: The district court concluded that the statute was constitutional, however, the court of appeals reversed.

Ex: The district court concluded that the statute was constitutional; however, the court of appeals reversed.

d. Use a comma (or commas) to set off a phrase or clause that is interrupting or "non-restrictive"—that is, when it provides information inessential to our understanding of the main clause. Do not use a comma if the information is essential—if the phrase or clause is "restrictive." (For the proper use of "that" and "which," see Part A, 13.)

Ex: The testator left his assets, which were in Utah, to his wife. (Non-restrictive: assets incidently located in Utah.)

Ex: The testator left to his wife his assets that were in Utah. (Restrictive: *only* those assets in Utah.)

e. Do *not* put a comma between subject and verb. The temptation to make this mistake most often arises in a sentence that is top-heavy with an overly complex subject. (See Part A (4), Complex Subjects.)

Not: *The principle of the existence of a reasonable expectation of privacy in documents shredded into small pieces by the defendant prior to disposal*, was traditionally assumed by the courts.

f. Put a comma before a phrase tacked on to a sentence like an afterthought.

Ex: The negotiations were prolonged, not to mention vehement.

EXERCISE 7(B)(3)

Correct the comma errors in the following sentences, using tight punctuation.

1. The executive offices were located in New York where the Board met regularly.

2. Mr. Wood lives and works in Chicago, holds a Chicago driver's license and voter registration card and gets all his mail in Chicago.

3. Because it was buried in his junk mail Wood didn't see the summons for some time.

4. The appellant appealed his conviction and sentence to the Court of Appeals which used the Supreme Court balancing test that weighs the public interest against the individual's right to personal security from arbitrary interference by law enforcement officers.

5. To protect products, at the cost of usurping the rights of prior good faith trademark owners is not something most countries are willing to do.

4. SEMICOLONS

a. Use semicolons in a list of three or more items if one or more of the items contains an internal comma.

Ex: The court weighs such factors as distance from the home itself; efforts, if any, to screen the area from view; and the type, frequency, and duration of occupation.

b. Use a semicolon to join two independent clauses, especially when you wish to connect or contrast their meanings. This is one way to correct the run-on caused by a comma splice. You must be certain, however, that *both* clauses could stand alone as complete sentences.

Ex: This decision is both edifying and cautionary; it simultaneously shows the court at its best and at its worst.

Not: This decision is both edifying and cautionary; the court at its best and at its worst.

EXERCISE 7(B)(4)

Correct the punctuation errors in the following sentences.

1. The TRIPS agreement should be extended, as it currently stands, TRIPS is the only agreement with international implementation and it is vital not to jeopardize that.

2. Each party fully disclosed the extent of his or her estate, income, and financial prospects, was fully informed of the estate, income, and financial prospects of the other, was represented in the preparation of the separation agreement by independent counsel and was fully advised of his or her rights by such counsel.

5. COLONS

Use a colon to introduce a list if what precedes the list could stand on its own as a complete sentence.

Ex: Non-interpretive factors include the following: pre-existing common-law, legislative history, and local custom.

Not: Non-interpretive factors include: pre-existing common-law, legislative history, and local custom.

A colon is also used to introduce a formal question, quotation, amplification, or example.

Ex: The discovery rule is an equitable doctrine: a way to do justice between the parties.

6. DASHES

Use a long dash ("em dash") to set off interrupting or other nonrestrictive information, just as you would use commas. Dashes are particularly helpful to set off interruptions that contain commas or to tack on afterthoughts.

Ex: This is precisely the kind of issue—controversial, consequential, confounding—that scholars love and judges dread.

EXERCISE 7(B)(6)

Which commas could helpfully be replaced by em dashes?

The Operations Policy Committee, to whom the Board of Directors had delegated the responsibilities of general operations such as making policy decisions, hiring corporate officers, and supervising plant procedures, met in Pittsburgh.

7. APOSTROPHES

Use apostrophes to form possessives and contractions—but not plurals. Remember that singular possessives are ordinarily formed by the addition of " 's" to the noun while plural possessives are formed by an apostrophe alone.

Ex: don't (contraction)

appellant's contentions (singular possessive)

appellants' contentions (plural possessive)

Not: appellants' contended (plural)

When a name or other singular noun ends in "s," most authorities say you should form the possessive by adding " 's." Some writers, however, use an apostrophe alone.

Ex: Professor Williams's article

Professor Williams' article

Be sure to remember that the pronoun "it" is an exception to the general rule that singular possessives are formed with " 's." Do not confuse "its" and "it's."

Ex: It's a difficult course. (contraction of "it is.")

The course has its difficult moments. (possessive.)

You should also note that contractions are a feature of informal prose and are therefore not often used in scholarly writing.

EXERCISE 7(B)(7)

Correct the apostrophe errors in the following sentences.

1. Plaintiff sued Nan West and her company for defendant's alleged misappropriation of plaintiff's trade secret.
2. Walker served as Matthews Lamaze coach.
3. The court has twice noted it's refusal to rule on this matter.

8. QUOTATION MARKS

Put closing quotation marks outside of commas and periods, even when this does not reflect the punctuation of the quoted material.

Ex: In addition to serving as "laboratories for national law," state courts serve as "primary guardians of the liberty of the people."

However, closing quotation marks always precede colons and semicolons.

Quotation marks should not be used around "block quotes"—quotations of 50 words or more, indented, and single-spaced.

9. ELLIPSES

Indicate omissions in quoted material with dots ("ellipses"). Use three dots to indicate the omission of a word or words in the middle of a sentence and four dots to indicate that the end of a sentence has been omitted. Do not use ellipses to indicate that the beginning of a sentence has been omitted, however; the use of a lower-case letter or its replacement by a capital letter in brackets is sufficient to indicate the omission.

Ex: In conclusion, the court of appeals reiterated that its "responsibility . . . is not to advance the goals of law enforcement, but rather to stand as a fixed citadel of civil liberties. . . . [A]s Benjamin Franklin observed, 'those who give up essential liberty to purchase a little temporary safety deserve neither liberty nor safety.' "

Four dots may also be used to indicate the omission of a sentence or sentences in the middle or at the end of a paragraph. An entire omitted paragraph should be indicated by an indented line of four dots between the quoted paragraphs.

REVIEW EXERCISE

The following passage from a student paper has many errors in grammar, usage, and punctuation. Diagnose and correct the problems. Be sure to check for wordiness; sexist usage; faulty parallelism; noun/pronoun inconsistency; and problems with comma, semi-colon, and colon usage. The answer to this exercise is in Appendix B.

Fifty years ago, it was held by the United States Supreme Court in the case of *West Virginia State Board of Education v. Barnette* that compulsion on the part of the state that requires that public elementary school pupils engage in recitation of the Pledge of Allegiance in school is inconsistent with the meaning of the Constitution, however in 1979, the Illinois legislature enacted a statute, which provides that the Pledge "... shall be recited each school day by public elementary school pupils.

In 1989, Richard Sherman challenged the constitutionality of that statute on three grounds, arguing: 1) that it's plain meaning violated Barnette, 2) reciting the Pledge in public school is further unconstitutional because the phrase "under God" offends the Establishment Clause of the First Amendment, and 3) like prayers at school graduation, even if students are not compelled to recite the Pledge, children who do not wish to participate are coerced when teachers and willing students pledge allegiance. The district court ruled in favor of the defendant school board and the Seventh Circuit court of Appeals affirmed. They found that 1) in order to "save" the statute, they would read "shall be recited by pupils" to mean only teachers and "willing pupils" are required to recite the Pledge; 2) "under God" is a form of "ceremonial deism," that is protected from Establishment Clause scrutiny because it has lost through rote recitation any significant religious content and 3) recitation of the Pledge is not coercive because it is not like prayer but merely part of the public school curriculum, and if a pupil objects, he may select private education instead.

Chapter Eight

WRITING WITH STYLE

"Most people don't realize that writing is a craft. You have to take your apprenticeship in it like anything else."

-Katherine Anne Porter

Scholarly writers traditionally privilege those stylistic conventions that suggest disinterested objectivity. They distance themselves from the text by writing exclusively in the third person. They efface themselves by using abstract language, instead of their own distinctive and ordinary vocabularies: "Given the second-best nature of the zero transactions cost equilibrium, it should not be surprising that the introduction of transactions has complex and ambiguous effects on contract choice, welfare, and optimal default choice." They depopulate the text with passive voice constructions: "This conclusion was reached no matter what legal theory was applied." And if forced to admit a personal interest in the debate, they scrupulously distance themselves by using the dual perspective of irony, understatement, or double negatives: "The analysis suggested here is not altogether disinterested." The upshot of such stylistic practices is that readers are often as put off by the writer's prose as they are captivated by the writer's thoughts.

The worst of scholarly writing—prose that "sounds untouched by human hands, like a monstrous frozen dinner fabricated from sawdust and boiled crayons"[1]—can be avoided if you pursue a clean, clear style. To be readable, scholarly writers need only adhere to the prescriptive advice offered in Chapter Seven: avoid too many passives and nominalizations, make the grammatical subject the agent of the action, use forceful verbs, and keep the subject near the predicate and your modifiers near the modified. The prose that results will be concise and comprehensible and serviceable. It may also be faceless and flat. If you

1. DONALD HALL, WRITING WELL 126 (1973).

would like your prose to be not just competent, but to be special—to have a little panache and pizzazz—your task is harder. You will have to move beyond writing as communication toward writing as creative craft. You will have to develop your own style.

Good style is not mere idiosyncratic flourish; it is content. For example, we employ narrative style to root abstract discussions in a human context. We speak in the vernacular for straight talk. And when we change tone, vary diction, use metaphor, bend grammatical rules, we do so for a purpose. The stylistic technique underscores—even makes—our meaning. When it does not, when the technique is mere icing, we are better off sticking with the simple and efficient.

Good writing is above all honest writing that does not settle for cliches, jargon, hackneyed analogies, and worn-out metaphors. Rather, it is thoughtful and individual. Good writers are always present in their writing, however discreetly. The rest of this chapter focuses on some of the techniques writers use to leave an imprint on their texts.

A. MEMORABLE TITLES

What's in a name? That which
we call a rose,
By any other name would smell as sweet.

-William Shakespeare

A rose might smell as sweet regardless of its name, but authors, like expectant parents, are rarely deterred from a name debate. Indeed, titles are a challenge. First, they should contain terms likely to turn up in a reasonable search so that the articles are easy to find. Second, they should be descriptive so that researchers can determine at a glance whether the article bears on their topic of interest. Third, they should be intriguing so as to motivate browsers to read further. Ideally, they should also be memorable—so attention-grabbing that they spring to mind years later. It is not surprising then that titles tax the creative juices.

At a minimum, titles should alert the reader to the topic, as in *A Conceptual Model of Health Care Fraud Enforcement*[2] or *A Remedy for Abortion Seekers*.[3] Some authors add a subtitle that narrows the topic announced in the general title: *Reinforcing Representation: Congressional Power to Enforce the Fourteenth and Fifteenth Amendments in the Rehnquist and Waite Courts*.[4] These titles may not be the most scintillating, but they are helpful. They orient the reader and supply context. To

2. Joan H. Krause, *A Conceptual Model of Health Care Fraud Enforcement*, 12 J. LAW and POLICY 55 (2003).

3. Rachel L. Braunstein, *A Remedy for Abortion Seekers*, 68 BROOK. L. REV. 303 (2002).

4. Ellen D. Katz, *Reinforcing Representation: Congressional Power to Enforce the Fourteenth and Fifteenth Amendments in the Rehnquist and Waite Courts*, 101 MICH. L. REV. 2341 (2003).

do this effectively, however, titles must be comprehensible. Avoid titles that are lengthy or abstract, or that contain jargon or statutory or case citations:

- *The Tax Treatment of Boot Distributions in Corporate Reorganizations under* Section 356(a)(2)–Commissioner v. Clark, *The Latest or the Last Word*[5]
- *Anti–Diversion Rules in Antidumping Procedures: Interface or Short–Circuit for the Management of Interdependence*[6]
- *Termination of Public School Desegregation: Determination of Unitary Status Based on The Elimination of Invidious Value Inculcation.*[7]

Unless a case or statute is well known, avoid references to it since the name alone provides no useful information. Similarly, abstract terms and legal jargon are more apt to mystify than tantalize the uninitiated. You must also ensure that a descriptive title cannot be misread: *Rotating Japanese Managers in American Subsidiaries of Japanese Firms: A Challenge for American Employment Discrimination Law*[8] left us with visions of spinning executives.

If description is the bottom line, eclat is the goal. Many writers achieve both criteria by using the main title to excite the reader's curiosity and the subtitle to provide context. The title may use puns, humor or literary references to entice the reader.

- *Hearing* Voices*: Speaker Identification in Court*[9]
- *From Outlaws to In-laws: Issues Surrounding the Evolving Status of Lesbian and Gay Individuals*[10]
- *The Purloined Personality: Consumer Profiling in Financial Services*[11]
- *Scrutiny of the Bounty: Incentive Awards for Plaintiffs in Class Litigation*[12]

5. Robert A. King, *The Tax Treatment of Boot Distributions in Corporate Reorganizations under* Section 356(a)(2)–Commissioner v. Clark, *The Latest or the Last Word*, 11 Whittier L. Rev. 723 (1990). We found this title in an article on the subject of titles: Richard B. Cappalli, *The 1990 Rose Awards: The Good, The Bad, and The Ugly–Titles for Law Review Articles*, 41 J. Legal Educ. 485, 487 (1991).

6. Edwin Vermulst & Paul Waer, *Anti–Diversion Rules in Antidumping Procedures: Interface or Short–Circuit for the Management of Interdependence*, 11 Mich. J. Int'l L. 1119 (1990), cited in Cappalli *supra* note 6, at 487.

7. Kevin Brown, *Termination of Public School Desegregation: Determination of Unitary Status Based on The Elimination of Invidious Value Inculcation*, 58 Geo. Wash. L. Rev. 1105 (1990), cited in Cappalli, *supra* note 6, at 486.

8. Eileen M. Mullen, Note, *Rotating Japanese Managers in American Subsidiaries of Japanese Firms: A Challenge for American Employment Discrimination Law*, 45 Stan. L. Rev. 725 (1993).

9. Lawrence M. Solan & Peter M. Tiersma, *Hearing* Voices*: Speaker Identification in Court*, 54 Hastings L.J. 373 (2003).

10. Nan. D. Hunter, *From Outlaws to In-laws: Issues Surrounding the Evolving Status of Lesbian and Gay Individuals*, 89 Ky. L.J. 885 (2000–2001).

11. Janet D. Gertz, *The Purloined Personality: Consumer Profiling in Financial Services*, 39 San Diego L. Rev. 943 (2002).

12. Clinton A. Krislov, *Scrutiny of the Bounty: Incentive Awards for Plaintiffs in*

- *Honor at the Trough: The Ethics of Pork Politics*[13]
- *I See London, I See France: The Constitutional Challenge to "Saggy" Pants Law*[14]
- *You Say Yes, But I Say No: The Future of Third Party Consent Searches after Georgia v. Randolph*[15]

Reversely, some authors use the subtitle to intrigue: Lawrence v. Texas: *The "Fundamental Right" that Dares Not Speak Its Name.*[16] The main title identifies the article as a casenote, but leaves the context a mystery. The reference to a well-known quotation from Oscar Wilde in the subtitle, however, alerts us to the subject and gives the title literary and sociological resonance.

While you want your titles to be memorable, remember that cleverness can backfire. One law review vetoed as being in bad taste the title *Premature Discharge of Seamen* for an article on retaliatory discharge in the marine industry.[17] In addition, be careful not to create a title so intriguing as to be downright perplexing. A title like *When is Clinical Psychology like Astrology?*[18] can't help but engage our interest, but it is borderline—you certainly would not want to be any more enigmatic than this.

Like texts, titles may need to be edited. If the title contains jargon or is long and abstract, readers might avoid the text. See if you can shorten and clarify the title without sacrificing wit and informativeness.

B. INTRIGUING INTRODUCTIONS AND SATISFYING CONCLUSIONS

"Well begun is half done."

-Anonymous

"All's well that ends well."

-William Shakespeare

Given the relative brevity of introductions and conclusions, writers spend what might appear to be a disproportionate amount of time writing them. Such expenditure of energy is justified by their important

Class Litigation, 78 ILL. B.J. 286 (1990), cited in Cappalli, *supra* note 6, at 485.

13. Virginia A. Fitt, *Honor at the Trough: The Ethics of Pork Politics*, 25 J.L. & POL. 467 (2010).

14. William C. Vandivort, *I See London, I See France: The Constitutional Challenge to "Saggy" Pants Law*, 75 BROOK. L. REV. 667 (2009).

15. Jason Zakai, *You Say Yes, But I Say No: The Future of Third Party Consent Searches after* Georgia v. Randolph, 73 BROOK. L. REV. 421 (2006).

16. Lawrence Tribe, Lawrence v. Texas: *The "Fundamental Right" that Dares Not Speak Its Name*, 117 HARV. L. REV. 1893 (2004).

17. We thank Gail Stephenson for telling us this story.

18. Margaret Berger, *When is Clinical Psychology like Astrology?*, 33 ARIZ. ST. L.J. 75 (2001).

functions and prominent positions. It is upon them, after all, that our readers form their first and final impressions of our work. Indeed, if they are poorly written, some law review editors never read beyond them.

Introductions establish context. They delineate the perimeters of the forest while orienting the reader to some of the landmark trees; in other words, they identify the topic of the paper, locate the topic within the general literature on the subject, announce the thesis, and point toward the support offered and organization followed. If you manage to work all this essential information into the opening paragraphs, you have gone a long way toward fulfilling your readers' expectations, especially because readers of scholarly articles tend to have a prior interest in the topic and thus require little more motivation than clear exposition to peruse the piece. Nonetheless, some readers might need an additional incentive, and most readers appreciate a fresh presentation of the material. Thus a captivating, provocative opening is always worth a little extra trouble.

Similarly, the best conclusions end with a bang, not a whimper. As your last word on the topic, conclusions tend to be remembered, and thus deserve special crafting. While a conclusion is not the place to raise new issues, the best reach beyond brief restatement of your thesis and major arguments. Mere summary is anti-climactic. Instead, suggest avenues for additional investigation or emphasize the important implications of your analysis. Most of all, leave the reader excited about the subject matter and interested in exploring it further.

To put a little punch in your introduction or conclusion, you might want to try using narrative. Alternatively, you might want to open with a quote or with a forceful, provocative statement.

1. USE NARRATIVE

Increasingly, part of the context that must be established in an introduction is the human and social context out of which legal issues emerge. Often that context is best realized through narrative.

James Boyd White tells us that because all legal issues begin and end "in ordinary language and experience, the heart of the law is the process of translation by which it must work, from ordinary language to legal language and back again."[19] In thinking about this statement, we realized that some of the most engrossing casenotes and comments that we have read follow this pattern. The article opens with a narrative in ordinary language, sometimes even a first-person narrative, about a legal problem. The body of the article then translates the narrative into legal language and analyzes the legal issues. Finally, the conclusion returns us to the ordinary world and reminds us of the impact of the law on human lives.

19. James B. White, *Rhetoric and Law: the Arts of Cultural and Communal Life*, *in* The Rhetoric of the Human Sciences: Language and Argument in Scholarship and Public Affairs 305 (John S. Nelson et al. eds. 1987).

Personal narrative quickly engages the reader's interest in the following introduction to a student law review article on plagiarism and copyright infringement.

> A few years ago, while working as an editor, I was putting the finishing touches on a forthcoming book about an event from fifty years before, which had previously been chronicled by participants, observers, and scholars. The new book was nothing to get excited about, but it was well organized and comprehensive; it offered a new interpretation of the event; and its author, who had written several books before, had apparently done a competent job.
>
> One day the mass-transportation system broke down and I was unable to reach my office. Instead I went to my local library to verify some historical information for the book. As I browsed through one of the other books on the same subject in the library's collection, scanning the pages for names and dates, a passage caught my eye—a passage that was strangely, even disturbingly, familiar. The same passage appeared almost word for word in the manuscript I had been editing. With increasing agitation I paged through the remaining books. In the end, I identified five passages that my author appeared to have lifted from three different sources.[20]

Not all effective narrative is personal. Storytelling enlivens the introduction to an article finding a right in state constitutions for community treatment of the mentally ill.

> On January 17, 1993, Christopher Battiste, a homeless man from New York, was arrested for bludgeoning eighty-year-old Doll Mamie Johnson to death in front of her church in the Bronx. Mentally ill for much of his life, Battiste had spent years "drift[ing] in and out of jails, homeless shelters and psychiatric emergency rooms." Less than two months later, Larry Hogue, notorious for his very public and very bizarre behavior on the Upper West Side, was ordered by a state appeals court to be civilly committed for six months in a psychiatric center in Queens. At the same time that these events were transpiring in New York, similar stories were being told in cities across the United States.[21]

Many conclusions also make impressive use of narrative, returning the reader—after whole sections of abstract analysis—to the impact the analysis might have in human terms. Personal narrative is effectively used in the conclusion of the following casenote to ground its criticism of a decision upholding a state's right to display the Confederate flag.

20. Laurie Stearns, Comment, *Copy Wrong: Plagiarism, Process, Property, and the Law*, 80 Cal. L. Rev. 513, 514 (1992).

21. Antony B. Klapper, *Finding a Right in State Constitutions for Community Treatment of the Mentally Ill*, 142 U. Pa. L. Rev. 739, 741 (1993).

> It is the spring of 1984 in Atlanta, and the groundskeeper at Franklin Delano Roosevelt High School is starting his morning routine. In my twelfth grade homeroom we have finished the morning business—attendance has been taken, the announcements have been made. We are simply waiting for the bell to signal the start of the first class period. As I wait, my eyes return to the groundskeeper, who is carefully unfurling and raising a series of flags. First is the American flag, last is the Atlanta Public Schools flag, and sandwiched between the two is the Georgia State flag. I am drawn to this flag, particularly to its wholesale incorporation of Dixie. . . .
>
> . . . My eyes close tightly, my fists clench, and I slowly force from my mind images of the flag, of the Ku Klux Klan, of Bull Connor and George Wallace—of black people in chains, hanging from trees, kept illiterate, denied the opportunity to vote.
>
> The bell has rung. My teacher is calling my name: "James, are you ok?" I look up, startled. "Yes ma'am, I'm fine," I say, as I collect my books and head for class. . . . But overcoming the flag has taken a piece of me—a piece that I will not easily recover.[22]

2. OPEN OR CLOSE WITH A QUOTATION

A striking quotation is a stylish way to begin—whether you use it as an epigram or in your opening sentences. Either way, the quotation is meant to spark the reader's interest by being either reflective and learned, or impertinent, humorous, and provocative (as in the example that follows).

> "Poetry is indispensable," Jean Cocteau once said, "if only I knew what for." Nearly everyone seems to agree that blackmail is an indispensable part of a well-developed criminal code, but no one is sure what for.[23]

Similarly, one effective way to close a piece is with a provocative, wise, or humorous quotation. Your own extended analysis can often be strikingly reinforced by an apt comment made by another author.

(1)

> Perhaps this pluralistic emphasis reflects the bias of someone who is struggling to finish the second edition of a treatise that tries to embrace the clash of competing constitutional visions. But I think my emphasis reflects something deeper than that. For me, the Constitution's greatness is in large measure its resistance to ideological reductionism—its resistance to neat encapsulation in any one grand tradition that defines the aspi-

22. James Forman, Jr., Note, *Driving Dixie Down: Removing the Confederate Flag from Southern State Capitols*, 101 YALE L.J. 505, 526 (1991).

23. Leo Katz, *Blackmail and Other Forms of Arm–Twisting*, 141 U. PA. L. REV. 1567 (1993).

rations of some of the dispossessed as outside the boundaries of the constitutive and defining charter of the society.

Is the Constitution, then, sometimes at war with its own premises? Perhaps it speaks in the words of Walt Whitman: "Do I contradict myself? Very well then, I contradict myself. I am large, I contain multitudes."[24]

(2)

It is only when "there are too many pigs for the teats," as Abraham Lincoln once said, that aggregate pork spending is thoroughly criticized.[25]

3. BEGIN QUICKLY AND END FORCEFULLY

Many solid papers begin informatively. They open with statements about the significance of a subject, they provide essential summaries of background information, or they review relevant literature in order to highlight the contribution of the present work. Such introductions are competent—but slow.

It is a refreshing change to read a piece that begins quickly and forcefully. Good openings have a little drama. They may start with a "punchy" controversial statement, as in the following statement, which appeared in a symposium volume honoring the very decision the author seemingly deflates.

> *Goldberg v. Kelly* does not rank with the most important decisions in the history of the Supreme Court. It did not establish judicial review, as did *Marbury v. Madison*. Nor did it usher in the Civil War, as did *Scott v. Sandford*. It did not legitimate Jim Crow in the South, as did *Plessy v. Ferguson*, nor did it help undo it as did *Brown v. Board of Education*. It did not stand testimony to substantive due process or economic liberties, as did *Lochner v. New York*, nor did it create a constitutional right to abortion as did *Roe v. Wade*. *Goldberg v. Kelly* did not launch a war or define a generation. Although thundering greatness shall forever elude it, *Goldberg* nonetheless rates at the top of the second tier of great Supreme Court cases....[26]

A good introduction may also challenge established critical positions and fundamental assumptions.

> Wifely submission is risky business in the 1990s. Gone is the day when a wife could depend on her husband's labor to maintain her at home, "secure and safe." Today is the day of

24. Laurence H. Tribe, *The Idea of the Constitution: A Metaphor-morphosis*, 37 J. Legal Educ. 170, 173 (1987).

25. Fitts, *supra* note 13, at 467.

26. Richard A. Epstein, *No New Property*, 56 Brook. L. Rev. 747 (1990).

> divorce at will and equality rhetoric, which means that if her marriage ends, the homemaker wife will be catapulted into financial independence, and probably ruin. Such is the 1990s price tag for choosing to "play with dolls."[27]

Good introductions may be a bit unconventional—as in the following opening, which trades on surprise, if not shock.

> What is pornography or obscenity? Except for those who profit by selling pictures of vaginas, the Supreme Court's various definitions of obscenity have been unsuccessful, at least in practice.[28]

Humor can also be good bait to hook your reader.

(1)

> Banking law appears to be the preferred habitat for a peculiar genre of legal doctrine, the oxymoron. We have the nonbank bank, the nonthrift thrift, the nonbranch branch, even, as of 1992, the nonstatute statute. In this paper, we examine another oxymoron in banking law, the nondeposit deposit, by which we mean an instrument or account that fulfills the functional purposes of a checking account deposit but is not treated as a deposit for purposes of federal deposit insurance, Federal Reserve Board requirements, or both.[29]

(2)

> Defying good advice, I entitled this lecture "Surviving Victim Talk." I wanted to call it "Beyond Victim Talk," but one friend told me she never reads anything that begins with "beyond." Another said he once attended a lecture entitled "Beyond Nihilism" and thought nothing of it. Still another friend reports that titles that begin with "beyond" or "towards" are like restaurants that say "all you can eat" or "a meal in itself"—all to be read as warnings to stay away.[30]

Conclusions also gain strength when they offer a fresh perspective on the familiar.

> Most individuals enter into employment contracts with hopes and dreams. Few enter with the end of the relationship clearly in mind. Still fewer anticipate that their employer will be able to prevent them from working elsewhere should they wish to leave. Would employees willingly enter employment relationships that so compromised their satisfaction, their personal

27. Cynthia Starnes, *Divorce and the Displaced Homemaker: A Discourse on Playing with Dolls, Partnership Buyouts and Dissociation Under No-Fault*, 60 U. Chi. L. Rev. 67, 69–70 (1993).

28. James Lindgren, *Defining Pornography*, 141 U. Pa. L. Rev. 1153, 1155 (1993).

29. Jonathan R. Macey & Geoffrey P. Miller, *Nondeposit Deposits and the Future of Bank Regulation*, 91 Mich. L. Rev. 237 (1992).

30. Martha Minow, *Surviving Victim Talk*, 40 UCLA L. Rev. 1411, 1412 (1993).

> autonomy, and maybe even their dignity if the situation unexpectedly deteriorated? Or would they enter these relationships only if they had no real choice, if they were impelled by necessity to work, and if they were unable to influence the terms? Perhaps, they would remain, despite unsatisfactory working conditions, only for the income or for love of the work, if the alternative was not to be able to do the work at all. But that is a far cry from the American ideal of free labor.[31]

Another effective closing is to use the conclusion to encourage the reader to explore other promising avenues of discussion.

> But as we reread and rewrite, we wonder whether we are proposing too much too late: too much because integrating even half of the close-reading practice we describe would radically transform the traditional two-credit advanced writing syllabus. (Might it find a place in a three-credit advanced writing course or a whole new course in Reading and Writing the Law?) And do our suggestions come too late in that we have accepted too readily an unexamined, perhaps ungrounded, assumption that critical reading can effectively be taught only after the first-year student's initiation into the discourse community? (Should the teaching of close reading be integrated into Legal Writing? Into Legal Process?) As we continue to teach and to read, the need for ever earlier training in critical thinking seems ever more apparent and urgent.[32]

Finally, conclusions are memorable when they go out with some straight talk, rendered perhaps with a light touch.

> *The Bluebook* began as a simple concept: a short citation guide for those contributing articles to law reviews. It has grown, however, like poison ivy. *The Bluebook* now acts as a general citation manual, a style book, a brief-writer's guide, and a bibliographic resource for American, foreign, and international law materials. This is too much to expect of any temporary committee of students, no matter how gifted they may be.... In the next edition, instead of looking for new worlds of citation to conquer, perhaps *The Bluebook's* editors should just try again, but this time get it right. To paraphrase Harvard Law's own Professor Kingsfield (or was it John Houseman): The Bluebook should get respect the old-fashioned way—by earning it.[33]

31. Lea S. VanderVelde, *The Gendered Origins of the Lumley Doctrine: Binding Men's Consciences and Women's Fidelity*, 101 YALE L.J. 775, 852 (1992).

32. Elizabeth Fajans & Mary R. Falk, *Against the Tyranny of Paraphrase: Talking Back to Texts*, 78 CORNELL L. REV. 163, 204–05 (1993).

33. James W. Paulsen, *An Uninformed System of Citation*, 105 HARV. L. REV. 1780, 1794 (1992) (book review).

C. CREATIVE SYNTAX

1. THE SYNTAX OF CONVERSATION

There is a trend among nonfiction writers to use ordinary language, to recreate for the reader the writer's train of thinking, to speak as persons with acknowledged interest in the subject matter. Moreover, this trend is not the province of journalists or "docu-dramatists" alone; it is happening in academic circles. If you are writing an informal essay or commentary, if you are incorporating narrative into your text, or if you simply want to imbue your prose with some of the vibrancy of natural speech, you might decide to adopt a conversational style.

A conversational style requires you to write sentences that have the structure of spontaneous thought, that is, your sentences must produce the illusion of mind in action—its flashes of insight, shifts of direction and tone, subjective interjections. Paradoxically, a lot of revision is often required to produce a pointed, "natural" sentence; early attempts may simply sound vacuous. Here are some tips to help you get started.

a. To suggest a mind unpacking and refining an idea, use apposite rephrasings or cumulative modifiers that hone and extend the generalization of the main clause.

(1)

> Time and again, right-of-publicity plaintiffs are described by the courts as carefully "cultivating" their talents, slowly "building" their images, judiciously and patiently "nurturing" their publicity values—as working long and hard to make themselves famous, popular, respected, beloved.[34]

(2)

> The Constitution is many things, but it is first a written text, words arranged for all to read.[35]

b. To incorporate personal commentary on abstract ideas, tack it on to the end of a sentence or interject it into the middle.

(1)

> Simply put, are secret searches and seizures reasonable? Regardless of one's answer, at least one will be asking the right question—talking sense rather than nonsense.[36]

(2)

> The need for communal approbation—the ultimate vulnerability in writing—is, if anything, greater for judges than for other writers.[37]

34. Michael Madow, *Private Ownership of Public Image: Popular Culture and Publicity Rights*, 81 COLUM. L. REV. 125, 182 (1993).

35. Robert A. Ferguson, *"We Do Ordain and Establish": The Constitution as Literary Text*, 29 WM. & MARY L. REV. 3 (1987).

36. Akhil R. Amar, *Fourth Amendment First Principles*, 107 HARV. L. REV. 757, 803 (1994).

37. Robert A. Ferguson, *The Judicial Opinion as Literary Genre*, 2 YALE J. L. & HUMAN. 201, 217 (1990).

Notice how often punctuation marks are used to herald an author's personal commentary, rather than the more obvious use of the first person singular. Subjective remarks are surrounded by parentheses, set off with dashes, or preceded by commas or ellipses. Similar signals often alert readers to humorous or ironic remarks.

(1)

> Or, if prejudice is a word that signified only what existed "back" in the past, don't we need a new word to signify what is going on in the present? Amnesia, perhaps?[38]

(2)

> Victims can get on the agenda, the evening news, and the gossip circuit—victims get time.[39]

c. To record questions, sudden insight, strong emotion, or shifts of thought, create a sense of movement by using rhetorical questions, parentheticals, and, even, snippets of sentences.

(1)

> The Fourth Amendment today is an embarrassment. Much of what the Supreme Court has said in the last half century—that the Amendment generally calls for warrants and probable cause for all searches and seizures, and exclusion of illegally obtained evidence—is initially plausible but ultimately misguided. As a matter of text, history, and plain old common sense, these three pillars of modern Fourth Amendment case law are hard to support; in fact, today's Supreme Court does not really support them. Except when it does. Warrants are not required—unless they are. All searches and seizures must be grounded in probable cause—but not on Tuesdays. And unlawfully seized evidence must be excluded whenever five votes say so. Meanwhile, sensible rules that the Amendment clearly does lay down or presuppose—that all searches and seizures must be reasonable, that warrants (and only warrants) always require probable cause, and that the officialdom should be liable for unreasonable searches and seizures—are ignored by the Justices. Sometimes.[40]

(2)

> The canonical blackmail problem is quickly stated. Busybody says to Philanderer: "Pay me $10,000, or I'll reveal

38. Patricia J. Williams, The Alchemy of Race And Rights 103 (1991).

39. Minow, *supra* note 30, at 1414–15.

40. Amar, *supra* note 36, at 758–58.

your affairs to your wife." Busybody is guilty of blackmail. What is strange, however, is that if Busybody had actually revealed Philanderer's affairs, or if he had threatened Philanderer with doing so but not mentioned the money, or if he had asked for the money but not mentioned what he was going to do if he didn't get it—if he had done any one of these things, he would not be guilty of any crime whatsoever. Yet when he combines these various innocent actions, a crime results—blackmail. How odd; how mysterious; how come?[41]

d. To acknowledge a personal interest in the subject matter and to engage your reader, use the first person.

> I represent "bad mothers" because I need the truths they tell me concerning our common culture. They tell truths by exposing to me our likeness and our differences. I see myself reflected in them sometimes, recognizing in their gestures and their attitudes variations of ones familiar to me because they are my own. Beyond that though, in their *difference* they tell me truths. They tell me truths when they refuse to let me see who they are, when they hold a mirror facing me, between themselves and me, so that I confront that mirror as a barrier.[42]

2. THE SYNTAX OF CEREMONY

Although writers often begin conversationally—with a "hook," a narrative, anecdote, or joke, that draws attention—there are occasions and topics which seem to call for a deeper note. On these occasions, you may want to raise your prose to a fitting level of resonance and formality. Writers often achieve ceremonial elegance by writing lengthy sentences with tightly coordinated, parallel structures.[43] Here are some tips.

a. To give your sentences rhythm, balance phrase against phrase, clause against clause in symmetrical patterns. Such symmetry is useful in highlighting similarity and dissimilarity because the parallel sequences invite clear-cut comparisons.

> To assert that the judicial choice between honoring the dictates of conscience and affirming civic unity is an easy one is a sure sign of an impoverished imagination. To proclaim that in America today such questions of constitutional meaning are amenable to the formal methods of conventional legal argument is to misunderstand both the limits of legality and the nature of moral choice. And to

41. Katz, *supra* note 23, at 1567.

42. Naomi R. Cahn, *Inconsistent Stories*, 81 Geo. L.J. 2533, 2566 (1993).

43. For a sophisticated discussion, see Joseph M. Williams & Gregory C. Colomb, Style: Lessons in Clarity And Grace (10th ed. 2010).

confuse advocacy with scholarship only ensures that one will, in the end, fail at both.[44]

Symmetry can also be achieved if you balance the subject against the object.

(1)

[S]urely being so thick skinned as to withstand rhetorical jabs does not entail being so thick skulled as to withstand violent blows.[45]

(2)

[T]hose who deploy power in the struggle to achieve justice must . . . sometimes employ bad soldiers in the service of a good cause.[46]

b. Another way to achieve eloquence is to end sentences with a series of cumulative, parallel statements. When you are lengthening a sentence by attaching coordinate statements to the end, cadence improves if each element is longer than the one before it.

> In California, the death penalty is not just a ferociously contested moral issue but a political metaphor: for some, the penalty is a sign of the repressiveness of the state, of the cruelty of all constituted authority, perhaps even of man's overreaching, a kind of ultimate anti-ecological hubris; for others, opposition to the penalty is the emblem of the lax, indulgent, sentimental distaste for all authority, of the disposition to lavish concern on those who break society's rules at the expense of those who keep them, or a pseudoprofessionalism that finds excuses for every delict and deviation—in sum a last vestige of the dreadful sixties.[47]

c. Sophistication is the mark of sentences that conclude with a summative, resumptive, or free modifier that follows your main clause.[48]

A resumptive modifier repeats a key noun, verb, or adjective from the main clause and then goes on to elaborate on it.

> Finally, women should educate themselves about the typically simple *procedures* for filing complaints against taxi drivers who make harassing comments to *passengers*—

44. Paul F. Campos, *Advocacy and Scholarship*, 81 CALIF. L. REV. 817, 860 (1993).

45. Eric J. Grannis, Note, *Fighting Words and Fighting Freestyle: The Constitutionality of Penalty Enhancement for Bias Crimes*, 93 COLUM. L. REV. 178, 230 (1993).

46. Campos, *supra* note 44, at 849.

47. Charles Fried, *Impudence*, 1992 SUP. CT. REV. 155, 167 (1992).

48. For a useful discussion of resumptive, summative and free modifiers, see WILLIAMS, *supra* note 43, at 176–178.

> procedures that may result in suspension or deprivation of the cabdriver's license.[49]

A summative modifier sums up in a noun or phrase the main idea in the sentence and then elaborates.

(1)

> [T]he outcomes of the six cases were driven by a deep recognition of law's indeterminate nature and of the inherently creative role of judge and juror—a *vision* that cannot tolerate excluding people with divergent perspectives from the creative act of adjudication.[50]

(2)

> Basically, *The Bluebook* suffers from a bad case of federal parochialism—a pervasive *belief* that state courts simply are not important.[51]

Free modifiers follow the verb but comment on the grammatical subject of the sentence.

> *The law* is itself a product of the human creative process—*shaped* by centuries of tradition, renewed by the infusion of the new and the rediscovery of the old, continually rethought, reanalyzed, and reconstructed, as powerful and moving as any other work of literature.[52]

d. Correlative conjunctions can be effectively used for emphasis and balance. Correlative conjunctions are conjunctions used in pairs.

not only . . . but also . . .

either . . . or . . .

neither . . . nor . . .

both . . . and . . .

whether . . . or. . . .

Because they are used to emphasize that two items are involved, the two items connected with correlative conjunctions should be parallel in construction to emphasize the comparison, as in the sentence that follows.

> The creative process is one of change, *both* for the creators, who while transforming their raw materials into new, finished works find themselves transformed, *and* for their audiences, who in seeking knowledge and enlightenment

49. Cynthia G. Bowman, *Street Harassment and the Informal Ghettoization of Women*, 106 HARV L. REV. 517, 579 (1993).

50. Burt Neuborne, *Of Sausage Factories and Syllogism Machines: Formalism, Realism, and Exclusionary Selection Techniques*, 67 N.Y.U. L. REV. 419, 421 (1992).

51. Paulsen, *supra* note 33, at 1788.

52. Stearns, *supra* note 20, at 515–16.

assimilate and transform those works as part of their own creative process.[53]

e. Finally, eloquence improves when sentence length is varied and used to underscore the message. Short parallel sentences convey urgency, emphasis, and strong emotion.

> This is a true story. It is the story of how the law punished a man for speaking about his legal rights; of how, after punishing him, it silenced him; of how, when he did speak, he was not heard. This pervasive and awful oppression was subtle and, in a real way, largely unintentional. I know because I was one of his oppressors. I was his lawyer.[54]

Long sentences frequently achieve a cadence that suggests a sense of weightiness, high resolve, responsibility, and thoughtful exploration.

(1)

> When conventional language is inadequate, when the hope of achieving justice through law collapses, when despair is deepest, the lyric of the street and the shop floor may best reflect what it is like to work for a living in an era that has contempt for work, workers and their lives.[55]

(2)

> There is a glory, it seems, in the mystery of a language that can be deciphered only by initiates of the secret society; there is a great sense of power and an even greater actuality of power in controlling a language that in turn controls the most pressing affairs of individuals and communities; and there is a monopolistic safety in being able to manipulate a language which because it was part of the creation of legal problems must be part of their solutions as well.[56]

D. DICTION

"Cliches are little cinder blocks of crushed and reprocessed experience."

-Donald Hall

One of the central ways we are present in our writing is in our "diction" or choice of words and in our use of figures of speech. It is primarily with words that we establish tone—be it conversational or

53. *Id.*

54. Clark D. Cunningham, *The Lawyer as Translator, Representation as Text: Towards an Ethnography of Legal Discourse*, 77 CORNELL L. REV. 1298, 1299 (1992).

55. David L. Gregory, *Working for a Living*, 58 BROOK. L. REV. 1355, 1375 (1993) (book review).

56. George D. Gopen, *The State of Legal Writing: Res Ipsa Loquitur*, 86 MICH. L. REV. 333, 334 (1987).

formal. It is with words that we convey our attitude toward the reader and the subject matter. And it is in our choice of words that we either hit the nail on the head or—as in the following example—miss the mark.

> Much of the innovation in capital market contracts can be *decomposed* into three continuing developments.

One of the most important qualities of a writer is sensitivity to words—to their denotations (explicit meanings) and connotations (implicit meanings or associations). Connotation plays a central role in the following sentence.

> Seriously at risk are the heroines of the Betty Crocker culture, women who have already devoted their most career-productive years to homemaking and who, if forced into the labor market after divorce, suddenly will be viewed as modern dinosaurs.[57]

With a stroke, "Betty Crocker" conjures up women of the 1950s, an entire generation of mothers baking in kitchens that are kept clean with labor-savings appliances. And, with another stroke, such women are relegated to a past as distant as the dinosaurs.

If a picture is worth a thousand words, so the right figure of speech or metaphor will save you a hundred.

> Fourth amendment case law is like a sinking ocean liner—rudderless and badly off course—yet most scholarship contents itself with rearranging the deck chairs.[58]

It is because language can be so evocative and precise that Donald Hall, a poet and teacher, tells us quite rightly that there are no synonyms in English. "Some words," he says, "are close to each other in meaning, close enough to reveal that they are not the same."[59] Although "to emulate" and "to ape" may be listed as synonyms, he illustrates, emulation implies imitation for the purpose of self-improvement while "aping" suggests imitation for the purpose of mockery. A thesaurus, he warns, is useful mostly for reminding us of the denotative and connotative differences between words that resemble each other.[60] Thus, careful writers spend time finding the words that express rather than approximate their meanings. They search for words that accord with their style and message.

In the scholarly context, problems arise when a writer uses academic discourse deceitfully—or simply unthinkingly. An author who writes "The child care provision is needs-based and, arguably, will involve a grievous loss if improperly denied" is not considering the effect his prose will have on his reader. The habit of hiding one's feelings under the garb of academic discourse is so ingrained that the author may not even realize that some might find his good intentions blurred by the seeming callousness of "arguably will involve grievous loss."

57. Starnes, *supra* note 27, at 70.

58. Amar, *supra* note 36, at 759.

59. Hall, *supra* note 1, at 27–28.

60. *Id.*

One way to avoid insensitivity to language is to restate in the vernacular a point made in formal language: a grass roots explanation or illustration is often a healthy reminder of an argument's practical significance and a refreshing check on pomposity.

(1)

> Plagiarism dwells at the meeting place of two great human endeavors: literature and the law. It is the source of legal and critical disputes, an example of *"creativity gone bad."*[61]

(2)

> If most government decisionmaking were decentralized today, cities would selfishly seek to evade responsibility for problems ranging from the disposal of toxic waste to the location of centers for the homeless (*"Not In My Backyard"*).[62]

Beware also of confusing formal language, which is often appropriate, with language that is merely "fancy." Simple words are often dignified words, while fancy words are empty and pretentious. For example, "rich," "tool," and "ease," are simple yet formal, but "wealthy," "implement," and "facilitate" are fancy.[63] The elegance of ordinary language is demonstrated in the following passages.

(1)

> Nothing is of more immediate practical importance to a lawyer than the rules that govern his own strategies and maneuvers; and nothing is more productive of deep and philosophical puzzles than the question of what those rules should be.[64]

(2)

> [M]ost cases that reach the Supreme Court, at least, are hard—decent and intelligent people could vote either way and in fact have usually done so—and in an important sense what most distinguishes the work of a good judge is not the vote but the achievement of mind. . . .[65]

As for the deceitful use of language, its worth observing that even naive readers pick up false notes. Mock humility, insincere flattery, sarcasm, or fake candor are more likely to damage the author than the audience.

E. MIXING STYLES

"The secret of good writing is to say an old thing in a new way or to say a new thing in an old way."

-Richard Harding Davis

61. Stearns, *supra* note 20, at 514.

62. Jerry Frug, *Decentering Decentralization*, 60 U. Chi. L. Rev. 253 (1993).

63. Hall, *supra* note 1, at 127.

64. Ronald Dworkin, *Principle, Policy, Procedure*, *in* A Matter of Principle 72 (1985).

65. James B. White, *Judicial Criticism*, 20 Ga. L. Rev. 835, 837 (1986).

Some of the best writing combines the conversational and the formal, yoking formal language with casual syntax, or weaving street talk into sophisticated syntactical structures.

(1)

> At its most extreme, realism views a court not as a syllogism machine, but as a sausage factory, where it doesn't much matter what goes into the product as long as it tastes good. Under a sausage factory view of adjudication, a judge is not a skilled mechanic, but a short order cook. The value of her work is measured, not by the rigor of the search for proper ingredients, but by the extent to which the final product conforms to the tastes of the best customers.[66]

(2)

> It is precisely to resolve the most difficult, the most uncertain, disputes that we have judges. Compelled to decide such cases, many judges pretend—sometimes to themselves as well as to the world—that what they have done is added two and two and gotten four, so that anyone who disagrees with their decision is crazy, or that what they have done is chosen Right over Wrong, so that anyone who disagrees with the decision is morally obtuse.[67]

The varied texture of this kind of writing keeps the reader alert and interested. Carefully calculated shifts from the elegant to the vernacular and vice-versa can summon laughter, righteous indignation—or, as in the example below, eulogy.

> At least in the years I knew him, Thurgood Marshall wasn't hot on celebrations. He had a vast capacity for joy and for sharing joy, and a fierce pride in the advances that civil rights had made in his lifetime. But he was too intensely aware of the work yet undone to waste his time reflecting on the past except as prologue.[68]

A mixed style conveys passionate feelings about another subject in the following passage.

> If lawyers have, by their words, alienated the individual nonlawyer; if the threat of litigation now must coerce the straightforward discourse that Jefferson always used when addressing a lay audience; if potential clients now think twice before retaining a clumsy wordsmith to verbalize the sensitive moments in their lives—yet the profession faces even a greater

66. Neuborne, *supra* note 50, at 420.

67. Richard A. Posner, The Problems Of Jurisprudence 233 (1990).

68. Anthony G. Amsterdam, *Thurgood Marshall's Image of the Blue-Eyed Child in* Brown, 68 N.Y.U. L. Rev. 226 (1993).

risk regarding the outside world. The lawyer's place as the arbiter and the rhetorician of the nation's values may have been permanently surrendered. No longer does a James Madison or Daniel Webster or an Abraham Lincoln fashion the Republic's aspirations by linking them to simple but elegant speech.

No. For, as a result of a pitched battle across a decade and before television audiences of millions, the verbal struggle has been lost. And who now dominates the discursive center? Not the creative writers; their voices are dispersed and idiosyncratic. Surely not the preachers; they are in disarray or in jail. Not even the journalists, who have sacrificed whatever prose power they once had to the twenty-second sound bite and the pretty face. The winners and at least temporary rhetorical champions are . . . the military.[69]

F. SOME FINAL THOUGHTS

Like all things worth cultivating, a good prose style takes time and hard work. There is no guaranteed program, but three habits are almost certain to help. First, read as much good writing as you can. We instinctively imitate what we read—this is why first efforts at persuasive writing often sound like a judicial opinion—and if we read only sloppy, empty, and pretentious prose, that is what we will write. Second, write a lot, at the end of every school day if you can. By articulating in prose what you think you learned from the day's classes or clinics, how you feel about it, and what confuses you, you reinforce what you have learned, clarify your questions, and keep your writing and thinking muscles toned. Finally, when you edit and polish your own work, be a pitiless critic capable of throwing out whole pages that do not measure up. As writing teacher Peter Elbow points out, to be a good writer you have to be a big spender.[70]

69. Richard Weisberg, Poethics and Other Strategies of Law and Literature 217–18 (1992).

70. Peter Elbow, Writing Without Teachers 39 (1973).

Chapter Nine

THE LAW REVIEW PROCESS: EVALUATING AND EDITING THE WORK OF OTHERS

"The essence of editing a law review is bringing out the best each author has to offer. Although this may sound simple, do not be deceived.... More than one author has had chance to remark that it is the editor who takes it upon himself to separate the wheat from the chaff, and then prints the chaff."

-Michael J. Killeen

"People ask you for criticism, but they only want praise."

-Somerset Maugham

"Working on a law review is not as much fun as being a rock star. The big difference is that rock stars earn wads of cash for playing music to throngs of adoring fans, while law review members earn nothing and spend their time poring over manuscripts in some dark corner of the library. Other than that, the two jobs are pretty much the same."

-The Princeton Review

As a law review editor, you are a gatekeeper and midwife. As a gatekeeper, you must first become familiar with your journal's standards for membership and for publication, its readership, and—if applicable—its particular focus or slant. Then you must apply this knowledge to the selection of both articles for publication and new members to carry on the work of the journal. As a midwife, your job is to assist an author in delivering to the journal the best piece possible. In this endeavor, you and the author are allies, not adversaries—a divine state, if one fraught with peril. A productive collaborative relationship is best maintained by sticking to the editorial role—which is, experienced editors claim, "to bridge the gap between the author's intention and the reader's understanding."[1]

Editors are not writers, not even ghostwriters. They do not make or alter meaning. They do not impose their style upon others. Rather, they are intelligent, diligent, representative readers who can articulate what in the text might create a misunderstanding that diminishes the article's power and persuasiveness. Sometimes it takes a lot of work to figure out what is causing the confusion. Then it takes even more work to write out your thoughts in a clear and supportive manner. Editing a law review article is, therefore, surprisingly time-consuming and involves imagination, patience, tact, stress, and numerous phone calls and letters. And, after all this effort, do not expect to be universally appreciated. Authors, however seasoned and esteemed, tend to acknowledge constructive criticism mostly in retrospect. Thus you must be thankful for what the experience can offer you—true exposure to the intellectual life of a community, enhanced credentials, and a chance to hone your own editing skills and, by default, your own writing skills.

This chapter begins with some advice on scoring law review competition papers and continues with a description of the peer editing process. It then discusses the selection of articles by outside authors and the process of editing the work of experts. Part C offers some suggestions on how to write constructive comments. We conclude with some comments on editorial communication and cooperation.

A. STUDENT AUTHORS

1. GATEKEEPERS: SCORING LAW REVIEW COMPETITION PAPERS

If your law review or journal, like most, selects some or all of its members through a writing competition, you may be asked to score competition papers. Scoring competition papers draws upon many of the same skills central to selecting and editing law review articles. Yet the task also differs in some key respects. In all three enterprises, you need to be able to articulate and read for the characteristics of an excellent article. But scoring it does not require you to come up with editorial suggestions on how to strengthen the piece. It requires diagnosis and evaluation only. Moreover, evaluating competition papers is easier than selecting articles in that you have many papers on the same topic that enable you to make comparative judgments. It is also harder in some respects. The sheer number of papers that need to be read can be numbing. It can be hard to sustain concentration, hard to find distinguishing characteristics, and hard to maintain an overall perspective on

1. Sheila Barrows, *Establishing Collaborative Author/Editor Relationships: The Heldref Paradigm, in* Writing And Publishing For Academic Authors 289 (Joseph M. Moxley, ed. 1992).

the quality of submissions. Thus, after summarizing the characteristics of a good competition paper, we offer some suggestions on grading efficiently and fairly.

a. Characteristics of a Good Competition Paper

Selection depends first on the quality of the analysis. A good competition paper, like a good article, should have an original thesis, one that goes beyond the court's analysis and that is not stated in any of the materials provided in the competition packet. A good competition paper should also have creatively supported and developed analysis displaying a writer's ability

- to generate at thesis;
- to maintain focus and logical development of ideas;
- to draw meaningful analogies;
- to draw on important facts and connect them to the thesis;
- to make an appropriate variety of arguments: policy, doctrinal, jurisprudential;
- to distinguish adverse material effectively;
- to distinguish the relevant material from the irrelevant;
- to read carefully and report accurately; and
- to make and support meaningful recommendations.

The paper need not focus on all or many of the major substantive issues, but it does need a detailed discussion of at least one of the major issues

The quality of the writing is another major concern. You need to look for introductions that establish context, announce a thesis, and provide a roadmap. The background section/s of casenote competition papers must clearly and accurately set forth the material facts, holdings, reasoning, and procedural history. It might also need sections giving historical background or summarizing relevant literature. The analysis section should clearly articulate and support its thesis and should have a clear issue/subissue organization and logical order. You should also check that paragraphs have unity, coherence, and topic and transition sentences; that sentences are clear and grammatical; that citations are accurate and in substantially appropriate Bluebook or ALWD form; and that the writer made good-faith proofreading efforts.

b. Tips on Scoring

Before you begin to score, the entire editorial board should agree on what the scores mean. To merit further consideration, must the paper receive an "Excellent" or "A" or is a "Very Good" or "A-" or "B+" sufficient? Every reader should know the implications of the score being given. In addition, it is important to establish relatively consistent standards of evaluation. To achieve this, some journals provide readers with a scoring checklist or with model answers—poor, fair, and good. Some journals impose a curve or median to achieve a useful distribution of scores. Still others require all scorers to grade individually a couple of competition papers. A comparison of tallied scores and a discussion of the reasons for the results could put all the editors on the same page when evaluating a competition paper.

If these suggestions cannot be practically implemented, or even if they are, it is a good idea to skim your papers to get a sense of the range of quality before you start filling out score sheets or checklists. If you have not been given model answers, pull out the first competition paper that fulfills almost all your expectations for a comment. This should set your standard of excellence. Pull out the weakest paper. Keep your copy of the excellent and weak paper on the side. Because it is easy to lose your sense of perspective when scoring many papers, reread these whenever you need to regain your standards. For example, if you have read five superficial papers in a row, the sixth, which may in fact be only average, might seem very solid. To check on your perception, compare it with the excellent paper you have put aside. A couple of other techniques might help you to maintain perspective and concentration. First, when you've reread the same page three times without remembering what it said, take a break. Second, if you cannot take a break because time is running out, note down your impressions as you read. Then articulate in a sentence or two your bottom line assessment of that paper, your basic reason for scoring it as you did. This too will force you to concentrate.

Since few papers will be excellent in all respects, you will need special criteria for the many borderline papers. Here are some tips.

- Give special weight to innovative arguments even if the paper has other flaws. You may be surprised at the general uniformity of analysis and feel inclined to give extra credit to a fresh approach.
- Seriously consider a paper that displays careful analysis even if it seems to have no thesis. (The thesis may be implicit or, with more time, the author might have arrived at one.)
- Seriously consider a paper that has a thesis even if it is well supported in only one section of the analysis.
- Reject any paper where organizational flaws or unclear expression make it difficult to evaluate an author's analytic ability. As a rule of thumb, score candidates with a view to your own skills as editors. Since it may fall to you to guide new journal members through drafts, you have an interest in selecting students who have weaknesses which you feel competent to address. Thus low scores should be given not only to papers with radical and identifiable flaws, but also to papers where you cannot articulate the problem—better safe than sorry.

Once you have finished scoring your papers, you need to assess your overall curve. Sort the poor, average, and excellent papers into piles. Compare them to each other. Do any seem misplaced? If so, compare them to papers in the pile you think they might belong and re-score them if necessary. This final comparative assessment is the best way of ensuring you graded the submissions consistently and fairly.

2. MIDWIVES: PEER EDITING

The editor of student articles has four primary functions, the first two of which you share with faculty advisors.

In principle, both you and the faculty advisor serve as topic editors. Although, in an ideal world, you would at this stage help steer writers to relevant and appropriate topics, methodologies, and, perhaps, literature, there is a good chance you do not have the expertise or the time to do this. Moreover, the student's faculty advisor is uniquely suited to help at this stage. But even if you lack expertise in an area, you are qualified to function as a *substantive editor*, acting as a sounding board and critical reader, seeing to it that the writer avoids logical flaws, digressions, ambiguity, inadvertent omissions, weak reasoning, and poor organization. In addition, you are a *manager*—you set tasks and deadlines so that the writer stays in sync with the publication's production schedule. And finally, you serve as a *copy editor*. You want to pinpoint confusing transitions and constructions as well as grammar and bluebook errors, but you need to control an editor's acquired—but recurrent—impulse to render every thought in your own style.

To understand these roles, it is important to realize that the editing process tracks the writing process: just as a writer limits her concerns at each writing stage to avoid frustration and paralysis, so too an editor limits his area of concern so as to conserve energy and encourage, rather than discourage, the author.

The writing process tends to be a four-step process (reading and exploring, drafting, revising, polishing), and as primary editors of student articles, your editing will correspond to these four stages.[2] With student authors, the first two stages in both the writing and editing process are writer-based, that is, you and your editee focus on figuring out the problem. The second two stages are reader-based, that is, both parties focus on communicating the ideas to the article's intended audience. Keep in mind that although editing can be described as a four-stage process, one or all of the stages may need to be repeated: the analytic or organizational problems of an early draft may, for example, persist into later drafts and require you to repeat an earlier step.

a. Beginning (The Reading and Exploring Stage)

Your primary role at the beginning of the writing process is to serve as a topic editor. Finding and narrowing a topic, developing a thesis, and creating arguments are the hardest stages for any writer since they

2. We are indebted to Jessie Grearson, John Marshall Law School, for sending us materials from her presentation to the SOFTWARE LAW JOURNAL that outlined the four steps in editing that we recommend here. For a discussion of how these four steps relate to the writing process in general, see Jessie Grearson, *Process to Product: Teaching the Writing Process in Law School*, 9 THE SECOND DRAFT 1 (1993).

require considerable familiarity with the subject and relevant literature. Thus the most helpful thing you may be able to do here is to encourage students to seek the assistance of your faculty, whose expertise can be most profitably used at this stage. If they can help steer students to viable topics, help them to narrow their topics, and prevent them from wasting time on dead-end issues, they are making a valuable contribution to their journals, and one for which their knowledge makes them truly qualified. In these early stages of a writing project, it might be also be helpful to hold some workshops for new journal members. Invite a research librarian, a writing teacher, and a faculty member interested in scholarship to describe the enterprise. (See Appendix C.)

Your research librarians are particularly qualified to direct writers to appropriate sources for topics and to introduce them to resources that will ensure that their brainstorming activities are situated within the general framework of literature on that topic. This will prevent writers from pursuing avenues already preempted or dismissed as insignificant (see Chapter 3). Remind writers to use several search methods: they need to look at a variety of Internet databases beyond that of LEXIS and WESTLAW and to vary terms- and-connectors searches with natural language searches and online queries with index searches.

After topic and thesis have been chosen, your first major task is to assist your writers in "seeing" their own ideas. An informed, vigorous dialogue is a terrific source of inspiration. Ideally, before you meet with your editees, you would do some preliminary research so that your comments can be informed and sensible. But even if you are too pressed for time to do this, you can be a sounding board. Say back to your writers what you hear them saying. Then ask questions about the topic that might help your writers to probe deeper and hone their thinking. And continue to encourage your editees to discuss their topics and theses with their faculty advisors. The faculty will know better than you whether the topic has been reviewed exhaustively or is close to resolution. In addition, your journal could think about putting your editees into peer writing groups and letting them brainstorm as a group. (See Appendix C.) Posting ideas on blogs is another way journal members might get useful feedback.

Finally, remind your editees that reading and writing are not purely sequential. Writers need to read to find a topic and thesis, but they may need to write to refine their topic and this refinement may send them back to research. Moreover writers must keep an eye on the area as they write: they must stay current so as to respond to developments and to avoid preemption.

b. Drafting (Getting Ideas Down on Paper)

By the drafting stage, the writer has articulated a thesis and is trying to get out the supporting arguments. The editor's primary role at this stage is substantive—you need to respond to the breadth, depth, development, originality, and credibility of the paper's ideas. You should not worry at this point about their expression. Because the article is still in its childhood, and will develop in ways yet unknown, it is a waste of your energy and the author's emotions to perfect the material.

To generate comments on the viability and sufficiency of the analysis, to get a sense of the "Big Picture," try these techniques.

- Read through the entire draft without stopping. When you are finished, write down the thesis and the key arguments in support of the thesis. If you cannot do this successfully, it is likely that either the thesis or the arguments (or both) require clearer articulation.
- Assess the originality of the thesis. If the analysis is always being attributed to another, there is a high chance the piece is not original. Similarly, if there is little analysis of primary sources, but a great many summaries of secondary sources, the piece is probably not original. In these cases, the author has to go back to stage one.
- Outline the draft and then make notes about discrepancies, ambiguities, and digressions. Where is the analysis incomplete because of missing links in reasoning? Where is it unsupported? Where are there unhelpful digressions? Where is background needed?
- Read the article again, playing devil's advocate. Does the author have a grasp of the relevant literature? Did the author ignore germinal sources, depend on unreliable sources, or improperly document sources? Are the author's summaries of case law and secondary authority inaccurate? Does the author seem familiar with relevant theoretical and jurisprudential concepts? Has the author overlooked crucial factual, doctrinal, or policy considerations? Has the author recognized and responded to opposing arguments? Are there logical mistakes—like confusing coincidental relationships with causal ones? Are the author's examples and illustrations ineffective? Are solutions adequately tested?[3]

Once you have made notes on your observations, review your data. What does it amount to? What are the most serious problems? What is working out well? Write up your conclusions.

c. *Revising (Writing for Readers)*

Increasingly, law professors post their papers on SSRN once they have a viable draft. Often they get valuable feedback that helps them to refine both their arguments and their presentation. Time permitting, student authors might want to do similarly, but whether or not you do so, now is the time for both the editor and the author to turn their

3. Anne Enquist, *After the Fact Outlines: An Old Idea Put to New Use*, 6 Wash. Eng. J. 29 (1984). We are also grateful to Anne for sending us unpublished materials on law review editing that included many of these editing techniques.

attention to the article's potential audience—to the reader. As a careful reader who is knowledgeable about your journal's expectations, you are in a good position to notice both where the piece is difficult to follow and what has to be done to bring it up to publication standards. Your responses at this point should not center around the originality or credibility of the discussion (your central concerns in the first editing stages), but on how clearly the ideas are being communicated to the reader.

Here too it is helpful to make a topic sentence outline that will assist you in getting an overview of organizational and substantive problems. Ask yourself these questions.

Organization

- Did outlining become difficult at any point? Did you encounter places where you wondered whether an idea was subissue B or issue II?
- Is each part mutually exclusive? Are the issues clearly separated or are some blurred together? Are arguments intertwined or repeated?
- Is the sum of the parts equal to the whole? Are there missing steps in reasoning or missing arguments?
- Are the issues in order of importance? Is that order logical?
- Is the organization of each section internally logical? Does the writer move from what the reader knows (old information) to what the reader doesn't know (new information)?
- Does each section have its own introductory roadmap paragraph and conclusion?
- Are there topic and transition sentences?

Substance

- Are the thesis and arguments clearly explained and supported?
- What is discussed in detail, and what is summarized? Is the balance appropriate?
- Were relevant issues were ignored?
- Are there still internal inconsistencies, digressions, or gaps?
- Are there remaining mistakes in logic or problems with premises or reasoning?
- Are there missing footnotes? Should some footnotes go in the text? Should some text go into footnotes?

You should also raise the following questions in order to sensitize your editee to the rhetorical situation—to the article's purpose, audience, and tone.

Rhetorical Considerations

- Do the article's introduction and conclusion reflect the same purpose? Should either or both be changed to better reflect what the author has actually done?
- Is the paper responsive to the needs and expertise of a law-school-educated reader? Does it properly balance how much information readers have against how much they need?
- Has the author established an appropriate tone? Is it consistently maintained or does the author inappropriately lapse into sarcasm, pomposity, or indecision?

After asking these questions, review their import and write up your conclusions.

d. Polishing

By the time you arrive at the fourth stage, the paper is just about finished. The last step is to remove all the surface glitches to ensure a pleasurable reading experience. You serve as a copy editor here, catching all the mechanical errors and awkward expressions.

Although you have already commented on topic and transition sentences, check them again. In addition, examine paragraphs for unity and cohesion. Is there more than one idea in a paragraph? If so, divide it. Are the sentences in the right order? If not, re-order. Are the connections between sentences clear? If not, add transition words and use dovetailing. (See Chapter Five, Part E.)

Spend some time thinking about the author's writing style. Some writers might adopt a rather conversational tone while others have a formal tone. Such choices are an author's to make. But you should comment on any stylistic traits that interfere with comprehension. Does the author use clear sentence structures? Vary sentence length? Use language precisely, concisely, and appropriately? (See Chapters Seven and Eight.)

Finally, correct mechanical errors—that is, errors in grammar, punctuation, quotation, and citation (though this is often done separately)—and proofread for typographical mistakes. (See Chapter Seven and Appendix B.) To aid your concentration when proofreading, copy editors suggest (1) that you read the pages of a document out of order or backwards, (2) that you move a ruler under each line as you read, (3) that you double check cross references, words in a different typeface, and names, titles, and numbers in footnotes, (4) that you search for the second half of quotation marks, brackets, parentheses, and dashes, and (5) that you check headings for consistency of formatting and agreement with the table of contents (if you have one).[4]

4. For more on copy editing, see Carolyn B. Bagin & Jo Van Doren, *Everyone is a Proofreader: How to Check Your Documents, in* WRITING AND PUBLISHING, *supra* note 1, at 261–64.

Line editing is appropriate at this stage, but you may want to write some overall comments if you think there are some persistent problems on the paragraph or sentence level that the writer needs to address throughout the text.

B. OUTSIDE AUTHORS

1. GATEKEEPERS: SELECTING ARTICLES FROM OUTSIDE AUTHORS

Law review editors report that electronic forms of submission like ExpressO have made the volume of submissions overwhelming. Top tier law journals receive over 2,000 articles yearly. Lower tier journals have also experienced increased volume.[5] As a result, as an editor, you will be forced to make decisions expeditiously, sometimes rejecting articles you consider poorly written and reasoned "within 5 to 30 minutes of reading"[6] and never going beyond the cover letter or abstract, introduction or conclusion.[7]

This reality explains most journals' reliance, or over-reliance, on authors' credentials—where they teach, received their J.D.s, and have published. Editors hope that credentials are a quick and reliable guide to the quality of the scholarship—a particular boon if they are unfamiliar with the topic and unsure how to evaluate it.[8]

This practice makes it more difficult for beginning scholars to get published, especially those who write in an area or from a perspective disfavored by top tier journals, because they cannot establish an impressive publication record.[9] In addition, there is some empirical evidence showing that journals are biased against 'outsider' scholarship that addresses race, gender, ethnicity, or sexual orientation.[10] Finally, one study has shown selection is biased against women authors.[11] Thus some academics urge law reviews to practice "blind" selection, removing all identifiers from a submission to level the playing field.

Although some peer review journals and a smaller number of law reviews do blind reviews, it will probably be some time before this more equitable system becomes a more common practice. This does not mean, however, that as an editor of a journal that relies on traditional selection

5. Leah M. Christensen & Julie O. Oseid, *Navigating the Law Review Selection Process: An Empirical Study of Those With All Power—Student Editors*, 59 S.C. L. Rev. 175, 204 (2007).

6. *Id.* at 198.

7. *Id.*

8. Rachel J. Anderson, *From Imperial Scholar to Imperial Student: Minimizing Bias in Article Evaluation by Law Reviews*, 20 Hastings Women's L.J. 197, 219 (2009).

9. Topics not favored include tax, civil procedure, admiralty, professional responsibility, law school pedagogy. *Id.* at 196.

10. *See* Anderson, *supra* note 8; Jonathan Gingerich, *A Call for Blind Review: Student Edited Law Reviews and Bias*, 59 J. Legal Educ. 269 (2009).

11. *See* Minna Kotkin, *Of Authorship and Audacity: An Empirical Study of Gender Disparity and Privilege in the "Top Ten" Law Reviews* (July 13, 2009) (Brooklyn Law School Legal Studies, Research -Papers), *available at* http://ssrn.com/abstract=1140644.

criteria you will use credentials as the sole grounds for publication decisions. Also important are an article's substantive contribution to the law; its readiness for publication; its topic; its thoroughness, importance, and originality; and its quality of prose and persuasiveness.[12] The topic does not have to be "big," but it should be fresh, timely, and worthwhile. The thesis needs to be valid, innovative, practical, and not self-evident.

These characteristics rule out articles that rest upon moot or stale issues or that pose questions already definitively answered. Preemption checks must be conducted to determine whether there is new law or a prior publication that renders the article moot. (For tips on conducting preemption checks, see Chapter 3.) It is also a good idea to see if there are other submissions on the topic that must be weighed against the one under your consideration.

One good way to make efficient and informed decisions about submissions, despite volume, unfamiliarity with the topic, and the risk of bias, is to read articles with an eye toward identifying the particular contribution of the piece. For example, an article might raise a new, important, or difficult problem—even if it does not suggest ways of resolving it. As one law professor noted, "there are multiple stages to legal scholarship," and identification of an issue may the first step, one that may be followed by explorations of remedies, critiques of those remedies, and preferred solutions.[13] For example, empirical research may result in an identification of a problem, even if the article summarizing the research does not resolve the problem. Other articles may have different strengths.

- The article may address issues of direct relevance to practitioners, thereby undermining the perception that academic scholarship is increasingly divorced from legal practice.
- The article may demonstrate that the law advantages certain interests or groups at the expense of others. A piece addressing the consequences of this can lead to eventual remediation.
- The article may be theoretically important, proposing a new legal theory or paradigm that may in time move the law in new directions.

If the article makes any of these contributions, it deserves serious consideration. The next step is to contemplate the appropriate criteria for evaluating that article. If the piece is practical or theoretical, the editor must decide whether the relevant historical, social, political, and legal contexts were explored, whether all competing arguments and evidence were considered and reasonably rejected, and whether the proposed remedy or theory will really operate as predicted. If the piece is empirical, its methodology must be examined: was the survey sampling representative and sufficiently large and were the survey questions

12. Christenson, *supra* note 5, at 201.

13. Anderson, *supra* note 8, at 236. We are indebted to Professor Anderson's article for identifying the virtues of different kinds of articles, as described here.

worded neutrally? If the article takes an "outsider" perspective on law, the editor must guard against bias. This kind of close reading will not only help with publication decisions, but it is also the first step in generating global comments.

Above and beyond preemption and contribution to the profession, publication decisions rightly depend upon an article's execution. Journals are plagued by "premature submissions,"[14] by authors who, in their rush to publish, fail to do the revision that turns a mere paper into a polished professional article. Editors report almost universal surprise at the quantity of mediocre submissions.[15] Thus, editors are quick to reject articles when they fail to do what they say they are going to do, or when the writer's methods, examples, arguments, or sources are suspect or inadequate. Some journals may be inclined to reject articles when their tone is intemperate, the style turgid, or the organization confusing. Excessive length, absent or sloppy citation, and grammar errors may also be factors in publication decisions because a journal may not have the time or resources for fixing the text.[16] Nonetheless, it is rare to receive an article so perfect you can immediately put it into production. When the flaws are not fatal, the topic is ripe, and the arguments cogent, you may well want to extend an offer.

Article selection may also depend on whether a journal has selection predilections or a special focus. Some journals eschew articles of only local interest; they seek pieces of national or international import. Some journals are reluctant to publish big "think" pieces or theory-building articles if authored by anyone less than a veteran in the field. Other journals may label themselves as interdisciplinary, feminist, or subject-specific and restrict publication accordingly. Some journals are particularly receptive to articles by practitioners; others look to legal scholars. But don't be bound by conventional ideas about your journal's bent; sometimes it is good to push a journal in a new direction.

Different issues arise with theme and symposium issues. Symposium issues provide several benefits. They enable you to solicit and interest experienced practitioners and scholars to write for your journal. Moreover, if you are fortunate enough to secure a few articles from prestigious authors, you can use those contributions to encourage articles from other respected authorities in the field. In addition, general announcement of a specialty volume often brings in a number of high quality unsolicited manuscripts. Thus, less well-known journals often find this is an effective way to enhance their reputation in the legal community.

Theme issues can be important for another reason: they are widely read. Someone interested in a particular topic is more likely to pick up a volume devoted entirely to that subject than a volume with only one

14. Gary A. Olson coins this phrase in *Publishing Scholarship in Humanistic Disciplines: Joining the Conversation, in* WRITING AND PUBLISHING, *supra* note 1, at 61.

15. Christensen, *supra* note 5, at 201.

16. Of course the editors of some specialty journals, like those in international law, often deal with authors who are not native English speakers. These editors need to spend considerable time editing the text.

relevant article. Thus theme issues can be of special value for journals trying to expand their readership.

Although symposia may reduce anxiety over the quality of your unsolicited manuscript pool, they pose their own problems. One disadvantage of theme issues is that they may require you to reject interesting unsolicited articles on other topics or prevent you from responding to other current developments. In addition, variety has the payoff of ensuring a broad audience. Moreover, it is inevitable that some symposium authors renege on publication promises while other articles arrive late or in "rough" condition. The authors may not have had the time or incentive to transform their oral presentations into published pieces. Unless your journal has reserved the right not to publish, however, it may think it has committed itself and is thus obliged to expend a great deal of time and effort getting the piece into shape. So be very careful to articulate the journal's role in further work on a symposium article. Establish a clear understanding with the author about what needs to be done to make the work publishable, and how much work the staff is willing and able to contribute. Sometimes authors expect the journal staff to function as an unnamed "co-author," doing more work than an editorial staff should or can do. Thus, many journals prefer a mix of open and special issues.

One final article selection problem comes from the practice of "trading up." With reappointment and tenure so dependent on prestigious publication, an acceptance catapults professors hoping for a "better offer" into frenzied requests for expedited reviews. This not only puts a journal's work on that article on hold, but it delays a journal from accepting other articles. In an attempt to avoid this, some editors put considerable thought into acceptance letters—explaining their interest in the article and their qualifications for, and enthusiasm about, editing it. This personal touch sometimes achieves what a journal ranking cannot.

2. MIDWIVES: EDITING THE WORK OF EXPERTS

Editing the work of experts is both easier and harder than editing the work of peers. Presumably, outside authors have maneuvered through the prewriting and drafting stages on their own, and if their efforts are unsuccessful, their articles do not merit your serious consideration. You should only accept pieces that meet your basic standards. Thus, the editing process for outside authors should be quicker, concentrating on the communication rather than generation of ideas and on manuscript preparation.

Editing experts is harder in that outside authors have greater legal expertise than law review editors and probably more writing experience as well. Although professionals are likely to give your suggestions mature consideration, they are also in a better position than a student author to evaluate your own evaluation and to take it on its merits. Knowing this, article editors must exercise good judgment and tact to avoid the kind of criticism leveled by this well-known law professor:

> Audiences for law reviews are rarely the reading public, but rather those who are already familiar with the issue and vocabulary of the substantive area under discussion. In this sense, the assumed congruence of identity between editor and reader is mismatched; the editor necessarily reads as an ingenue while the actual reader—likely a professor, lawyer, or judge—will already have the basics in hand. A consequence of this disparity is that editors often ask authors to simplify, define, and clarify words and arguments (the meaning of "fair use" in a symposium on copyright; an explanation for "capitalization" in a sophisticated article on corporate finance) that are unfamiliar to the editor but not necessarily to the intended audience.[17]

Thus, after a full interchange between editor and author, legal professionals would, as a rule and with good reason, like to have final authority over text on which they put their names and for which they are accountable.

Nonetheless, editors who exercise intelligence, common sense, and diplomacy are a valuable resource to a writer. Closeness to text often makes it difficult for authors to notice an infeliticious phrase, a gap in logic, or an error in logic, fact, or organization. And any author worth her salt should be grateful when an editor points out these problems or shares some of her speculations, questions, and reactions with the author—pushing the writer to achieve the best piece possible. If both parties focus on their commitment to legal scholarship and truth, and agree that reason and flexibility are the best means to that end, positive author/editor relationships can evolve.

To that end, article editors should extol a manuscript's strengths and triage the problems, focusing on the ones most fatal to the piece. To do this effectively, editors must truly understand the topic before offering suggestions. They should then focus on the big picture, not minor irritants. Substantive comments are the ones that writers are most grateful for, while extensive line editing is often resented. Take care then not to make changes for the sake of change. Be sensitive to the way small rewordings can singly or in tandem alter meaning or tone. Legal writers are increasingly sensitive to narrative and style and do not want their prose unthinkingly homogenized and flattened. So, short of error or confusion, defer to the author's judgment.

Most importantly, always let the author see your editorial suggestions in order to evaluate them. The quickest way to anger an author is to change text without consultation. An author is likely to bristle over unauthorized changes—even if, in another context, she would be likely to agree with your suggestions.

Finally, be polite. (See Part C.) You may encounter difficult authors while serving as an articles editor: authors who do not return phone calls, contest every editorial suggestion, disregard deadlines, rewrite

17. Carol Sanger, *Editing*, 82 Geo. L.J. 513, 519 (1993).

without end, or fail to provide obscure sources. One way to reduce aggravation is to try to avoid it in the first place. Work on establishing some initial rapport by showing your enthusiasm for the article, your eagerness to help, your willingness to accommodate the author: solicit information about the best means of contact, give information about the editorial process and schedule so the author can plan accordingly, request the author's help on obtaining obscure sources and meeting production deadlines, and address his or her special concerns. If you can figure out how the author likes to work, you may be able to adapt and avoid conflict.

In the two-sided equation of editing and being edited, it is, of course, not only editors who bear responsibility for acting with maturity and efficiency. Authors have a duty to move past defensiveness, denial, and anger and to consider comments with an open mind and commitment to improvement. They should not expect staff members to do the author's job of revision, nor should they obstruct the production process by slowing down cite and source checks through failure to provide obscure sources that are needed for authority and attribution. Nor should they delay in inspecting and returning page proofs.[18] Failure to cooperate with a publication schedule is nothing short of destructive, threatening both the journal's publication record and the author's. Whether editing or being edited, it is important to keep your eyes on the prize—the timely production of a piece of which both parties are proud.

C. WRITING CONSTRUCTIVE COMMENTS

1. EDITING PROTOCOL

As we just noted, most authors harbor fantasies of an editor saying: "This piece is dazzling. Let's send it straight to the printer." But, in reality, such a response is not likely, nor is it truly expected. As long as you take a writer seriously, and word your recommendations courteously, most authors put on a brave face and react positively.

The first maxim when it comes to writing up your appraisal is always to temper criticism with praise. An entirely negative critique is demoralizing and counter-productive. If you point out the strengths of the article, you are not only helping the writer to recognize your standards, but you may be dissipating antagonism and resistance.

The second maxim is to focus your comments on the article's future readers and on the article itself, instead of on the writer's performance.[19]

18. *See* Michael L. Closen and Robert M. Jarvis, *The National Conference of Law Reviews Model Code of Ethics: Final Text and Comments*, 75 Marq. L. Rev. 509 (1992).

19. Mary B. Ray & Jill J. Ramsfield make this very sensible suggestion in Legal Writing: Getting it Right and Getting it Written 89 (2nd ed. 1993).

In other words, do not focus on the mistake, shift the focus to the effect the mistake will have on the reader's reaction or understanding. Do not write: "Your explanation here is very unclear." Instead, write: "Our readers might find this explanation clearer if you explain how X relates to Y." It is always a good idea to re-read your comments, trying to hear them from the writer's point-of-view.

The third maxim is do not edit what you do not have to, i.e., do not step over the line by usurping the writer's role. It is the author's job to determine the content and to set the tone (as long as it does not antagonize the reader)—not the editor's job. Exercise restraint.

2. TYPES OF FEEDBACK

When you write up your comments, you should be aware that there are different types of feedback—exploratory, descriptive, prescriptive, and judgmental.[20] Your comments should ultimately be a combination of all four. Although these different types of responses are all helpful to a writer, some may be more appropriate for peer editing than for outside authors and some are more relevant at one stage in the editing process than at another.

a. Exploratory Feedback

Exploratory feedback is especially helpful in the earlier stages of writing. By raising interpretations, meanings, choices, and strategies other than those presented in the draft, the editor helps the writer to explore the problem thoroughly and to refine the thesis. Exploratory feedback is collaborative brainstorming; it prevents premature thesis selection and simplistic analysis. Although exploratory feedback leads writers to the missing evidence and analysis that would improve the work, it is neither prescriptive nor judgmental.

b. Descriptive Feedback

When an editor reacts as a reader and describes as neutrally as possible her reactions to the text, she is providing descriptive feedback. An editee needs to know how a reader reacts to the text in order to determine whether the text accurately and easily communicated the writer's ideas to the reader or whether revision is needed. Although descriptive feedback is non-judgmental, since it simply reflects the meaning that was conveyed, it also prepares the ground for revision. Descriptive feedback is helpful in the early and late stages of writing.

c. Prescriptive Feedback

Prescriptive feedback is based on the editor's diagnosis of the cause of ineffectiveness. It offers suggestions on how to revise. It is sometimes difficult to decide how directive or non-directive to be. Your decision will probably depend on the editee. For some, especially outside authors,

20. Kristin Woolever & Brook K. Baker, *Diagnosing Legal Writing Problems: Theoretical and Practical Perspectives for Giving Feedback*, Panel Presentation at the Legal Writing Institute Conference, Ann Arbor, Michigan, July 28, 1990.

strategy-provoking questions will be enough for a writer to figure out what to do next. For others, explicit instructions might be necessary.

d. Judgmental Feedback

An editor must eventually offer an opinion on the quality of the writing submitted. Outside articles must be selected or rejected. New journal members need to know how close or far they are from producing a publishable piece of work. But, to be fair, editees need to be exposed to professional standards early enough in the writing process that they may identify their proficiencies and deficiencies and improve their skills. Thus, editors must articulate their standards, realizing that

- judgments should be based on shared, objective criteria;
- judgments should be geared to the particular stage of the writing process (first drafts should not be judged by the same standards as final drafts);
- judgments should be positive as well as negative; and
- judgments should be impersonal, not personal; they should be couched in terms of the document and the journal's needs, not in terms of the writer's abilities.

In the edit that follows, we annotate an editor's comments on an article on loss of consortium in wrongful death actions to show how these different types of feedback mingle. The comments were offered while the writer was in the early stages of drafting.

Sample Critique (Early Stage)

> This draft shows the depth and breadth of your research . . . you probably don't need to do more, at least until you've developed your thesis. Moreover, between the footnotes and the text, the draft is full of ideas (*positive feedback*). Nonetheless, the note is still descriptive, not analytic. Your very organization reflects this: you have an introduction, followed by three summaries and a conclusion. First, you summarize the general development of the wrongful death action, then its development in New York, then its status in other states. You do not even have an analysis section; rather you move directly into your conclusion. You have a point of view, but you do not have clear arguments in support of it (*primarily descriptive feedback*).
>
> You have a couple of options in rethinking and rewriting your note. Your analysis could be organized around the arguments in support of recovery for loss of consortium. Much of your research is usable, but raise cases cited in support of arguments rather than in an historical narrative. (Note that many arguments are implicit in your footnotes.)

- the illogic of allowing recovery in personal injury but not wrongful death
- the illogic of allowing children recovery for loss of services but not spouses (see footnote 10 & page 17)
- the general willingness of the judiciary to act in tort areas (give other examples in this cause of action [see footnote #23] and others)
- social changes that dictate a new policy
- trends in related causes of action and allied areas

You could narrow your topic to some of the problems that may have retarded recovery and try to pose solutions.

- what courts have done in other instances of legislative inaction
- difficulty in calculating damages (although this is a bit of a straw man argument)
- concern about excessive damages (page 21)
- how to handle claims for loss of consortium when the marriage is incompatible (fn 38)

You could focus on what a valid test for determining damages might be, as you start on page 13 (*primarily exploratory feedback*).

Obviously when you find your angle, you will need to rethink the sections of your note. In writing each section, remember to begin with an introductory thesis paragraph. Your reader will find it much easier to follow your points if the text has introductory paragraphs that establish the context and foreshadow the discussion (*prescriptive feedback*).

Overall, good start. But to be published, you still need to decide on one angle and then pursue it singlemindedly (*prescriptive and judgmental*).

3. ORGANIZING YOUR COMMENTS

Law review editors are notoriously fond of line edits, and indeed, there is a time and place for those. Line edits are never, however, a replacement for "global," big-picture comments. Marginal comments are rarely absorbed with the same ease as overall comments, nor are they credited with the same seriousness. Nor can you routinely substitute conversation for a letter or memo. Although conversation can stimulate exploration, some of your finest perceptions may be forgotten when the telephone receiver is replaced or door closed. Thus, you should give your editees a written assessment of their work.

Moreover, if you want your editees truly to benefit from your comments, and to incorporate them into their rewrites, you must organize your critique. A critique that is stream-of-consciousness is probably as confusing as an article that is stream-of-consciousness, and will likely produce a rewrite that is differently but equally stream-of-consciousness.

How you organize your comments depends on where you are in the editing process and what problems exists. In the beginning, you may want to write *overall comments* that are directed to the analytic substance of the piece, to its focus (thesis) and scope (arguments). Later, you may want to add a section on *large-scale organization* in which you discuss the division of arguments, the order of arguments, the separation of issues and subissues, and the presence of introductions and conclusions. If there are persistent problems with paragraphing, syntax, diction, or mechanics, you may want from the beginning to include a *writing* section so that certain mistakes are not carried through draft after draft. Otherwise, you may leave this for later edits, or for a line edit.

When you are further along in the process, you might want to comment on each part of the article separately—focusing in turn on the content, analysis, and large- and small-scale organization of each section, as well as on paragraphing and prose.

What follows is, we think, a thorough, well-organized, thoughtful critique of an article in the later stages of development. You can play with and adapt its format until you find one with which you are comfortable. In addition to its encouraging tone, note especially the specificity of its description of problems and of its suggested solutions.

Sample Critique (Revision Stage)

This piece is beautifully written, very interesting and on the timely topic of state constitutionalism. Nonetheless, as this memo describes, I have several suggestions that I hope will make it even stronger.

I. Synthesis

In a significant way, the paper reads like two different pieces. The problem results, I think, from your analytic framework. Sections IV A & B have too few over-arching ideas; in short, both sections should be subsets of a larger analytical whole.

Thus, I suggest you edit each section with an eye toward highlighting the common themes in the sections themselves and in the introduction. For example, section A's discussion of the retrenchment of rights in Oliver and Burger makes for easy cross reference as part of B's discussion of the history of the new federalism, i.e., as examples of Supreme Court restriction of federal constitutional rights that inspired state Supreme Courts to give teeth to state constitutional provisions.

II. Section A

A couple of points here. First, an observation in regard to references to the fourth amendment. Since the fourth amendment itself recognizes and balances the interests of individual rights with society's interest in crime prevention (in proscribing unreasonable searches and seizures), a statement like "Burger's central concern . . . is efficient law enforcement, not the fourth amendment" is not quite right. Concern for law enforcement is not trumping the fourth amendment, it is trumping individual rights. The criticism is where the Court draws the line between the competing values inherent in the fourth.

Second, some readers might find your treatment of Powell "unfair." Powell, though concededly pro-government on criminal matters, on a variety of civil cases is famous for concurrences in 4–4 splits where he agonizes over the precedents, searching for a principled way out. Thus, the following statement is too sweeping: "For Justice Powell, any two assertions of the Court's authority are inherently consistent."

Nonetheless, this section works; it has several keen insights.

III. Section B

This section might benefit from some reorganization. My suggested organization of this section is as follows:

i. Introduction of New Federalism. Here give history: incorporation doctrine, expansion of federal rights and application to actions by state government, retrenchment, the Brennan and Marshall dissents calling state courts to action, the S.Ct. response and changed presumption under adequate state ground doctrine.

ii. Then give arguments on both sides, including discussion of Gardner now on p. 95.

iii. Then, as an example of how one court has gone, insert discussion of New Jersey opinions here.

iv. Finally, in distinction to how N.J. got it right, show how N.Y. got it wrong.

Again, despite these suggestions, this section is a strong contribution to moving the debate forward in a fascinating area. The article is very promising.

Please call me with any questions you have about these comments.

D. CHAIN OF AUTHORITY: EDITORIAL COOPERATION & COMMUNICATION

Journals have a hierarchical, but interdependent structure. Staffed as they are by people who are also students, spouses, parents, paid employees, and job hunters, their successful operation is fraught with distraction. They can thrive only if members understand the chain of authority, the publication process, and their own role within that process.

Communication is essential. Each person must be clear about his or her responsibilities and schedule. Everyone needs to know what everyone else is doing, when they are doing it, and what they are saying to authors if the journal is to stay on top of the production schedule. Because every piece goes through a number of editing levels—from the first notes and comments editor to the senior editor, for example—it can be frustrating, repetitive, and counterproductive if one editor does not know what the other has done. Comments, revisions, critiques need to be documented, and the people involved in the process need to receive a copy of everything so the comments of both the writer and the editors can be tracked. If problems and delays cannot be easily resolved, they must be reported up the ladder so that each editor is in the picture and decisions made about how best to ameliorate negative consequences.

Mentoring and training are also essential. New members must learn how to do careful source and cite checks and how to proof pages. They must be told to avoid the temptation to rush the process in the belief that some one else will catch the errors. Third-year editors must learn how to conduct both substantive and technical edits. Training sessions to supplement the advice given in this book are an excellent idea. Give new members source and cite check exercises and workshops on the scholarly writing process. (See Appendix C.) Give third-years an editing workshop, perhaps with a member of your writing faculty. But, regardless of training, in the end, all members must also act with motivation, diligence, good will, flexibility, and humor.

Every year, journal boards have problem members—members who miss deadlines and meetings, submit substandard work, refuse work, unfairly burden some members more than others, or misuse journal equipment and supplies. This is unfortunate because poor performance on a journal can damage both a student's reputation and the reputation of the school—one slacker can torpedo the ship. Each member of a publication must be made aware of the journal's expectations and its disciplinary procedures for, and the consequences of, non-compliance. The prestige of law review membership does not come without a price, namely, the willingness to labor in the fields of scholarship to produce publications that are a credit to your school and yourself. When this commitment is made, participation in the collaborative process of publishing can be rewarding and—even—enjoyable.

Chapter Ten

GETTING MILEAGE: WINNING AWARDS, PUBLISHING YOUR WORK, AND JOINING THE CONVERSATION

You're done at last. You've found your topic and thesis, researched, drafted, revised, and polished; you discovered something that needed saying, documented it carefully, and said it as clearly and elegantly as you could. If your piece was written for your school's journal, and it has been accepted for publication, congratulations! But if your paper was written for a seminar or written for law review and not accepted, there's no reason to limit yourself to the satisfaction of a job well done. Good ideas deserve to be disseminated and talent recognized. And there may be a journal or writing competition waiting for your submission. Not only would your sense of satisfaction increase, but you would be gaining recognition, adding an important credential to your resume, even (in the case of writing competitions) winning a cash award.

There are numerous writing competitions sponsored each year by bar associations, professional associations, foundations, legal defense funds, law institutes, and international organizations. The competitions cover a wide range of subjects. Even if you did not write your paper with a competition in mind, you may be able to tailor your work to fit the competition requirements. The chance of winning is worth the effort. Most competitions assume you are submitting work written under faculty supervision, and the fact that you may have received substantive and editorial assistance is therefore not ordinarily a problem. Read the competition rules carefully, however, so that you do not violate any ethical obligation.

The career centers of most law schools compile information about writing competitions and this is one good place to start. The other is a simple online search. We Googled "legal writing competition" and found both the websites of many individual competitions and, even more useful, numerous websites, mostly hosted by law schools, compiling lists of such competitions and providing links to them. The lists are not identical or comprehensive, however, so be sure to check more than one.

In addition, you should not rule out publication in a law review. If you are not a journal member, it is worth trying to publish your seminar paper in your own school's journals. See if the professor who supervised your paper is willing to recommend it to an executive editor of one of your journals. When editors are told by a professor that a piece is truly special, they will often consider it.

Also try journals at other law schools. Publication in another school's journal can be even more prestigious than publication in one of your own journals, especially if your article is accepted by a journal that is ranked above yours. There are more than 500 law journals; many are willing to publish articles by students from other schools. Each year, some student articles are published: why shouldn't one of them be yours? First, determine when to send out your manuscript. The traditional windows for submissions are March–May and August–October, though some experienced writers would narrow this to August to mid-September and mid-February through March. The optimum periods for submissions vary somewhat from school to school and from year to year, but in general, early spring and early fall are when most editors are actively looking for articles to fill the upcoming issues. If you submit at other times, the issues may have already been filled and your article rejected regardless of its merit. Nonetheless, if timeliness is an issue, send it out as soon as and whenever you can. Or, if you are a third-year student, consider waiting until after you graduate so that your work will be considered in the professional category.

Next, determine how and where to submit. As to the "how," you have two choices: you can submit to the journals of your choice by uploading your paper just once to a submission application, like ExpressO (http://law.bepress.com/expresso/), or you can compile your list, check the submission requirements for each individual journal, and send off your paper in the appropriate format, electronic or hard-copy. ExpressO, which is part of the Berkeley Electronic Press ("bepress"), has institutional subscription rates for law schools as well as individual rates. ExpressO offers institutional student accounts as well as the traditional accounts used by faculty. Check to see whether your school has such an account. When you use such an account, ExpressO will submit your paper only to law reviews that will consider student work. Of course, if your school does not have a student ExpressO account, you can still subscribe individually and pay a fee for each submission. SSRN, the Social Science Research Network (http://www.ssrn.com), also has a submission service; it is free, but is serves fewer law journals than ExpressO.

Whichever route you choose, you will need to decide which journals to submit to. Lists of law reviews and their rankings by *U.S. News and World Report* and other ranking authorities can be found online, for example, on ExpressO, and in your law school's library. You certainly want to submit to any specialty journals in your subject area and to numerous general topic journals in addition. How high (or low) you wish to go in the rankings is a difficult question. Common sense might suggest eliminating, for example, the thirty or so most highly ranked law reviews, even if they do not explicitly rule out student work. These schools may not give your piece considered attention, given the serious competition you face from well-known scholars. You have a better chance at the journals of schools ranked lower. On the other hand, why sell yourself short? The very first article written by the authors of this text was published by a top-ten law review, despite the unlikelihood of such a journal publishing an article on legal writing by novice scholars from a non-top-ten law school. If you believe in your work (and if you will not have to pay mailing costs or individual ExpressO rates for each submission), you may wish to start at the top. Talking to a faculty member—someone who has published in your field or someone whose advice you value—might help here.

Once you have compiled a list of journals, write an abstract or cover letter, depending upon the journals' submission requirements. Each should be written carefully and thoughtfully. Because electronic forms of submission have made it easy and inexpensive to send out articles, law journals have become flooded with manuscripts. As a result, they make some publication decisions solely on the basis of the cover letter or abstract, introduction or conclusion. If these do not whet the interest of the reviewer, the article is often discarded.

The clearest abstracts track the content and structure of an introduction—in briefer form. They begin by introducing the topic and narrowing the article's focus. If necessary, they supply some background. Then they describe the thesis, typically a problem in the law that needs to be remedied. Finally, they conclude with a short summary of the main points.

Topic	Legislative ethics is a largely untreated area of legal and policy scholarship.
Topic Narrowed	Focusing on the case of pork barrel spending projects, this Article examines legislative ethics in practical application.
Background	Pork projects are not illegal, and they are well within the bounds of how the legislative game is played. Yet, collectively, spending on pork projects is widely unpopular, often derided as inefficient and self-interested.
Problem	Against such conventional wisdom, this Article argues that pork projects can serve valuable real and institutional purposes and that such projects are typically ethical, despite their aggregate unpopularity. For example, pork projects can serve a representative's constituency and forge alliances that maximize a representative's power to serve that constituency.
Solution	The Article also drafts initial guidelines to open the debate for evaluating when pork is and is not ethical. It proposes a tiered system

> of responsibility that can serve as a framework for determining when the use of earmarks for pork barrel spending is justified.[1]

Abstracts are not only used for publication decisions. Some journals print them at the beginning of articles or post them on their websites so that researchers can determine if the article is necessary reading for their own work. They serve the same function on databases like SSRN. Thus a good abstract can help you find a publisher and a readership.

Like abstracts, cover letters can convince law review editors that an article is worth reading closely. Many cover letters emphasize an article's contribution to an ongoing debate in the law and its timeliness and originality. Often they provide a brief summary of the thesis and major arguments. In addition, cover letters include necessary contact information, and if relevant, personal information establishing any special credential you may have that bears on your article—related work experience, for example, or a joint degree in urban planning, business administration, or ethics. A more controversial question is whether you must inform a journal of your student status. We think that the failure to be candid about your status provides journals with an excuse not to publish, especially when many hesitate to publish students who are not members of the journal or students of its school. Indeed, we know of one journal that revoked its offer to a student who failed to inform it of her status. Thus we suggest you be candid and let your work stand on its merits.

[Date]

[Recipient's address]

Dear [salutation]:

Topic's Importance	Since the heated debates during the last presidential campaign, pork barrel spending has been a hot topic, but also one little understood. Pork projects are not illegal, and they are well within the bounds of how the legislative game is played. Yet, collectively, spending on pork projects is widely unpopular,
Problem	often derided as inefficient and self-interested.
Thesis	Against such conventional wisdom, this Article argues that pork projects can serve valuable real and

1. Adapted from Virginia A. Fitt, *Honor at the Trough: the Ethics of Pork Politics*, 25 J.L. & Pol. 467 (2010).

institutional purposes and that such projects are typically ethical, despite their aggregate unpopulari ty. For example, pork projects can serve a representative's constituency and forge alliances that maximize a representative's power to serve that constituency. The Article also drafts initial guidelines to open the debate for evaluating when pork is and is not ethical. It proposes a tiered system of responsibility that can serve as a framework for determining when the use of earmarks for pork barrel spending is justified.

Solution

Second contribution

In addition to providing guidelines for pork project decisions, this article will hopefully trigger greater interest in legislative ethics, a neglected area of legal and policy scholarship, but one of some importance.

I would be happy to answer any questions you may have about the article. I look forward to hearing from you.

Sincerely Yours,[2]

[Contact information]

In the first few weeks after submission, you will get a number of acknowledgments of receipt. The entire selection process can be slow, however, since decisions are often vetted by several levels of editors. Expect the process to take about four to twelve weeks. If you are fortunate enough to receive several offers at once, you will have a delicious decision to make. You can ask for, and may receive, a few days or weeks to make your choice. It is not part of legal culture to renege on an offer once you have accepted, however. It is also considered courteous to inform the other journals once you have placed your article so as to save them unnecessary toil.

If your paper is not accepted by a traditional law review—don't be too disappointed. There are still other ways to make yourself and your ideas known: join the online conversation of scholars, practitioners, students, and others who think seriously about the law. Many law reviews have open-access online supplements—often with quirky names like "Pocket Part" (Yale Law Journal) or "CONNtemplations" (Connecticut Law Review)—that publish shorter, less formal articles, most often on timely topics. With a bit of editing, your paper might fit right in. You can also post your paper on the Legal Scholarship Network of SSRN, the Social Science Research Network (http://www.ssrn.com). Uploading and downloading are free; this is a good way to put your ideas and talents out there and to get feedback. (Indeed, some writers post

2. Based on Virginia A. Fitt's article, supra *note 1.*

works in progress for the express purpose of getting feedback.) Another similar site for archiving and sharing scholarship is provided by the Legal Repository of bepress (http://law.bepress.com/repository). Finally, no matter how timely or how obscure your topic, somewhere in the blogosphere, it the subject of an animated and educated conversation. Some blog-posts are so substantial that they are really short, informal articles. There are hundreds of law-related blogs; you are sure to find at least one where you can post comments and meet like-minded scholars. You can also email them and offer to share your paper. Although blogging and online posting in open-access archives like SSRN do not have the same prestige in the legal academy as publication in a traditional journal, they are becoming ever more accepted, and as you begin your career, they can provide you with an invaluable entry into your community of interest within the law.

Appendix A

SAMPLE CASENOTE/COMPETITION PAPER

What follows is a sample law review competition paper. Such papers often bear a strong resemblance to casenotes written for publication, differing in length, scope, and development rather than approach and format. The constraints under which a competition paper is written might compel the writer to focus on a single issue, while a casenote might likely analyze all the issues raised in the opinion. A casenote requires original research, much of which will appear in footnotes and be incorporated into a background section. In contrast, writing competitions will usually provide a student with a careful selection of relevant materials. Absent the extensive research of casenotes, competition papers tend to have fewer footnotes than casenotes and sometimes dispense with background sections.

Generally, both competition papers and casenotes for publication follow the traditional casenote outline discussed in Chapter One, Part B(2) and Chapter Four, Part B(1). One difference is that competition papers usually use endnotes, while casenotes are footnoted. The paper that follows, however, uses footnotes instead of endnotes in order to make it easy for the reader to see how authority, attribution, and textual footnotes relate to the text. (See Chapter Six.)

The competition paper that follows analyzes a decision upholding a statute that requires willing public school children to recite the Pledge of Allegiance. As you read, note the writer's careful work at two critical stages of the scholarly writing process. First, the writer's thesis is original—it does not just paraphrase the court's reasoning. The writer argues that, although correctly decided, the case is poorly decided. By reading critically, the writer has found a logical flaw in the court's reasoning: the court assumed the truth of a proposition (that the Pledge is "curriculum") that should have been proven. Second, having found a thesis, the writer organized the paper effectively into background and analysis sections, using reader-friendly headings.

Reading, Writing, and Reciting the Pledge of Allegiance: *Sherman v. Community Consol. Dist. 21*

Introduction

Fifty years ago, the Supreme Court held in *West Virginia State Board of Education v. Barnette*[1] that a State may not compel children to recite the Pledge of Allegiance. In 1979, the Illinois legislature enacted a statute which provides that the Pledge "shall be recited each school day" by public elementary school pupils.[2]

In 1989, Richard Sherman challenged the constitutionality of that statute on three grounds, arguing 1) that its plain meaning violates *Barnette*; 2) that recitation of the Pledge in public school is further unconstitutional because the phrase "under God" offends the Establishment Clause of the First Amendment; and 3) that even if recitation is optional and the phrase "under God" is constitutional, recitation of the Pledge by teacher and willing pupils, like prayer at a school graduation, unconstitutionally coerces children who do not wish to participate.[3] The district court found for the defendant school board, and the Seventh Circuit Court of Appeals affirmed. The court held that 1) in order to "save" the Illinois statute, the court would read "shall be recited . . . by pupils" to mean that only teachers and "willing pupils" are required to recite the Pledge;[4] 2) "under God" is a form of "ceremonial deism" that is protected from Establishment Clause scrutiny because it has lost through rote repetition any significant religious content;[5] and 3) recitation of the Pledge is not coercive, because it is not like prayer, but merely part of the public school curriculum, and those children who object may select private education instead.[6]

As religion-clause jurisprudence, *Sherman* is easily within the mainstream of Supreme Court precedent. The Seventh Circuit's interpretation of the language of the Illinois Pledge statute renders it consistent with *Barnette*. Further, the court is undoubtedly correct in its conclusion that the Supreme Court would not strike "under God" from the Pledge of Allegiance. Finally, in concluding that recitation of the Pledge by willing students in the presence of unwilling students violates no constitutional right, the court recognizes correctly the simple truth that religion is different from speech for the purposes of constitutional analysis.[7] However, although *Sherman* is correctly decided, it is nonetheless, on all three issues, poorly decided.

First, the court's statutory interpretation is tortured.[8] Moreover, the court's discussion of the Establishment Clause issue is superficial: nei-

1. West Virginia State Bd. of Educ. v. Barnette, 319 U.S. 624, 642 (1943).

2. ILL. REV. STAT. ch. 122, para. 27-3 (1990).

3. *Cf.* Lee v. Weisman, 505 U.S. 577 (1992) (establishment clause forbids prayer at public high school graduation ceremony).

4. Sherman v. Cmty. Consol. Dist. 21 of Wheeling Twp., 980 F.2d 437, 442–43 (7th Cir. 1992).

5. *Id.* at 447 (quoting Lynch v. Donnelly, 465 U.S. 668, 716 (1984) (Brennan, J., dissenting)).

6. *Id.* at 444–45.

7. *See infra* text accompanying note 22.

8. *See infra* note 18.

ther the majority's argument that "under God" is inoffensive because it is meaningless nor the concurrence's argument that it is only a *de minimis* violation of the Constitution seems a good enough justification for its presence in the Pledge. Finally, the court's conclusion that recitation of the Pledge is not "coercive" is reached through the unexamined assumption that the Pledge is just an ordinary part of the school curriculum. This third and most troubling aspect of *Sherman* is the subject of this Note. Not only did the Seventh Circuit beg the question by equating Pledge and curriculum, but its assumption is faulty: the recitation of a patriotic oath is in fact more like prayer than like learning to add and subtract. This Note concludes that while the analogy to religious ritual may not be so perfect as to require the conclusion that recitation of the Pledge "coerces" belief in non-reciting elementary school children, the likeness is strong enough to have warranted more thoughtful analysis by the court.

Part I of this Note sets out factual and procedural background to the issues raised in *Sherman* and details the reasoning of the majority and concurring opinions. Part II examines the court's analysis of the coercion issue in greater detail and then discusses its failure to confront the oath/prayer analogy.

I. Sherman v. Community Consol. Dist. 21

A. Factual and Procedural Background

In 1954, the Pledge of Allegiance was amended to include the words "under God."[9] In 1979, thirty-six years after the Supreme Court forbade mandatory recitation of the Pledge,[10] the Illinois legislature enacted the statute in question here, a statute which provides that public elementary school children "shall" recite the pledge, although it provides no penalty for refusing to pledge.[11] The legislative history of the Illinois statute suggests that some members of the Illinois General Assembly believed that the statute would mandate recitation of the Pledge, and that it would thus defy *Barnette*.[12]

By his father, Robert Sherman, elementary school student Richard Sherman filed suit in federal district court in 1989 alleging that the statute violates both the Free Exercise and Establishment clauses of the First Amendment. School officials filed affidavits responding that no pupils were ever compelled to recite the Pledge. Richard's teacher said she permits no "hazing" of students who decline to participate.[13] Richard's father stated in his affidavit, however, that the principal asked Richard to stand with his hand over his heart and recite the Pledge, and that other students "hassled" Richard in the playground for refusing to

9. *See* 36 U.S.C. § 172 (1988).

10. *Barnette*, 319 U.S. at 642.

11. ILL. REV. STAT. ch. 122, para. 27–3 (1990).

12. *Sherman*, 980 F.2d at 443.

13. *Id.*

say the Pledge. Since the father did not allege that he knew these facts of his own knowledge, the evidence was deemed inadmissible.[14]

The district court granted summary judgment for the defendant school district,[15] and plaintiffs Sherman appealed to the Seventh Circuit Court of Appeals.

B. The Majority Opinion

Judge Easterbrook's opinion for the Seventh Circuit begins with a famous quote from Justice Jackson's *Barnette* opinion, followed by a somewhat confusing and incomplete statement of the issues presented:

> "[N]o official, high or petty, can prescribe what shall be orthodox in politics, nationalism, religion, or other matters of opinion or force citizens to confess by word or act their faith therein." *West Virginia State Board of Education v. Barnette*, 319 U.S. 624, 642 (1943). A state therefore may not compel any person to recite the Pledge of Allegiance to the flag. On similar grounds, *Wooley v. Maynard*, 430 U.S. 705 (1977), adds that a state may not compel any person to display its slogan. Does it follow that a pupil who objects to the content of the Pledge may prevent teachers and other pupils from reciting it in his presence? We conclude that schools may lead the Pledge of Allegiance daily, so long as pupils are free not to participate.[16]
>
> . . . .
>
> We held in *Palmer v. Board of Education*, 603 F.2d 1271 (7th Cir. 1979), that states may require teachers to lead the Pledge and otherwise communicate patriotic values to their students. The right of the school board to decide what the pupils are taught implies a corresponding right to require teachers to act accordingly. *See also Webster v. New Lenox School District*, 917 F.2d 1004 (7th Cir. 1990). Richard Sherman, who attends elementary school in Wheeling Township, Illinois, and his father Robert challenge the premise of *Palmer* that schools may employ a curriculum including the Pledge of Allegiance among its exercises. Since 1954 the Pledge has included the words "under God," 68 Stat. 249, which the Shermans contend violates the establishment and free exercise clauses of the first amendment.[17]

The court first addresses the statutory construction issue: whether the statute is mandatory and therefore facially unconstitutional, or discretionary and therefore constitutional. For the court, the issue is whether "pupils" in the statute means "some pupils," "willing pupils," or "all pupils."[18] The court notes preliminarily that when the Supreme

14. *Id.*

15. Sherman v. Cmty. Consol. Dist. 21 of Wheeling Twp., 758 F.Supp. 1244 (N.D. Ill. 1991).

16. *Sherman*, 980 F.2d at 439.

17. *Id.* at 439–40.

18. *Id.* at 442. This seems a strange way to describe the statutory construction problem here. Surely the real problem is whether "shall" should be given its plain meaning or be construed as "may." But neither "shall" nor "pupils" seems even remotely ambiguous.

Court of Illinois is called upon to resolve a statutory ambiguity, it adopts the reading that will save rather than destroy the state law. The court thus resolves the problem:

> Given *Barnette*, which long predated enactment of this statute, it makes far more sense to interpolate "by willing pupils" than "by all pupils." School administrators and teachers satisfy the "shall" requirement by leading the Pledge and ensuring that at least some pupils recite. Leading the Pledge is not optional, *see Palmer*, but participating is. This makes sense of the statute without imputing a flagrantly unconstitutional act to the State of Illinois.[19]

According to the court, this understanding is consistent with the actual non-compulsory practice in the school district. The court deems the legislative history "unenlightening" and inconclusive. The anti-*Barnette* comments made by at least two state senators are in the court's view merely "juicy tidbits," politicians "bring[ing] obloquy upon themselves."[20]

The court then sets aside for last the issue of whether "under God" in the Pledge is an Establishment Clause violation, although logically that issue would seem the next to be resolved. Instead, the court assumes the Pledge to be entirely secular, and discusses the coercion issue by considering *Barnette* in light of *Lee v. Weisman*.[21] The court asks whether, given that no one may be compelled to pledge (*Barnette*), and given that an optional graduation prayer led by a member of the clergy has an unconstitutionally coercive effect on unwilling students (*Lee*), the recitation of the Pledge by willing students has a similarly coercive effect on those who object to the Pledge. The short answer is that "[t]he religion clauses of the first amendment do not establish general rules about speech or schools; they call for religion to be treated differently."[22]

The court concludes that so long as students are not formally compelled to profess belief in the content of the Pledge, they have no valid objection; recitation by the teacher and willing students is not in itself impermissibly coercive.[23] "Objection by the few does not reduce to silence the many who *want* to pledge allegiance to the flag 'and to the Republic for which it stands.' "[24]

Finally, the court reaches plaintiff's claim that " 'under God' makes the Pledge a prayer, whose recitation violates the Establishment Clause."[25] While the Supreme Court has never squarely decided whether such theistic invocations violate the Establishment Clause, in recent years it has several times indicated in dicta that such mottoes are consistent with the Establishment Clause—not because their import is

19. *Id.* Yet, if the court's interpretation indeed "ensur[es] that at least some pupils recite," it is inconsistent with *Barnette*, which gives *every* student the right to refuse to pledge.

20. *Id.* at 443.

21. *Lee*, 505 U.S. 577. The Seventh Circuit's reasoning on the issue is described more fully in Part II, A., *infra*.

22. *Sherman*, 980 F.2d at 444.

23. *Id.* at 445.

24. *Id.*

25. *Id.*

de minimis, but because they have lost any true religious significance.[26] Thus, the *Sherman* majority concludes that like the Christmas tree, "under God" is secular, having lost its religious significance.[27]

C. The Concurrence

Judge Manion writes separately only to take the majority to task for concluding that "under God" is constitutional because it is meaningless "ceremonial deism."

> Such an approach implies that phrases like "in God we trust" or "under God" when initially used ... violated the establishment clause because they had not yet been rendered meaningless by repetitive use.[28]
>
> . . . .
>
> Another problem with the concept of "ceremonial deism" is that it selects only religious phrases as losing their significance through rote repetition. Why only "under God?" Why not "indivisible," "liberty and justice for all?"[29]

According to Judge Manion, "under God" is constitutional not because it is meaningless, but because it simply does not rise to the level of an establishment of religion.[30]

II. The Pledge of Allegiance: Curriculum or Coercion?

The Seventh Circuit is too quick to conclude that recitation of the Pledge of Allegiance by teacher and "willing" elementary school pupils does not have an unconstitutionally coercive effect on children who wish not to pledge. The court reasons that the Pledge is part of the school curriculum and therefore cannot be meaningfully analogized to voluntary school prayer, which is forbidden in public schools because of its inherent coercive effect. In so reasoning, the Seventh Circuit correctly points out that religion is quite simply "different" for the purposes of constitutional analysis. However, the court fails to see that swearing a patriotic oath is not like studying geography—a reality the Supreme Court recognized when it forbade forced recitation of the Pledge long ago in *Barnette*.

A. Religion is Different

Once the court in *Sherman* jumps the *Barnette* hurdle by interpreting the words "[t]he Pledge of Allegiance shall be recited by pupils" to mean "shall be recited by willing pupils,"[31] the next issue is whether voluntary recitation of the Pledge violated the First Amendment by coercing recitation from unwilling pupils. This issue the court frames as whether "a pupil who objects to the content of the Pledge may prevent teachers and other pupils from reciting it in his presence."[32] The court

26. *Id.* at 446–47.

27. *Id.* at 447.

28. *Id.* at 448.

29. *Id.*

30. *Id.*

31. *Id.* at 442.

32. *Id.* at 439. It seems unlikely that this is plaintiff Sherman's framing of the issue. The court's recasting of the issue foreshadows its conclusion. Ironically, the

concludes that "schools may lead the Pledge of Allegiance daily, so long as pupils are free not to participate."[33]

The court begins its analysis by asking whether "[n]otwithstanding the lack of penalties or efforts by teachers to induce pupils to recite," the First Amendment is offended by the social pressure on students to participate in the daily recitation of the Pledge and their "sense of exclusion when [their] beliefs enforce silence during a ceremony others welcome."[34] In answering this question, the court postpones consideration of plaintiff's argument that the words "under God" transform the Pledge into a prayer and considers it simply as a secular expression of patriotism.

To analyze the issue, the court relies on two lines of cases. The first line begins with *Barnette*, which struck down a regulation requiring public elementary school students to recite the Pledge of Allegiance each day in school.[35] The Supreme Court held in *Barnette* that under the Free Speech provision of the First Amendment, the state may no more compel the profession of belief than it may forbid it.[36]

The second line of Supreme Court cases on which the Seventh Circuit relies begins with *Engel v. Vitale*,[37] and includes most recently *Lee v. Weisman*.[38] *Engel* held that the daily recitation of a brief, denominationally neutral prayer required in New York public schools violated the Establishment Clause of the First Amendment despite the fact that student participation was voluntary.[39] The majority held that "[t]he Establishment Clause, unlike the Free Exercise Clause, does not depend upon any showing of direct governmental compulsion and is violated by the enactment of laws which establish an official religion whether these laws operate directly to coerce nonobserving individuals or not."[40] The court went on to acknowledge, however, that while a finding of an Establishment Clause violation does not require coercion, in fact laws officially prescribing a particular form of religious worship, such as the New York public school prayer, are coercive: "When the power, prestige and financial support of government is placed behind a particular religious belief, the indirect coercive pressure upon religious minorities to conform to the prevailing officially approved religion is plain."[41]

court's framing of the issue is similar to the framing of the issue in *Minersville v. Gobitis*, 310 U.S. 586 (1940), which was overruled by *Barnette*. In *Gobitis*, Justice Frankfurter transformed the plaintiff's contention (that it was unconstitutional to force a child with religious objections to pledge) so that it asked "whether ... the authorities in a thousand ... school districts ... are barred from determining the appropriateness of various means to evolve that unifying sentiment without which there can ultimately be no liberties...." *Id.* at 597. Like Justice Frankfurter, Judge Easterbrook asks a question to which there seems to be just one right answer. *See* Robert A. Ferguson, *The Judicial Opinion as Literary Genre*, 2 YALE J.L. & HUMAN. 201, 209 (1990).

33. *Sherman*, 980 F.2d at 439.

34. *Id.* at 443.

35. *Barnette*, 319 U.S. at 642.

36. *Id.*

37. Engel v. Vitale, 370 U.S. 421 (1962).

38. *Lee*, 505 U.S. at 577.

39. *Engel*, 370 U.S. at 424.

40. *Id.* at 430.

41. *Id.* at 431.

The Supreme Court again recognized the inherent coerciveness of state-sponsored prayer in *Lee*. In that case, the Court held that a public school may not provide for a non-sectarian graduation prayer to be given by a clergyman selected by the school.[42] The court recognized "heightened concerns with protecting freedom of conscience from subtle coercive pressure in the ... public schools" and concluded that "prayer exercises in public schools carry a particular risk of indirect coercion."[43] It continued, "[w]hat to most believers may seem nothing more than a reasonable request that the nonbeliever respect their religious practices, in a school context may appear to the nonbeliever or dissenter to be an attempt to employ the machinery of the state to enforce a religious orthodoxy."[44] Combining *Barnette's* Free Speech reasoning with *Lee's* Establishment Clause reasoning, Sherman's argument was that "[i]f as *Barnette* holds no state may require anyone to recite the Pledge, and if as the prayer cases hold, the recitation by a teacher or rabbi of unwelcome words *is* coercion, the Pledge of Allegiance becomes unconstitutional under all circumstances, just as no school may read from a holy scripture at the start of class."[45]

In rejecting this argument, the *Sherman* court correctly points out that "[t]he religion clauses of the first amendment do not establish general rules about speech or schools; they call for religion to be treated differently."[46] Indeed, in *Lee* the Supreme Court stressed that:

> The First Amendment protects speech and religion by quite different mechanisms. Speech is protected by insuring its full expression even when the government participates, for the very object of some of our most important speech is to persuade the government to adopt an idea as its own. [citations omitted] The method for protecting freedom of worship and freedom of conscience in religious matters is quite the reverse. In religious debate or expression the government is not a prime participant, for the Framers deemed religious establishment antithetical to the freedom of all. The Free Exercise Clause embraces a freedom of conscience and worship that has close parallels in the speech provisions of the First Amendment, but the Establishment Clause is a specific prohibition on forms of state intervention in religious affairs with no precise counterpart in the speech provisions.[47]

Thus, the Seventh Circuit reasonably concludes that the school prayer cases decided under the Establishment Clause do not compel the conclusion that voluntary, school-sponsored patriotic recitations offend the Free Speech clause.

B. What's in a Pledge?

As argued above, *Sherman* is "correctly" decided in the sense that it does not directly conflict with any Supreme Court holdings. However,

42. *Lee*, 505 U.S. at 593.

43. *Id.* at 592.

44. *Id.*

45. *Sherman*, 980 F.2d at 444.

46. *Id.*

47. *Lee*, 505 U.S. at 591.

although the court's conclusion in *Sherman* is consistent with Supreme Court precedent, its analysis ignores the special nature of pledging.

Rather than examining the constitutional implications of daily subjecting students to the ritual state-sponsored recitation of patriotic oaths by their peers and teachers, the court assumes that the Pledge is just an ordinary element of the school curriculum. The court makes this assumption on the basis of a strained and questionable definition. Deeming the Pledge "patriotic expression,"[48] the court defines "patriotism" as "an effort by the state to promote its own survival, and along the way to teach those virtues that *justify* its survival."[49]

Having thus given patriotism a pedagogical component absent from its dictionary definition,[50] the court is then free to call the Pledge "curriculum." Having called the Pledge curriculum, the court can then easily conclude, citing *Lee*, that schools may legitimately expose students to ideas that they find "distasteful or immoral or absurd or all of these" as part of their education.[51] The court explains that the government "retains the right to set the curriculum in its own schools and insist that those who cannot accept the result exercise their right ... [to] select private education at their own expense.... '[S]chool boards may set curricula bounded only by the Establishment Clause' even though pupils may find the books and classroom discourse offensive or immoral."[52]

By thus equating the Pledge with books and classroom discourse, the court easily dismisses the claim of coercion. Moreover, the equation permits the court to make the dire prediction that "[a]n extension of the school prayer cases could not stop with the Pledge of Allegiance. It would extend to the books, essays, tests, and discussions in every classroom."[53] The court reasonably concludes such accommodation of individual beliefs would be impossible.

However, both the court's conclusion that recitation of the Pledge is not coercive and its slippery-slope warning are based on the faulty premise that the Pledge is an ordinary part of the elementary school curriculum. In fact, a state-sponsored patriotic pledge is far more clearly analogous to state-sponsored prayer than it is to a classroom discussion or a reading assignment about a controversial subject. To pledge allegiance is to make a "solemn promise"[54] of "loyalty owed to one's country,"[55] an utterance with great emotional resonance.

Indeed, the difference between pledging and learning is implicit in the *Sherman* court's opinion. For while the court points out that students may be required to "write essays about [ideas that conflict with

48. *Sherman*, 980 F.2d at 444.

49. *Id.*

50. An authoritative dictionary defines patriotism as "loyal support of one's country." Oxford American Dictionary 490 (1980).

51. *Sherman*, 980 F.2d at 444.

52. *Id.* at 445 (quoting Mozert v. Hawkins Cnty. Bd. Of Educ., 827 F.2d 1058, at 1080 (6th Cir. 1987) (Boggs, J., concurring)).

53. *Id.* at 444.

54. Oxford American Dictionary, *supra* note 50.

55. *Id.* at 17.

their beliefs] and take tests—questions for which their teachers prescribe right answers, which the students must give if they are to receive their degrees,"[56] it acknowledges, as it must, that students may not be forced to recite the Pledge.

This distinction is evident in caselaw concerned with the rights of teachers. The Seventh Circuit has held that teachers are not free to teach or not teach particular subjects according to their religious beliefs in disregard of the prescribed curriculum. In *Palmer v. Board of Ed.*,[57] that court held that the First Amendment did not support the claim of a Jehovah's Witness who refused to teach about President Lincoln and why we observe his birthday on grounds that to do so would be idolatry. In *Webster v. New Lenox Schl. Dist.*,[58] the Seventh Circuit similarly held that the school board had the right to prohibit a teacher from teaching a nonevolutionary theory of creation. In sharp contrast, however, is the Second Circuit's ruling that a teacher may not be required to lead the Pledge of Allegiance.[59]

Distinctions can certainly be made between an official prayer and a secular pledge based on the difference between the Establishment Clause and the free speech provisions of the First Amendment. Yet it is hard to reconcile the Supreme Court's recognition in *Engel* that the inherent coercion of school prayers offends the Free Exercise clause[60] (which is analogous to the free speech provision of the First Amendment) with the conclusion that recitation of the Pledge is not also coercive. Coerced patriotism would appear to violate *Barnette's* warning that "no official, high or petty, can prescribe what shall be orthodox in politics, nationalism, religion, or other matters of opinion or force citizens to confess by word or act their faith therein."[61]

Conclusion

The Seventh Circuit's analysis of the coercion issue in *Sherman* is more than disappointing. Asked whether state-sponsored recitation of a patriotic oath by school children could ever be truly voluntary, the court begs the question by replying that the Pledge of Allegiance is mere curriculum. The thinness of the court's analysis is particularly troubling because the real-life story of *Sherman* is played out in the minds of very young children. But unlike the Supreme Court in *Engel* and *Lee*, the Seventh Circuit shows no interest in whether, in fact, children who wish not to recite the Pledge feel themselves to be the subjects of "an attempt to employ the machinery of the state to enforce ... orthodoxy."[62]

56. *Sherman*, 980 F.2d at 444.

57. Palmer v. Bd. of of City of Chicago, 603 F.2d 1271 (7th Cir. 1979).

58. Webster v. New Lenox Sch. Dist., 917 F.2d 1004 (7th Cir. 1990).

59. Russo v. Cent. Sch. Dist., 469 F.2d 623 (2nd Cir. 1972).

60. *Engel*, 370 U.S. at 430–31.

61. *Barnette*, 319 U.S. at 642.

62. *Lee*, 505 U.S. at 592.

Appendix B

ANSWERS TO EXERCISES

A. CHAPTER 5 ANSWERS

EXERCISE 5.1

IV. Constitutional Challenges
   A. Plaintiff's Challenge
      1. The Takings Clause
      2. Substantive Due Process
      3. Procedural Due Process
      4. Equal Protection
   B. Defendant's Challenge
      1. The Excessive Fines Clause
      2. The Double Jeopardy Clause
   C. State Constitutional Challenges
      1. The Right to a Jury Trial
      2. The Remedy Clause
      3. Separation of Powers
      4. The Single Subject Clause

The basic problem here is one of division: sub-issues A, B, and C divide the issue by party (A and B) and by type of constitutional challenge (C), creating an illogical outline. The writer should choose type of challenge or party as her basic principle of division. Two sample revisions follow.

IV. Constitutional Challenges
   A. Federal Constitution
      1. Plaintiff's Challenges
         a. The Takings Clause
         b. Substantive Due Process
         c. Procedural Due Process
         d. Equal Protection

      2. Defendant's Challenges
         a. The Excessive Fines Clause
         b. The Double Jeopardy Clause

B. State Constitution
  1. Plaintiff's Challenges
     a., b., etc. [List plaintiff's challenges]
  2. Defendant's Challenges
     a., b., etc. [List defendant's challenges]

IV. Constitutional Challenges
  A. Plaintiff's Challenges
    1. Federal Constitutional Challenges
       a., b., etc. [List the challenges]
    2. State Constitutional Challenges
       a., b., etc. [List the challenges]
  B. Defendant's Challenges
    1. Federal Constitutional Challenges
       a., b., etc. [List the challenges]
    2. State Constitutional Challenges
       a., b., etc. [List the challenges]

EXERCISE 5.2

The optimal penalty theorists' approach to sanctioning convicted criminals assumes that it is better to impose fines than jail sentences. This view is based upon the economic rationale that the best option for solving a problem is the one that preserves the most societal resources. From an optimal theorist's perspective, the imposition of optimal fines creates as much deterrence as the imposition of a prison sentence; therefore, it is better to impose a fine, because doing so conserves resources that would have been expended to incarcerate the convicted criminal.

Add an intro summarizing position of opt. pen. folks on the statute - 2 objections

Good intro to opt. pen. doctrine - but define "optimal fine"

Given the legislative history of the recent legislation, optimal penalty theorists likely will argue that political expediency superceded rationality in the furor to ensure enactment of a package that creates the impression that politicians are tough on corporate fraud. The number of politicians who, in speaking about the new law to the press, focused on the enhanced prison terms for corporate criminals, bolsters their

This seems like the secondary objection - move to the end

argument. For example, upon signing the bill, the President commented that " there will be no more easy money for corporate fraudsters, just hard time." The Speaker of the House similarly was quoted as warning "If you lie, cheat, or commit some other white collar crime, you'll face the same consequences as a street criminal." Optimal penalty theorists will cite comments like these as an indication that Congress and the President were not motivated by rational judgments, but rather, that they included enhanced penalties for white-collar criminals in the legislation as a way to show their voters that they are opposed to corporate wrong-doing.

While incarceration has the obvious effect of constraining a convict's freedom, optimal penalty theorists argue that the main purpose of incarceration is to protect the public. Optimal penalty theory suggests that this goal is not very important in the context of white-collar crime because white-collar criminals pose no threat of physical harm. They discount the deterrent effect flowing from loss of liberty because white collar criminals are unlikely to serve lengthy sentences. Other psychological effects of incarceration, such as shame or loss of reputation, optimal penalty theorists argue, are ineffective deterrents because they are too costly to achieve– contrary to fines, they do not yield any revenue. Moreover, optimal penalty theorists resist the idea that such stigma effectively attaches as a result of sentencing, maintaining that whatever stigma does attach to a felon does so as a result of conviction, not of sentencing.

Topic sentence needed

Optimal penalty theorists argue that white-collar defendants are more likely than other offenders to make decisions from a cost-benefit point-of-view. Therefore, imposing fines directly deters undesirable behavior among this group. By contrast, non-monetary sanctions, whether jail sentences or corporate probation, are an indirect method of curbing undesirable behavior and therefore provide a less effective deterrent. Optimal penalty theorists would only impose non-monetary deterrents, such as jail time, when collecting fines is likely to be a problem.

Topic Sentence needed

Optimal penalty theorists were hostile to efforts to impose criminal liability on corporations themselves. They argued that corporations convicted of fraudulent business practices should not receive corporate probation. Corporate probation (in which the government monitors a convicted corporation for a specified number of years) was subjected to the criticisms that it 1) wasted societal resources in comparison to fining and 2) did not have a deterrent effect greater than fining. From an economic point of view, punishment of individuals or corporations that is costly to the government can only be produced by irrational motivations like personal political gain.

Relevance? Our topic is individual Δs, not corps. Omit

A different topic

This draft passage needs clearer organization, an introductory sentence, and transition sentences. Clarity is even more than usually important here, because the ideas are unfamiliar to most readers. In this draft, the ideas are almost impossible to follow. The outline that follows would increase readability.

I. Introductory paragraph on basic optimal penalty theory. (Fill gap by defining "optimal fine.")

II. First objection to jail sentences for corporate criminals in new legislation: ineffective deterrent and costly to government. (Omit discussion of corporate probation—not relevant to our topic)

III. Second objection to jail sentences in statute: irrational decision by politicians, motivated by desire for votes.

EXERCISE 5.3

In the sample revision that follows, a topic sentence summarizing the passage has been added—brackets indicate its optional placement at the beginning or end of the passage. Additionally, transitions (indicated in italics) and dove-tailing (indicated by underscore) aid comprehension.

[The original rationales for spousal maintenance have eroded over time.] The law of maintenance has its origin in England. Under English ecclesiastical law, although divorce was forbidden, spouses were permitted to live separately. In cases of separation, the husband's duty to support his wife formed the rationale for awards of maintenance. *When* courts in the United States *later* applied the English practice to divorce as well as separation, the rationale became somewhat shaky, *because* divorce logically negates the existence of a spousal support duty. *Yet* until the advent of no-fault divorce, maintenance still retained some principled bases. Punishment and deterrence of wrong-doing could be seen as grounds for awards of spousal maintenance. *Once* no-fault divorce became the norm, *however*, those rationales, *too*, were undermined. [*Thus* have the original rationales for spousal maintenance eroded over time.]

EXERCISE 5.4

G. POLISING: PROOFREADING

"Nobody is prefect."
- The authors

Proofreading someone else's work is a demanding job that calls on highly specialized skills; proofreading your own work is that and simple misery. The only thing worse is discovering all those humiliating typographical errors after you have handed in your work. Moreover, even the friendliest reader is turned off by typographical errors and typographical inconsistencies (inconsistent spelling capitalization, or use of hyphens. Fairly or not, he effect of work that is carefully researched, thought out and written can be compromised if you do not allow enough time for an equally careful proofreading.

The first rule of proofreading is more in the nature of a warning: your computer's Spell-check program is just a beginning. Spell-checkers are a congenial time and embarrassment saver for all writers, and a positive blessing for people who simply can not cope with the eccentricities and infidelities of english spelling. But your spell-checker cannot detect wrong words or missing words. For instance, it will not fault you for typing "he" for "the" or "their for "there" In addition, spellcheckers do not speak the language of the law. For example, your computer will be undisturbed by "judgement" (a variant spelling aceptable in Standard American English) although in the American legal culture, "judgment" is the *only* correct spelling.

The second rule is harder to observe: read every word, do not skim. Reader anticipation is the enemy of proofreading: we see the words we expect to see. One of the most useful anti-browsing techniques simply to move a ruler or a sheet of blank paper under each line of text as you read, so that your eye can go no farther than the end of one line. Some writers force themselves to start at the end of their texts and read sentence-by-sentence toward the beginning. Whether you choose to endure this particular from of torture or not, it is a good idea to proofread the latter sections first, because they are more likely to have undetected errors. Be sure to proofread headings and epigrams as well as text. And check specifically to see that quotation marks, parentheses, and brackets all have their partners.

If you are writing for publication you *must* profread for typographical consistency as well as for accuracy; even if you are not writing for publication, you *should* read for consistancy. Foolish consistency may well be the hobgoblin of small minds, as Emerson said, but inconsistency certainly gives your paper an air of carelessness and unprofessionalism that puts off a serious reader and complicates a copy-editor's job. Be sure that all headings of equal weight are treated the same way. Be sure that your use of capitalization is consistent (If you are writing for Law Review, your capitalization must of course follow Bluebook or ALWD style. And be sure that compound terms are consistently, as well as *correctly*, rendered: hyphenated, one word, or two words. When no prefered form can be found, choose one form and stick to it. For instance, westlaw and lexis can be described as "online" or on-line" services and one of their major uses as "fulltext" or "full-text" searches. We use "online" and "full-text," largely because the latter, a newer coinage, looks strange to us as one word. But in any event, you should make a list of recuring difficult words or terms so that you can refer to it as you proofread. (You can also use your computer to search and replace inconsistent usage.)

As you may have noticed, this section on proofreading is plaqued by common typos. As Exercise 5.4, go back and proofread it carefully. Then look at the corrected version in appendix b. If you missed more than one, your proofreading skills need polishing.

B. CHAPTER 6 ANSWERS

EXERCISE 6.1

Authority

Mass. Const. Art. 15

In all controversies concerning property and in all suits between two or more persons, except in cases in which it has heretofore otherways been practised, the parties have a right to a trial by jury; and this method of procedure shall be held sacred....

Dalis v. Buyer Advertising, 636 N.E.2d 212, 214 (Mass. 1994)

The jury system, as the "sacred" method for resolving factual disputes, is the most important means by which laypersons can participate in and understand the legal system. *Commonwealth v. Canon*, 368 N.E.2d 1181, 1193 (Mass. 1977) (Abrams, J. dissenting). It brings the "rules of law to the touchstone of contemporary common sense." *Id.*, quoting 1 W. Holdsworth, A History of English Law, 348–349 (3d ed. 1922). "Jurors bring to a case their common sense and community values; their 'very inexperience is an asset because it secures a fresh perception of each trial, avoiding the stereotypes said to infect the judicial eye.'" *Parklane Hosiery Co. v. Shore*, 439 U.S. 322, 355 (1979) (Rehnquist J., dissenting), quoting H. Kalven & H. Zeisel, The American Jury 8 (1966).

Stonehill College v. Massachusetts Commission Against Discrimination, 808 N.E.2d 205, 233 (Mass. 2004) (Sosman, J., concurring)

Laws prohibiting workplace discrimination against racial and ethnic minorities, women, and homosexuals were enacted precisely because prejudices against, or stereotypical assumptions concerning, those persons were so widespread and deeply held. When the legislature first authorized private suits to redress discrimination in 1974, the Legislature could reasonably have been of the view that plaintiffs asserting their rights under [the anti-discrimination statute] would face reluctance or even downright hostility from jurors.... (By way of historical reference to illustrate the point, 1974 was the first year of court-ordered busing to desegregate the Boston public schools, a time of terrible racial strife within the city.) That discrimination claims were to be handled either by [an administrative agency] ... or by the court ... reflected the practical reality of the times....

Draft

The right to a jury trial in civil cases is "sacred" in Massachusetts.**1** It provides laypersons with an opportunity to participate in the legal system and, in the words of Holdsworth, brings the "rules of law to the touchstone of contemporary common sense."**2** But though the right may be sacred, juries themselves are not always pure. Discrimination in many forms—racism, ethnic hatred, sexism, homophobia—pervades our society,**3** and when jurors "bring to a case their...community values," those values are not uniformly positive.**4** Thus, in drafting Massachusetts' anti-discrimination statute in 1974, a year of terrible racial strife in Boston, the Legislature deliberately did not provide for trial by jury, fearing that "plaintiffs asserting their rights under [the statute] would face reluctance or even downright hostility from jurors."**5**

---

1. Mass. Const. Art. 15.
2. 1 W. Holdsworth, A History of English Law 348-49 (3d ed. 1922).
3. *Stonehill College v. Massachusetts Commission Against Discrimination*, 808 N.E.2d 205, 233 (Mass. 2004) (Sosman, J., concurring).
4. *Parklane Hosiery Co. v. Shore*, 439 U.S. 322, 325 (1979) (Rehnquist, J., dissenting).
5. *Stonehill College*, 808 N.E.2d at 233 (Sosman, J., concurring).

need quotes here – distinctive language

1. Proper use of "no signal" cite for four square authority

2. Improper – should cite to source where the quote was found – not create the impression Holdsworth was read

3. Improper – the judge was referring to attitudes in 1974, not today. Also, the opinion of a historian would carry more weight here.

4. Improper – although "no signal" cite is appropriate for a quote, this quote is out of context, distorting meaning that Rehnquist intended. Also writer should cite Dalis, where she found quote.

5. Improper – although "no signal" is appropriate for quote, the context exaggerates the meaning. The judge said it would have been "reasonable" for legislature to fear jurors' reluctance.

EXERCISE 6.2

Sample A

Many ethical lapses here!

In the last twenty years or so, defendants have asserted that routine police questioning has forced them to make false confessions.**1** Psychological studies have demonstrated that when routine questioning techniques are used on people who are especially vulnerable to the pressures generated by these techniques, the result may be a coerced-compliant or a coerced-internalized false confession.**2** In a coerced-compliant confession, the suspect confesses to stop the questioning or gain some other benefit. Coerced-internalized confessions occur when the suspect actually comes to believe in his own guilt.**3**

Whenever there is a real possibility that the circumstances of interrogation will produce a false confession, a confession so obtained should be deemed untrustworthy. "A false confession may be defined as one in which the facts admitted in the confession appear to be either totally incorrect or materially inaccurate. An untrustworthy confession, on the other hand, should be defined as one that is obtained under circumstances that provide significant doubt as to its accuracy."**4**

Direct paraphrase with no attribution to Prof. White

Another paraphrase lacking attribution to Prof. White, with no quotes around original language and 5 consec. words

Here, the writer steals White's ideas

Properly shown to be a quote, but should be in block format

---

1. *See, e.g.*, CONVICTING THE INNOCENT, (Donald S. Connery, ed., 1996) (claiming that Richard Lapointe, a brain-damaged defendant who was convicted of the murder of his wife's grandmother, falsely confessed to the murder following several hours of intensive police interrogation); Sharon Cohen, *"Ringmasters" Unlock Truth, Free Man who Confessed to Murder*, L.A. TIMES, Mar. 31, 1996, at A2 (recounting case of Johnny Lee Wilson, a retarded defendant who was convicted of murder after falsely confessing to a crime that subsequent evidence showed he did not commit). See generally Gisli H. GUDJONSSON, THE PSYCHOLOGY OF INTERROGATIONS, CONFESSIONS AND TESTIMONY 235-40, 260-73 (1992) (analyzing several British cases and one American case in which defendants were charged or convicted on the basis of confessions later shown to be false)....
2. GUDJONSSON, *supra* note 26, at 228.
3. *Id.*
4. Welsh S. White, *False Confessions and the Constitution: Safeguards against Untrustworthy Confessions*, 32 HARV. C.R.-C.L.L. REV. 105, 109 (1997).

"Lifting" this fn. is also plagiarism. It was compiled and written by White.

White's original use of this source must be attributed.

Attribution here is ok, but it gives false impression that this is White's only contribution to this piece.

Sample B

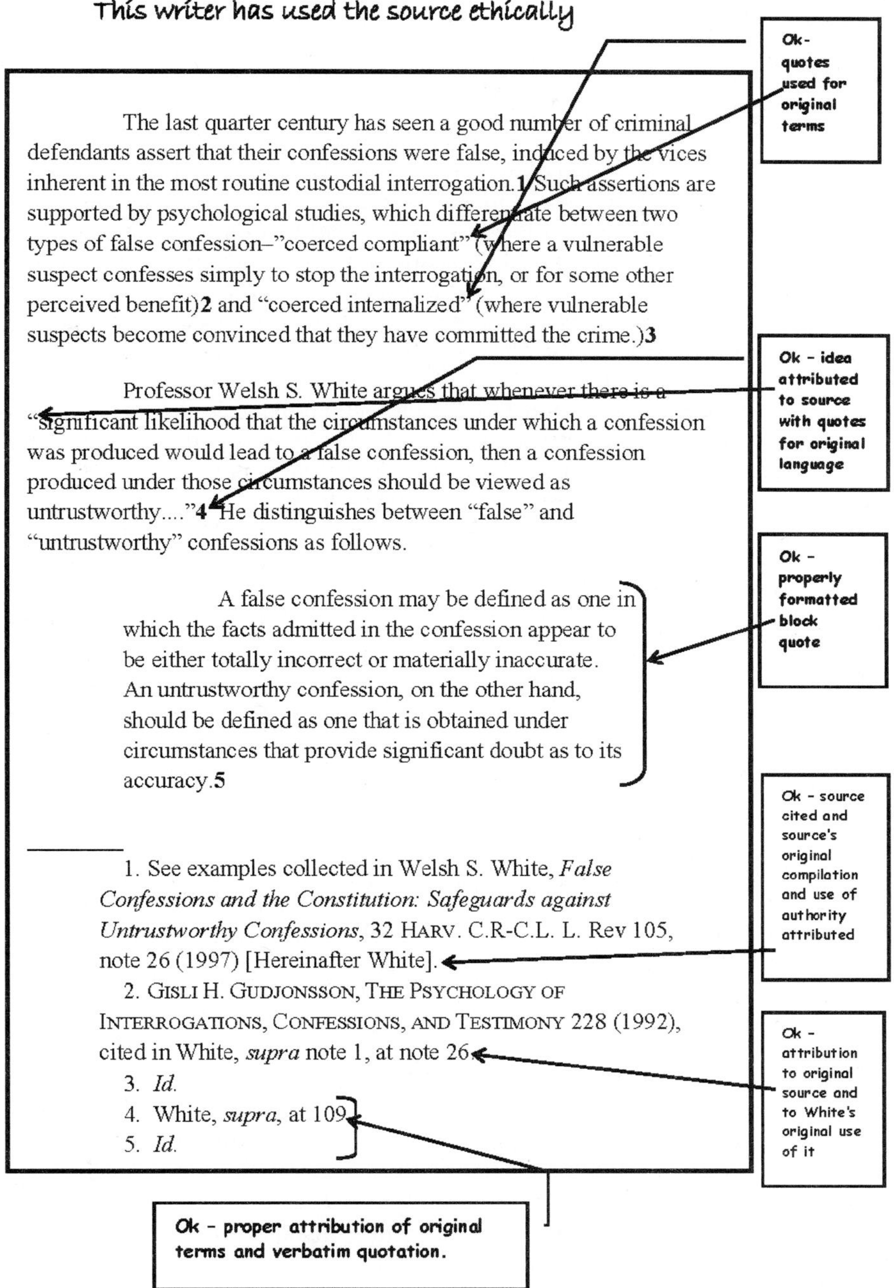

The last quarter century has seen a good number of criminal defendants assert that their confessions were false, induced by the vices inherent in the most routine custodial interrogation.1 Such assertions are supported by psychological studies, which differentiate between two types of false confession–"coerced compliant" (where a vulnerable suspect confesses simply to stop the interrogation, or for some other perceived benefit)2 and "coerced internalized" (where vulnerable suspects become convinced that they have committed the crime.)3

Professor Welsh S. White argues that whenever there is a "significant likelihood that the circumstances under which a confession was produced would lead to a false confession, then a confession produced under those circumstances should be viewed as untrustworthy...."4 He distinguishes between "false" and "untrustworthy" confessions as follows.

> A false confession may be defined as one in which the facts admitted in the confession appear to be either totally incorrect or materially inaccurate. An untrustworthy confession, on the other hand, should be defined as one that is obtained under circumstances that provide significant doubt as to its accuracy.5

---

1. See examples collected in Welsh S. White, *False Confessions and the Constitution: Safeguards against Untrustworthy Confessions*, 32 HARV. C.R-C.L. L. Rev 105, note 26 (1997) [Hereinafter White].

2. GISLI H. GUDJONSSON, THE PSYCHOLOGY OF INTERROGATIONS, CONFESSIONS, AND TESTIMONY 228 (1992), cited in White, *supra* note 1, at note 26.

3. *Id.*

4. White, *supra*, at 109.

5. *Id.*

EXERCISE 6.3

1. Although practitioners might point out that reusing the facts is permissible in practice, it is unlikely to be found so in an academic setting, especially because a writer's selection and perspective on the facts of a case may indeed be original. To take the exact words of another without attribution is plagiarism. Clear cases of this are borrowing the facts from a case or commentary.
2. In an article, it is permissible to reuse work if you acknowledge your past work with a footnote. Scholars often cite earlier work in a paper because ideas frequently build upon each other. In a seminar paper, it would be academic dishonesty to try to get new credit for work for which you already received credit unless you received permission from your professor by demonstrating why its use is important to your current work. You would need to cite it even then.
3. Using exact words without quotation marks is plagiarism, even if you provide a citation. There is language plagiarism and idea plagiarism. Here, the ideas were credited, but the writer lets the reader believe the words were her own.
4. This isn't plagiarism, but it may be a different kind of academic dishonesty. First, it misrepresents the writer's research. Second, since the student doesn't know if the second author was correctly summarized, the student could be charged with misrepresenting the source.
5. The foreign student has committed plagiarism, but the student shouldn't be punished unless he or she had been made aware of U.S. conventions.
6. It is plagiarism. Writers should never let this happen. They should print out all internet sources and retain hard copy, so if the site disappears, they have a record. Indeed, readers frequently see citations in law reviews that say this material is on file with the author or journal.
7. This is plagiarism. In legal scholarship, it is conventional to acknowledge the first person who expressed an idea, though you may explain that you came independently to that same conclusion.

EXERCISE 6.4

The first sentence changes a lot of language and is a legitimate paraphrase, although the rule needs to be cited because it sets out the court's standard. In addition, the legally significant term "physically present" used by the Court should be in quotes.

The language in the second sentence discussing exigent circumstances is identical to the source and should be written as an altered quotation, using quotation marks, an ellipsis, and a citation, as shown below.

To determine the validity of a warrantless search, a court must regard as dispositive a physically present co-inhabitant's clear refusal to permit a search. *Cite.* Moreover, here, as in *Georgia v. Randolph,* the state does not "claim that the entry and search should be upheld . . . [because] of exigent circumstances, owing to apprehension . . . that . . . [the defendant] would destroy evidence of drug use before any warrant could be obtained." *Cite.*

C. CHAPTER 7 ANSWERS

EXERCISE 7(A)(2)

Use the plural: Common sense suggests that when patients are injured in the hospital, they should promptly notify their attorneys.

Use an article and who: Common sense suggests that a patient who is injured in the hospital should notify an attorney.

Use "you": Common sense suggests that when you are injured in the hospital, you should notify your attorney.

Use the passive voice: Common sense suggests that when a patient is injured in the hospital, an attorney should be notified.

EXERCISE 7(A)(4)

The fourth amendment permits the arrest and conviction of a suspect for failing to identify himself during a lawful Terry stop.

EXERCISE 7(A)(6)

1. *(Dangling modifier)* Applying this test to the facts of the case, the court held the defendant's interest was minimal.

2. *(Misplaced modifier)* The defendant had a scar that resembled a crescent moon on his left cheek.

3. *(Misplaced modifier)* One reason why we accept statutes as legitimate is that our legislators are democratically elected. *(No matter where we put "in part," the ambiguity remains—so rewriting is in order.)*

EXERCISE 7(A)(7)

The Supreme Court has not indicated that it is constitutional to require identification. (Or; . . . to require suspects to identify themselves.)

EXERCISE 7(A)(8)

1. Reasonable efforts to maintain secrecy include **putting** the recipe in a locked office, **storing** parts of the recipe in separate locations, or **establishing** a continuing course of conduct that creates a confidential relationship.

2. Part II of this note will discuss the historical background of agreements leading up to the TRIPS agreement, the scope of other agreements, and the reasons for limiting geographical protection.

EXERCISE 7(A)(10)

1. Because Frost held Clemente at gunpoint and explicitly threatened to shoot him, Clemente never had an opportunity to escape. Moreover, Clemente tried to refuse to participate in the offense when he said "no

way'' would he rob Sheldon. Thus, Clemente can establish imminence of threat.

2. When the anti-discrimination statute was enacted in 1974, it was reasonable for the Legislature to believe that juries should not decide suits filed under the statute. In enacting the statute, the Legislature had sought to provide redress for workplace discrimination against racial minorities, women, and homosexuals that was based on widespread prejudice and stereotyping. Thus, the Legislature could reasonably have believed that jurors hostile to the protected groups would frustrate plaintiffs' assertions of rights under the statute.

EXERCISE 7(A)(11)

(A violation can't grant jurisdiction) A violation of a federal statute **gives rise to** jurisdiction if the statute authorizes a private right of action.

EXERCISE 7(A)(12)

Move ''properly'' to follow ''situation,'' but leave ''carefully'' where it is. If ''carefully'' appears after ''weigh,'' it is unclear if it modifies ''weigh'' (''weigh carefully'') or modifies ''planned improvements'' (''carefully planned improvements'').

To assess the situation properly, you have to carefully weigh planned improvements against anticipated results.

EXERCISE 7(A)(13)

The ''who'' modifier should be restrictive; it is restricting the reference of ''children'' to a particular group. Do not use commas.

EXERCISE 7(A)(15)

1. *(Object of preposition)* Rhetorical analysis asks, ''For **whom** is this document intended?''

2. *(Subject of verb)* The Committee decides **who** should be nominated for a judgeship.

3. *(Object of verb)* The defendant, **whom** we knew, was convicted of fraud.

4. *(Subject of verb ''had gone'')* She asked him **who** he thought had gone.

5. *(Object of verb)* Is there no one **whom** we can trust?

6. *(Subject of Infinitive—we should get* ***him*** *to alter)* **Whom** should we permit to alter our civil liberties?

EXERCISE 7(B)(3)

1. *(Afterthought comma needed)* The executive offices were located in New York, where the Board met regularly.

2. *(Serial commas needed)* Mr. Wood lives and works in Chicago, holds a Chicago driver's license and voter registration card, and gets all his mail in Chicago.

3. *(Introductory comma needed)* Because it was buried in his junk mail, Wood didn't see the Summons for some time.

4. *(Comma before the non-restrictive "which" phrase.)* The appellant appealed his conviction and sentence to the Court of Appeals, which used the Supreme Court balancing test that weighs the public interest against the individual's right to personal security from arbitrary interference by law enforcement officers.

5. *(Close interruption or make restrictive.)* To protect all products, at the cost of usurping the rights of prior good faith trademark owners, is not something most countries are willing to do, **or** To protect all products at the cost of usurping the rights of prior good faith trademark owners is not something most countries are willing to do.

Note that loose punctuation would omit the comma before "and gets" in 2.

EXERCISE 7(B)(4)

1. *(Semicolon between independent sentences.)* The TRIPS agreement should be extended; as it currently stands, TRIPS is the only agreement with international implementation, and it is vital not to jeopardize that.

2. *(Semicolons to separate elements with internal commas.)* Each party fully disclosed the extent of his or her estate, income, and financial prospects; was fully informed of the estate, income, and financial prospects of the other; was represented in the preparation of this Agreement by independent counsel; and was fully advised of his or her rights by such counsel.

EXERCISE 7(B)(6)

The Operations Policy Committee—to whom the Board of Directors had delegated the responsibilities of general operations such as making policy decisions, hiring corporate officers, and supervising plant procedures—met in Pittsburgh.

EXERCISE 7(B)(7)

1. *(Plural possessive)* Plaintiff sued Nan West and her company for defendants' alleged misappropriation of plaintiff's trade secret.

2. *(Singular noun ending in 's')* Walker served as Matthews's (or Matthews') Lamaze coach.

3. *(No apostrophe with possessive pronouns.)* The court has twice noted its refusal to rule on this matter.

REVIEW EXERCISE

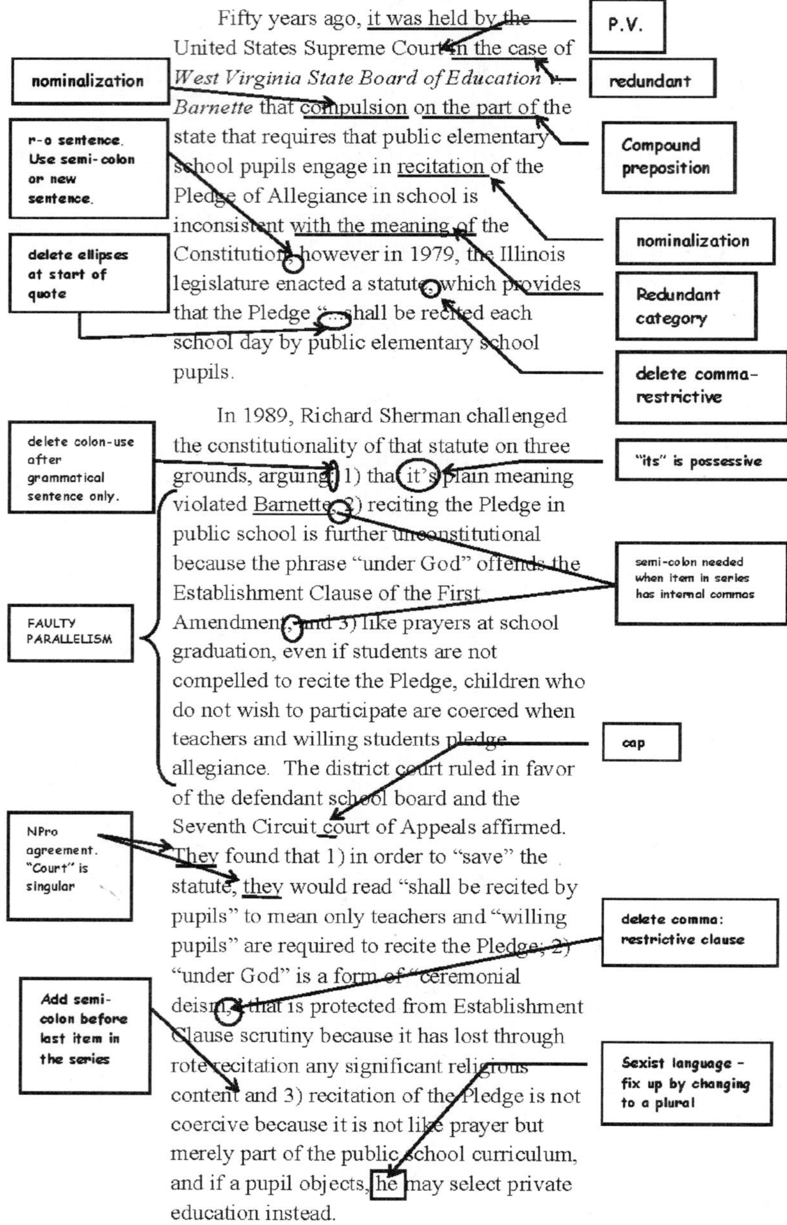

Fifty years ago, it was held by the United States Supreme Court in the case of *West Virginia State Board of Education v. Barnette* that compulsion on the part of the state that requires that public elementary school pupils engage in recitation of the Pledge of Allegiance in school is inconsistent with the meaning of the Constitution, however in 1979, the Illinois legislature enacted a statute, which provides that the Pledge "...shall be recited each school day by public elementary school pupils.

In 1989, Richard Sherman challenged the constitutionality of that statute on three grounds, arguing: 1) that it's plain meaning violated Barnette, 2) reciting the Pledge in public school is further unconstitutional because the phrase "under God" offends the Establishment Clause of the First Amendment, and 3) like prayers at school graduation, even if students are not compelled to recite the Pledge, children who do not wish to participate are coerced when teachers and willing students pledge allegiance. The district court ruled in favor of the defendant school board and the Seventh Circuit court of Appeals affirmed. They found that 1) in order to "save" the statute, they would read "shall be recited by pupils" to mean only teachers and "willing pupils" are required to recite the Pledge; 2) "under God" is a form of "ceremonial deism," that is protected from Establishment Clause scrutiny because it has lost through rote recitation any significant religious content and 3) recitation of the Pledge is not coercive because it is not like prayer but merely part of the public school curriculum, and if a pupil objects, he may select private education instead.

1 A corrected version of this text appears at the beginning of the sample casenote/competition paper in Appendix A.

Appendix C

SCHOLARLY WRITING WORKSHOPS AND COURSES

This book is mostly addressed to student authors, but it has as a secondary audience the teachers and law review editors who supervise student scholarly writing. The suggestions we have made to that latter audience in this book are limited to the interaction of individual supervisors with individual writers. In our law review editing chapter, we also discuss techniques for writing constructive and supportive comments.

In this appendix, we go beyond the writer/supervisor context to suggest curricular and institutional changes that can also help nurture student scholarly writing: first, the institution of workshops on scholarly writing; second, the institution of scholarly writing courses, especially full-year courses; and third, the use of peer writing groups. We also provide sample syllabi and schedules.

A. WORKSHOPS

One efficient way to disseminate information on scholarly writing is to offer a workshop or series of workshops on legal scholarship and on the process of scholarly writing to new law review members or for students writing seminar papers.

The first workshop could be devoted to a discussion of legal scholarship. Ask one of the active writers on your faculty to speak about the kinds of topics, issues, and articles that are of interest to the legal community. Then invite a librarian to talk about research strategies for scholarly writing. In the law review setting (and in the classroom), you may be able to give the librarian a list of your writers' topics so he or she can tailor suggestions to those areas. A third workshop could be on the brainstorming and writing process itself. One of your legal writing faculty may be especially competent to describe the scholarly writing process. A fourth session might familiarize students with the conventions of legal scholarship, with particular emphasis on footnotes and the ethical use of borrowed material. A review of the mechanics of writing might also be helpful—grammar, usage, punctuation, and manuscript preparation.

This mini-course on scholarly writing could be open to, or required of, all students beginning writing projects, whether new journal members or upperclass students writing seminar papers. It could be done in an all-day format or half-day format or spread out over a few weeks. The workshops could be an all-school or all-journal event or every constituent body could organize its own. International law journals may need their own international research strategy sessions, for example. Ideally, each workshop would be given at the beginning of each semester, and each session or topic covered by a different person, someone with expertise in that particular area. This way no one person would feel overburdened.

B. SCHOLARLY WRITING SEMINARS

Courses on scholarly writing are becoming more common as teachers find that beginning scholars often need more supervision than a student gets when writing a paper in a doctrinal seminar or for a journal. These courses, focusing exclusively on the scholarly writing process, are models of active learning. As the following syllabi show, class time is used for group brainstorming, editing, and presentation. We provide a syllabus for the traditional one semester course as well as a syllabus for teachers who might assign our book as a required reading for students writing seminar papers in a doctrinal course. We also provide a syllabus for the more novel two-semester course, the model we prefer.

We believe that if student writing projects, including "term" papers, were routinely of a year's, not a semester's, duration, the process might be more meaningful and the product more substantial. The great majority of expert scholarly writers would have difficulty teaching and producing a piece of serious writing in one semester, yet professors most often expect students to produce an original and polished paper in three and a half months. Requiring two semesters of work for upperclass writing credit would undoubtedly be awkward, particularly for students writing papers for traditional one-semester courses, but we think it would be worth the administrative and curricular flexibility entailed. Most other kinds of writing projects—law review submissions, independent study projects, and writing connected with clinical experience—could quite easily be structured to require at least six months of work.

1. Syllabus: Two–Term Scholarly Writing Seminar

1. **Intro Class:** Legal Scholarship Introduction

Assignments:
- Chapters 1 & 2 in *Scholarly Writing [SW]*
- Work on Thesis Development
- Research Competitions

2. **Thesis Development**: Potential Topics and Theses

Assignment: Chapter 3 (Research) in *SW*

3. **Research** Advance Research Strategies (Invite Research Librarian)

Assignments:

- Robert C. Post, *Legal Scholarship and the Practice of Law*, 63 U. Col. L. Rev. 615 (1992).
- Research Topics
- Draft a One-page Proposal
- Identify Research Strategy
- Create Primary Reading Log (Due Next Class)

4. **Discovering the Law** Research Logs
Finding the Conflict
Integrating Theory Into Your Thesis
Building on the Work of Others

Assignment: Anthony d'Amato, *Can Any Legal Theory Constrain Any Judicial Decision?* 43 U. Miami L. Rev. 513 (1989)

5. **Topic Discussions**

Assignments:

- Excerpts from Students' Reading Logs
- Prepare Outline of Paper

6. **Outline & Writing Process Discussion**

Assignments: Chapters 4 & 5 in *SW*

7. **Outline** Presentation of Outlines and Readings

Assignments:

- Key Articles Circulated by Students on Their Topics and Excerpts from Classmates' Reading Logs
- Begin Working on Drafts

8. **Footnotes: Attribution & Authority**

Assignment: Chapter 6 in *SW*

9. **Presentations** Presentation of Outlines and Readings

Assignments: Key Articles and Excerpts from Classmates' Reading Logs

10.	**Presentations**	Presentation of Outlines and Readings
	Assignments:	Key Articles and Excerpts from Classmates' Reading Logs
	Paper Due:	First Rough Draft
11.	**Presentations**	Presentation of Outlines and Readings
	Assignment:	Key Articles and Excerpts
12.	**Presentations**	Presentation of Outlines and Readings
	Assignments:	Key Articles and Excerpts
	Paper Due:	Second Rough Draft
13–14.	**No Class—Individual Conferences** (Work on projects)	
15.	**Wrap-up Class (First Semester)** Third Draft Due	
16.	**Focusing on Structure**	
	Assignment:	Chapters 4 & 5 in *SW*
17.	**Focusing on Grammar and Style**	
	Assignment:	Chapters 7 & 8 in *SW*
18.	**Editing**	
	Assignments:	Chapter 9 in *SW* Interchange Draft with Peer & Edit
19.	**Fourth Drafts Due: Conferences**	
20.	Presentation 1	
21.	Presentation 2	
22.	Presentation 3	
23.	Presentation 4	
24.	Presentation 5	
25.	Presentation 6	
26.	Presentation 7	
27.	Presentation 8	
28–29.	No Class (work on projects)	

30. Wrap–Up Class—Final Papers Due

2. Syllabus: One–Term Scholarly Writing Seminar

Week 1	Topics and Theses Read: Chapters 1 and 2 in *Scholarly Writing*
Week 2	Research Process Read: Chapter 3 in *Scholarly Writing*
Week 3	Topics and Thesis: Initial Thoughts Due: Topic Selection and Research Log
Week 4	Tailoring Your Research
Week 5	Drafting and Revising Read: Chapters 4 & 5 *Scholarly Writing* Due: Outlines
Week 6	Footnotes Read: Chapter 6 in *Scholarly Writing*
Week 7	Polishing Read: Chapters 7 and 8 in *Scholarly Writing* Due: 1st Draft
Week 8	Conferences and Presentations (Exchange Paper with Peer and Edit) Read: Excerpts on Topic
Week 9	Conferences and Presentations Read: Excerpts on Topics
Week 10	Conferences and Presentations Read: Excerpts on Topics
Week 11	Conferences and presentations Read: Excerpts on Topics
Week 12	Editing Read: Chapter 9 in *Scholarly Writing*
Week 13–14	Release Weeks for Writing
Week 15	Wrap-up Class Due: Final Papers

3. Schedule for Writing Projects in a Doctrinal Seminar

Week 3 — Turn in Choice of Topic. Background Reading: Chapters One, Two and Three and Appendix A in *Scholarly Writing for Law Students.*

Week 5 — Turn in Reading Journals and a page or two describing your thesis and the results of some initial research. Don't just describe the case or topic—use your best and most original thinking. If you have trouble formulating your thesis, you may want to reread Chapter Two.

Week 7 — Turn in Detailed Outline. This should be standard "Roman" form, about 5 pages long, indicating not only the organization, but the substance of your project as well. It should be based on completed research. Background Reading: Chapter Four in *Scholarly Writing.*

Week 10 — First Draft. This should flow easily from your outline. It should be a complete draft, with footnotes or endnotes, and be the result of your best intellectual efforts. Background Reading: Chapters Five, Six, and Seven and Eight in *Scholarly Writing.*

Week 15 — Final Draft

C. COLLABERATIVE GROUPS

One last strategy for nurturing student scholarship is to set up peer writing groups. These would involve supervisors not as actors, but as stage-managers. Recent research suggests that peer writing groups are an exceptional teaching/learning tool. Writing groups contribute to important gains in critical thinking, revising and organizing skills, and confidence.[1]

Peer writing groups can be introduced in a number of ways. Substantive seminars can be structured so that the teacher is the facilitator of student projects—so that the class, or at a minimum one component of it, is, in fact, "about" works in progress on interrelated topics. Peer groups can be facilitated by teaching assistants or be facilitator-less. In this model, supervisors would provide exploratory feedback as the writing projects progress. Most descriptive and prescriptive feedback would happen within the group. Writing groups could be composed of students from the same course, or perhaps more ideally, they could be affinity groups—students writing papers and articles on securities law or intellectual property or white-collar crime. Peer writing groups can be introduced into law review in similar ways. Here too, groups could be composed of students working under the supervision of one editor, or divided into affinity groups.

1. See Bari R. Burke, *Legal Writing (Groups) at the University of Montana: Professional Voice Lessons in a Communal Context*, 52 MONT. L. REV. 373, 406 (1991).

Whatever their composition, peer writing groups need to be small, with a maximum of ten students, so as to promote active learning. Students can take turns presenting their research, or they can circulate outlines, or drafts, and then solicit discussion and reaction. The journal's advisor or the seminar teacher might be persuaded to attend some of these sessions and give feedback, or perhaps a faculty member with expertise in the area of the affinity groups could be persuaded to come. The journal of one major school has an editorial seminar which involves weekly or bi-weekly meetings with a faculty member.[2] Such interaction makes the writing process less isolating and more fun intellectually and socially and seems likely to produce better articles.

2. See James Lindgren, *Reforming the American Law Review*, 47 STAN. L. REV. 1125–27 (1995).

Index

References are to Pages

References are to Pages

†